Jemmy Jock Bird

James Bird Jr in 1855,
drawn by Gustav Sohon.
Washington State Historical
Society Sohon Collection

by John C. Jackson

Jemmy Jock Bird

Marginal Man on the Blackfoot Frontier

UNIVERSITY OF
CALGARY
PRESS

© 2003 John C. Jackson
National Library of Canada Cataloguing in Publication

Jackson, John C., 1931-
  Jemmy Jock Bird : marginal man on the Blackfoot frontier / by John C. Jackson.

Includes bibliographical references and index.
ISBN 1-55238-111-0

  1. Bird, Jemmy Jock. 2. Métis--Prairie Provinces--Biography. 3. Fur traders--Prairie Provinces--Biography. 4. Fur traders--Montana--Biography. 5. Hudson's Bay Company--Biography.
  I. Title.

E99.M47B57 2003   971.2'004973   C2003-905756-9

Published by the University of Calgary Press
2500 University Drive NW, Calgary, Alberta, Canada T2N 1N4
www.uofcpress.com

No part of this publication may be reproduced, stored in a retrieval system or transmitted, in any form or by any means, without the prior written consent of the publisher or a licence from The Canadian Copyright Licensing Agency (Access Copyright). For an Access Copyright licence, visit www.accesscopyright.ca or call toll free to 1-800-893-5777.

We acknowledge the financial support of the Government of Canada through the Book Publishing Industry Development Program (BPIDP) for our publishing activities.

 Canada Council for the Arts / Conseil des Arts du Canada

Cover design, page design and typesetting by Mieka West.

Contents

	Preface and Acknowledgments	vii
1	In a Gathering Darkness	1
2	The Floating Community of the Saskatchewan	11
3	War and Trade	21
4	The Blackfoot Barrier	31
5	Piikani Summer	37
6	Muddy Waters on the Upper Missouri	47
7	A Taste of Corporate Comeuppance	59
8	A Company Man Again	71
9	Marginal Man on a Closing Frontier	83
10	In the Shadow of the Cross	93
11	Under the Long Knives	107
12	White Man's World	119
13	Métis Politics	131
14	Prairie Calling	139
15	Treaty Number Seven	145
16	In a Gathering Darkness	153
17	Man or Myth?	165
	Bibliography	167
	Notes	175
	Index	195

Preface and Acknowledgments

As the end of the nineteenth century neared, the Canadian northwest was trying to rise above its raw fur trade origins. Victorians on the fringe of the British Empire had the indiscretions of the founders to sweep under the carpet. To their everlasting embarrassment, the son of chief factor James Bird, a pillar of the Red River community, returned. James Bird Jr was a half-breed who ran away with the Red Indians, a ghost of the past best forgot. As the nineteenth century neared an end, he was still out there on the prairies, blind and toothless, bumping around between Indian reserves in his rickety old cart. The way to soften the cultural affront was to wrap him in a cocoon of half-truth and myth.

But Jemmy Jock was a real person, a uniquely North American man who had lived by direct experience and was always indifferent to imposed boundaries. Although not quite an outcast, he didn't fit the expected patterns, not English, not Cree, not fully Niitsitapi. After almost a hundred years, the Piikani fellow traveler was unable to escape the shadows closing over the Indian world.

Tracing of a unique life owes much to those who have aided a fascinated researcher forced to become an author. The dossier that Anne McDonnell, Librarian of the Historical Society of Montana compiled for her notes to the Fort Benton Journal started the process. The late Pat McCloy, librarian for the Glenbow, provided data on a complex family. Beverly Bishop of the Missouri Historical Society found information on Bird's relationship with the American Fur Company. Former keeper of the Hudson's Bay Archives, Shirlee Ann Smith facilitated the readings that substantiate this study while moderating my wilder enthusiasms. Judith Hudson Beattie and Ann Morton uphold the tradition of a world-class research center. Trudy Nicks was generous with information opening a new understanding of the Métis claims. Fellow historians and writers Richard Wright and David Smyth have also followed this convoluted trail, and David R. Miller made an early reading of this manuscript and gently nudged it toward a better presentation. Editor Walter Hildebrandt encouraged telling the story as it should be told and the staff of the University of Calgary Press saw that it was with impressive efficiency.

The inspiration to recover the man behind the myth radiates from my rediscovered kinswoman, Jemmy Jock's great-granddaughter, Nettie Burd Connell. Nettie is the example of those manly-hearted women who held the Piikani together through all the tough times. This book is dedicated to Nettie and the memory of the never defeated Big John the Griz.

In a Gathering Darkness

For three weeks the *niitsitapi* had been coming to set up their lodges in the long meadow beside the Bow River, smoke with old friends, and sing and drum into the night. But this was another kind of sun dance and the bands of the Gens du Large were assembling to hear the words of the great English Mother's men. They knew that treaty papers had already corralled the Cree, the Assiniboine, even the elusive Atsiina. Across the Medicine Line, their brothers lived in a shrinking world. What the queen's men had to say could mean grave changes.[1]

The first Siksika and few Kainaa to arrive camped on the south side of the Bow River and turned thousands of horses loose to graze on what the British described as the "excellent herbage on hill and dale." Not entirely confident of a friendly reception, Sarcees, Stoneys, and Bobtail Cree located on the north side of the river keeping the camps of the traders and the mixed-bloods between them and potential trouble. Although the presence of the mounted police discouraged peddling liquor, the Hudson's Bay Company and American traders set up their canvas marquees in expectation of skimming off the expected payments. But a determined drinker could always find a bottle.

On 15 September, eighty North West Mounted Police rode in, driving supply wagons, wheeled guns, and a herd of cattle. Setting up camp they placed a gun on a commanding position on the heights, not an unreasonable precaution as their contingent was less than half of the number of bluecoats that the Sioux had done for on the Little Big Horn.

The commander of the mounted police was Colonel James Macleod, who was known to many tribesmen who visited his post. As one of the two commissioners his words could be trusted. The arrival of the lieutenant governor of the Northwest Territory on Sunday 16 September completed the official party. David Laird was not an entire stranger. Earlier in the month, he had stopped by the council grounds on his way to Fort Macleod.

It had been two years since worried Siksika asked for a meeting. Crowfoot had gotten a priest who lived with the bands to put those words on paper. For the past moon riders circulated among the scattered bands calling them to a council. Tribal differences soon arose when Fort Macleod was the designated location. Sensitive to the implications of being dominated by the redcoats, the Blackfoot leader, Crowfoot, held out for a gathering at the crossing of the Bow River. His demand prevailed, Crowfoot and his followers were among the earliest to arrive. But the Bloods who followed Red Crow were hunting in the south near the Medicine Line, and it would take them longer to get there. At night, the *niitoyis* (tipi or lodge) spread across the meadow were glowing cones of soft light. Deeply concerned people sat up late, feeding the small fires and worrying about what the redcoats meant to do. Too many strangers were crowding them.

The initial response from the new government assured the bands that their lands would not be taken without a consultation. But that hadn't stopped Crees and Métis from taking buffalo on their traditional hunting grounds, and whites from building houses. In the last two years thousands of *Pinaapisinaa* (Lakota or Sioux) fleeing from the bluecoats had crossed the Line and were now consuming the herds near the Cypress Hills. Other rumors said that *Komonoitapiikoan* (Nez Percé) were also coming north.

If those were dark times for tribes, it was even darker for the old man in the mixed-blood camp. James Bird was blind. He sat locked in a personal darkness, regretting that as a young man he had run with the dogs across blinding snowfields. There had been too many smokes, too many lodge fires, too many times blinking in the smudges that kept the damn mosquitoes off. Those times had finally claimed his eyes and all that he saw against his eyelids were memories.

In that darkness there were no dawns, no sunsets, no reason to sleep or call to wake beyond the stirring of those who shared the crowded lodge. Blindness left no way of calculating where the sun stood or the moon's phase in a night sky. He knew time as hunger, thirst, or the call of nature. Because his teeth were gone, the old woman even had to chew his meat for him, as she might have done for a baby. The old prairie ranger felt old, too old. He had come to that point in an increasingly difficult life where a man ceases to value years that only heap insults upon him.

In better moments he recalled that it had been a good life, lived with trustworthy friends, loving wives, and children. There was always new country to see when he locked his strong young legs around the barrel of a dancing pony, and gave it the quirt. Living by the hunt, riders killed buffalo in the heart-pounding glory of a run and the bloody triumph of butchering, biting the dripping liver, and making meat enough to feed family and friends. What he packed back to camp was shared with those who had no one to hunt for them. That was the way of it. Now he didn't even have a gun. Any daring dog could snatch a bone from his hand.

Those were times when meat was real meat and not some pre-chewed gob. Young men walked far to the camps of enemies and came back riding. Taking a beaver skin to trade meant powder and ball and blankets, maybe a little tea. He made sure that the women in his lodge were properly dressed and tinkled with hawks' bells as they strode proudly across the camp circle. Nights on the prairie, laying on a robe under the dome of stars, he hadn't thought much about the next day. Let others try to remake the world, he accepted it as his tribesmen did. Being alive was enough.

Although his father was an Englishman, and his mother Cree, he never thought of himself as a half-breed. Those who he grew up with at Edmonton or knew in the York Factory school also had Indian mothers. So did his stepmother Elizabeth and Uncle Nick Montour. Only a handful of company officers were English and most of the workmen were island Scots, Orkneymen. In most of the posts where he had grown up there were French Canadian voyageurs just across the fence.

As a factor of the great Hudson's Bay Company, his father had started him on the path of an apprentice clerk sent out to move between the post and the camps of the Cree beaver hunters. Those were times when the business demanded more and more pelts. As competition stiffened, the rival Montreal adventures resorted to violence and his father raged over their outrageous abuses. Still young when his father sent him to the Assiniboine River, he found the Nor'westers trying to convince the Métis that they were a tribe with rights to protect. Luckily, he escaped the war party that killed the Selkirk colony settlers at Seven Oaks.

The next years were murderous times. It couldn't go on and eventually the rivals agreed to merge their interests. But the new company felt no obligation to loyal servants or old engagees. The new governor ruthlessly turned out old hands, many children of the country or older officers like his father. The new regime preferred to bring in strangers from England or Orkney.

Father Nicholas Point's version of the free hunter. Washington State University

Finding more trustworthy friends among the *niitisitapi*, James turned to trapping and riding with the Piikani. Those Muddy River beaver hunters had always tolerated a random Cree so he found a place in that world bounded by mountains and the howling horizon, and became a plainsman. On that first trip south he remembered passing *Nee-tuck-kiss* the last lone pine that marked where the northern forest yielded to the grass. On the buffalo plains, he had learned to sleep in the breathing cone of a skin lodge. Those were the best years, free to hunt, to roam, to claim a wife. When his fellow tribesmen bumped against Snakes or Flatheads, there were exhilarating horse-capture adventures and an occasional fight. What a fine thing to be part of the Piikani world.

Being British or American didn't matter to plainsmen. What had he cared for the schemes of greedy company officers? For a time, John Rowand persuaded him to work against the encroaching Americans, but when they offered a better price, he took his friends and their beaver to Kipp and McKenzie. That was how the Upper Missouri robe trade started. Those hunters who traders disparaged as Slaves got the trading house they had always wanted, and became powerful.

Anyone who tried to put him in the middle soon learned that he was his own man. He faced down blustering Nor'westers, overbearing baymen, pushy Americans and even made the little Governor Simpson bite his thumb. Those little triumphs only made being blind more humiliating. He was completely dependent on others. What good was he to his old wife Sally, to his sons Tom or Philip? With their own futures to consider, those boys must think of him as just another baby to care for, to put to the moss.

Old Bird knew a bit about treaties. The family came to the Blackfoot Crossing expecting to get in on the presents that the Canadians would surely distribute. It was twenty years since he spoke for the Americans. Those Yankee treaty makers were a pompous bunch, full of themselves and jealous of each other. He helped explain to the Piikani that what they had drawn up required giving up some territory, but left more than enough good buffalo ranges. That was a reasonable compromise if it stopped the wars that tortured those who only came for meat.

What they did at the mouth of the Judith River in fifty-five divided the buffalo grounds. Why kill each other when there was meat enough for all? To keep hunting bands from fighting each other the southern ranges were set off for the western tribes and sufficient territory was guaranteed to the Gens du Large. At the time that seemed like the best thing to do, but later the Americans took more land until the Piikani were penned on a reservation.

Drawing boundaries had spoiled it for him. Taking the family he left the northern plains and went to the Red River settlement to become an Englishman like his

Kainaa, Piikani and Kutenai leaders at Fort McKenzie in 1833 by Karl Bodmer. Courtesy of Arthur H. Clark & Company.

father. Although their neighbors hadn't treated Sally as well as they should, the family learned to live under a roof. After eleven years, they went back to the prairies. By then his sight was going and bumping along in the back of a cart he had to imagine the long horizon. They were just another half-breed family ... but not quite the same.

Old friends they encountered told him that, despite the American treaty and the hope for peace, the murder games had gone on: Indians were killing miners and each other, bluecoats and whiskey traders killing Indians, everyone killing buffalo. Many of the peace-treaty chiefs went to the Sand Hills; Big Smoke killed by Crees, Middle Sitter by Big Bellies, Mountain Chief and Little Dog by their own people. At least Lame Bull died hunting. A year ago, his widowed daughter, Nancy, became the wife of a Blood named Medicine Shield. He was a warrior who got himself wounded while raiding horses with Red Crow.[2] So much for peace.

Blind as he was, in the camp along the Bow he sensed an ominous difference. Depressed hunters complained about the scarcity of buffalo. Although traders in the nearby camp bragged of taking in sixty thousand buffalo robes along the Belly and Old Man rivers, there were too many years when the herds were hard to find. To make it worse, the redcoats strolling around the camp were saying all the buffalo would soon be gone. How could that be? How could the *niitsitapi* live without meat?

He remembered animals scattered all over the plains. The vast herds churning the banks of the rivers into mud seemed to go on forever. What had the hunters done? Had the *niitsitapi* offended the master of life by taking so many robes, selling dried tongues that the traders shipped downstream by dozens, killing cows carrying unborn calves? After they ate the horses and the dogs, what would the Piikani do, eat fish?

The situation finally got bad enough to unify the Blackfeet. At a gathering two years ago they had a Canadian half-breed draw up a petition asking the government to do something. Most of the band leaders who took that desperate step had not even been born in his time. After the great chiefs were gone, it was men like Crowfoot, Red Crow, or Medicine Calf who made themselves considerable. And that was just fine with the Queen's men. When the redcoats first appeared, Crowfoot had gained their trust by being cooperative and being just the kind of leader that the treaty makers wanted to deal with. But he put off Red Crow by shifting the council ground from Fort Macleod to the Blackfoot Crossing.

Finally, the redcoats fired off their little canon. Tom and Phillip led him to hear the speeches, describing how fifty Mounties marched in and stood behind the officials while the band played. After smoking with Crowfoot, Lieutenant-Governor

Buffalo along the Missouri River
Courtesy of Arthur H. Clark & Company.

Laird shouted impressive words meant to reassure the apprehensive crowd. English speakers understood ... but the Indians didn't.

The mounted police interpreter chiselled the governor's speech down to a dry nut. Jerry Potts was just the spawn of a petty Fort Benton robe trader and some fort woman. The redcoats had taken the former whiskey peddler up because he knew a few words, and bragged of being a leader among the people. But his abbreviated restatements were too concise, blunt exchanges were no way to begin. If the bands were to save themselves, they had to find a way to accept what was thrust upon them as curt demands. Grave matters needed time to simmer while the elders smoked and thought, tried to wrap their minds around impossible concepts.

After the second meeting, the commissioners of the great English Mother realized that a better translation was necessary. He was surprised when they asked him to channel their words tomorrow. He suspected that before coming to the council the Canadians had already written out their paper. The commissioners were not entirely forthcoming in their initial statements and the chiefs surely guessed that what they might say would not count. Was he being brought in to mislead old friends? Unable to read the document he could only hope that a blind man's justice might prevail.

The Floating Community of the Saskatchewan

The waters of the Saskatchewan River were English by discovery and corporate by royal decree. Native inhabitants might have contested that conceit, but who were they to question the Ancient and Honorable Company of Adventurers trading into Hudson Bay. The company held the king's chartered monopoly on all the Indian trade in whatever country whose waters drained into the bay. For over a hundred years, those London gentlemen of commerce had insinuated their business into the tribal world. But after the conquest of New France, it became increasingly difficult to deny other British subjects access to the interior. In order to compete, the Hudson's Bay Company had been obliged to move inland from the bay in 1774.

The English who were responsible for difficult, often risky, field operations learned to live in shabby log hovels and endure often petulant Orkney *servants*. The difficult neighbors next door were canoe men of the rival Montreal traders who proudly called themselves "*hommes du nord*." Those ragtags bragged of being better paid than their British parallels, but a canny bit of calculation disproved the difference between a northwest *livre* and a shilling.

Leapfrogging competitive posts up the Saskatchewan, by fall 1799 the Hudson's Bay Company reached the high-tide line. The twenty-five-year-old English clerk, James Bird, established Acton House where the Clearwater River came in and named the rough place in sentimental memory of his Middlesex home. He did what he could to keep rival Nor'westers from becoming too intimate with the beaver trading Muddy River Indians.

James Curtis Bird was the product of a modestly genteel English background. He was born at Winchester in Hampshire before the family moved nearer to London. As the eldest son of a respectable Acton family, James had the opportunity to study with a physician uncle. When the profession of late eighteenth-century medicine didn't take, his disappointed father took him to the paneled offices in Beaver House where the London secretary of the Hudson's Bay Company engaged the lad as an apprentice for five years.[1]

After a couple of years as a writer at York Factory, the promising clerk was sent inland in 1790. Charles Thomas Isham, the mixed-blood son of a former officer, introduced him to the rigorous life of a fur trader. Two years in the Swan River country proved that Bird was capable of a more demanding assignment on the upper Saskatchewan River. His mentor would be William Tomison, the master to reside inland, whose post was Manchester House.

That trade was with Plains Indians who French voyageurs generalized as Gens du Large.[2] Most Plains bands were buffalo runners but ineffective beaver hunters. Mr. Tomison concentrated on the more productive Muddy River Indians by sending servants to winter with them.[3] In the next nine years, Bird rose from an apprentice clerk earning twenty pounds per annum to Tomison's successor in command on the upper river.

Trading on the Saskatchewan was mostly a transport problem. Merchandise for the Indians had to be hauled inland during the summer when the waterways were free of ice. If that failed, men and dogs had to draw toboggans over the ice. As soon as the ice broke next spring, canoes and boats carried out the peltry obtained from Indian hunters. Those seasonal rushes bracketed long winters at lonely posts. In that unforgiving environment, it was no surprise that officers and servants formed relationships with daughters of neighboring tribes. Beyond being agreeable bed companions those young girls were experienced helpmates. But, respecting the sensitivities of the London gentlemen, little was written in the letters or daily journals about *country* arrangements.

By the end of the eighteenth century, a community of commercial and tribal nomads was strung along the Saskatchewan. As brigades of boats crawled inland in the fall or floated downstream in the spring, the traders were reluctant to leave their families exposed to jealous tribesmen. Mindful of a massacre at the South Branch House in 1795, the women and children rode downstream with the boat brigades.

They were left at Cumberland Lake to subsist by fishing until the men returned. The seasonal rhythm of the floating community of the Saskatchewan included a pleasant summer outing. That must have been where a young officer found a Cree bride.

At least from the documentary record, the fur trade was a man's world. Women were not so much neglected as slyly obscured to spare the sensitivities of the genteel governor and committee of the Hudson's Bay Company. Early on, those gentlemen discouraged connection with Indian women as a post security measure, as a distraction from business, and as an unnecessary expense. As far as the London secretary was concerned, the less said about those matters, the better. Post journalists kept domestic comments out of the daily records. As little as possible was made about orders sent to London for private goods obviously intended for families.

James Bird made his first country arrangement shortly after Charles Thomas Isham took him into the Swan River Country. Isham pointed out that a helpmate was essential for living comfortably. Having a girl broke down barriers between a trader and her people. The arrangement with the Cree girl named Oomenahowish was made by 1794. Her name has been interpreted to mean "well-dressed woman" and may have reflected the advantages enjoyed by a white man's wife.[4] Oomenahowish was probably a daughter of the homeguard Cree who lived around York Factory, maybe even the country child of a former trader. Her Cree name would be recorded in the Mitcham, Surrey parish register in 1815 when their twenty-year-old son George visited his English relatives. James Bird's preference for the name Mary was a compliment to his sister Mary Bird Downes. When George was born in 1795, he was named in honor of James's younger brother.[5]

Three years later a second son was born at Carlton House on the middle Saskatchewan River.

James Bird wrote the Carlton House Journals from 1795 until spring 1798 and then from nearby Setting River during the winter 1798/99.[6] His son was born near present Prince Albert, on the Sturgeon River, which suggests that he left the family there when the trader went upstream to establish Acton House in 1799/1800.[7] When James Bird returned, he gave the boy his own name and that of his English grandfather.

The naming practices were English, but the spacing between births was consistent with the Indian practice of nursing children for two or sometime three years. The boys grew up in the household of a Cree mother who had learned some English, but resorted to her native language when husband wasn't around. The stories Oomenahowish told to the boys gathered around the fireplace in the master's house were those of her people, their ways. She set a Cree example for them.

The child's first voyage was probably made in the moss of a Cree cradle board tucked between his mother's knees as they rode upstream to Edmonton House. After four years, that was a relatively established place where the mother and children were safe when the master traveled to supervise his outposts. Mary's last son was born in 1806. Then she was gone; a victim perhaps of the influenza-like sickness that ravaged Indian bands on the upper Saskatchewan and across the Rocky Mountains about that time.

With a considerable young family to care for, the trader needed another housekeeper. He did not need to look very far; just across the fence that separated the compound that the company shared with its North West Company rivals. The new wife was the Métisse daughter of a founder of the rival company. Before leaving the country a few years before, Nicholas Montour *set off* her mother on an obliging *engagé* (for a price, of course). Montour took two of their sons out of the country to be educated. A baby sister was put with nuns in a Quebec convent but did not survive the transition. That proved the inadvisability of trying to take country children into an unfamiliar and often deadly environment. While her father lavishly made himself one of the nabobs of Montreal, Elizabeth Montour was far from being an heiress.

Her brothers, Nicholas and Robert dit Bonhomme, returned from outside schooling with enough education to qualify as North West Company clerks. By 1805 Nicholas was a *commis* (clerk) working in the Lower Fort des Prairies department on the Saskatchewan. He may have retrieved his mother and sister from their guardian. Did that family responsibility include the tribal right of approving a marital arrangement, even to a leading opponent?

At the age of eight, Jamey might have resented a stepmother but *Uncle* Nicholas was a man to capture boyish imagination. Montour was already an experienced traveler in the summer of 1806 when he helped cut the pack road that the North West Company would use to extend trade to the Pacific slope.[8] The rival posts of Edmonton House and Fort Augustus shared a common yard so it was relatively easy for Uncle Nicholas to step over to visit his sister and indulge her inherited brood of boys with his yarns. Jamey was very aware that beyond the palisades, beyond the confining banks of the river, loomed an intriguing horizon of distant mountains and a world of exotic tribesmen.

Understanding the necessity for good interpreters James Bird sent young men to live with the bands and learn their languages. Language lessons also took place around the family hearth. Despite a French family name the first language of the Montours was English.[9] Like most women of the floating community Elizabeth also spoke a mix of French and Cree and introduced her stepsons to the language of the *voyageurs*.[10] Being able to speak to them gave Jamey early access to the vital, expressive, sometimes disreputable world of the *hommes du nord*. Those chatterers exuded an élan that the staid Orkneymen generally lacked. From a childhood base of English, Cree, and French, he would eventually command eight languages.

Cree had been his mother's language. Young Jamey understood something of what the woodland, parkland, and Plains Indian hunters said when they visited Edmonton House. Most times, in the gravity of the trading situation, they simply ignored a boy. But a visiting elder, warmed with a welcoming drink, might wink knowingly. Young men flicking their quirts made threatening faces and then laughed at a good joke. The boy knew those exotic tribesmen as real individuals.

As the man in command, James Bird could not share his feelings with the men. He brought them to the family fireside, giving the three young boys a sense of their father's frustration with the distant York factor or his vulnerability to annual letters from a mythic place called London. Looking toward their future, or from fear of the infectious attraction of a mere hunter's life, he entered them on the company payroll as apprentices. That was a way to arrange for a proper education.[11]

Before spring 1798, Trader Bird had already applied for permission to send his three-year-old son George home to live with relatives and be educated. The boy was four when a letter from London confirmed the arrangement. Unfortunately, that came at a critical moment in the development of the Saskatchewan trade. Bird's promotion as chief on the Saskatchewan could not be refused, but that new duty prevented him from taking the boy to York Factory.[12] In what turned out to be a lackluster career, George was hampered by an inferior education. By the time that Jamey was old enough to leave the family, a school of sorts had been established at York Factory.[13]

According to the instructions addressed to the overseas officers, the governor and committee "thought it would be advisable to instruct the children belonging to our servants in the principles of Religion and teach them from their youth Reading, Writing, Arithmetic, & Accounts, which we hope will attach them to our Service, and in a few years become a small colony of very useful Hands."[14] In 1808, G. Geddes, a minister who was willing to act as a schoolmaster, arrived at York Factory. Geddes undertook the charge with the principles of religion close to heart and his small class was imbued with a lasting respect of Christianity as well as some skill in reading and writing. When that teaching began to bear fruits, the factor ordered the construction of quarters to be used as both a school and hostel for the children.[15]

In August 1809, Jamey entered the York Factory school along with two other country sons of officers, William Sinclair and Richard Colen. Although Jamey was older than the projected entry age of five years, his father was determined that he should have advantage of the opportunity. At the Albany Factory school to the south, another fur trader's son, William Mackay, was allowed to begin his schooling at the advanced age of fifteen. Three girls, Harriet Ballenden, Catharine Sinclair, and Mary Bunn were left over from the school's first year at York Factory. The proud schoolmaster was sending in examples of their scholarship as the second class arrived.[16]

It was a new experience for a boy raised in the shadow of the Continental Divide. The flat, swampy surrounding country had bushes instead of real trees. The up-country boy marveled that the waters of the bay drained away daily and then came rushing back across the mud flats. Jamey found *the factory* was a lonesome place of sagging old buildings put together from necessity rather than architecture, that had compounded over the years into a rotting rabbit warren of dark apartments and narrow passages. Turned inward by dreary surroundings, the homesick young scholar learned to read a bit, and to steer a pen through the convolutions of writing.

They came innocent of A to zed but Mr. Geddes taught his wild things how to press those letters together until the string made an idea. Those words were traced out on squeaky slates until they could be trusted with a real pen. Mr. Geddes' lessons included examples drawn from a Bible that seemed to recall the ancient experiences of another kind of tribe. Those mythic people lived in deserts with burning bushes and speaking stones. If teacher was to be believed, there was spirit power on those pages and visions hidden in the words not unlike those that their Cree mother told them.

Although Jamey showed progress, the teacher recognized that wild boys were not destined for a life of the mind. Born into the mercantile hierarchy, Jamey and his schoolmates were being prepped for places in company operations, as a *colony of useful hands*. After his brief schooling, Jamey returned to the upper Saskatchewan to begin the duties of an apprentice and junior clerk. He would share a lifelong affinity with the half sister Letitia who was born in 1810. Returning Nor'westers described fabulous Montreal where Elizabeth said that their wealthy grandfather spent his fortune, and died in debt.

Hunters and traders were locked in a symbiotic tradition. In the fall, tribesmen were outfitted to hunt, and support their families, with the expectation that they would return in the spring to repay those debts with the furs they took.[17] During the early years of rivalry with the Canadians, Bay men learned that they had to gain possession of returns before opportunistic rivals subverted the system. Edmonton trader Bird's annual agreements with his NWCo neighbor were no guarantee of fair play, so his son was soon put to work traveling through the parklands to collect debts before some ruthless, liquor dispensing opponent got them.

A winter traveler was abraded by pitiless winds and driven snow. Jamey's frozen leather coat became sculpted with ice. He inhaled ice crystals, or if the sun broke through, his eyes were seared by dazzling snowfields. He made those winter trips along the frozen rivers running on snowshoes with linked teams of dogs that were not far from wolfish ancestry and just as unmanageable. Harnessing a team, the driver waded into the snarling pack and subdued the worst with a club. Pitiless elements cut a young man down to sinew, muscle, bone, and tanned hide.

Summer was just as bad for a horseman charred by the high sun. Jamey Bird was a plainsman before he attained legal maturity, riding without stirrups by clamping his legs around the barrel of a pony that he mounted with a leap. Not as difficult as it might seem, as thirty or forty years later, the horses of the northern plains were still being described as small, ugly-headed mustangs. Riding to live, plainsmen considered them expendable. A rider roped and choked a half-broken animal into submission, locked on, and rode out the storm. Getting about on the northern plains was a painful reality of deadened hams, aching knees, bruised shins, and horse bites. There were times when a rider might doubt that being a horse was the grandest state of man.

Exhilarating experiences included a buffalo run. Racing on a fast runner across meadows rutted with buffalo trails and badger holes. Skirting the dust of a stampeding herd, Jamey reloaded on the run by spitting a ball on top of the powder and thumping the butt against the saddle. He shot down fat cows and rolled the warm carcass on its belly for butchering. The front legs were tucked under as supports so strips of dripping tenderloin and hump ribs could be hacked out. Reaching elbow deep into the bloody carcass he drew out the raw liver and claimed a hunter's first bite. Special delicacies like the tongue might be seared over a dry dung fire. That was protein on the hoof, mobile food stocks that insured tribesmen the freedom to roam and be independent.

Jamey's childhood and youth were unusual but not unique. Other sons and daughters of the floating community, the children of lesser officers or workmen, did not find much notice in the house journals or in letters to headquarters. The fur trade had created a subpopulation whose young lives were entangled in what was after all just a business. They were subject to its floods and ebbs.

Before Jamey was sent to school, the Nor'westers crossed to the Pacific slope. When he returned, Uncle Nicholas Montour was across the mountains helping develop the Kutenai and Salish trades. The American beaver trappers who tried to establish a post on the Upper Missouri River were driven off by the Bloods and the Big Bellies. In spring 1812, James Whitway was sent to live with the beaver-hunting Muddy River Indians. He would learn their language while keeping an eye on

Beaver along the Missouri River
Courtesy of Arthur H. Clark & Company.

American activity on the Upper Missouri. At the beginning of December Whitway returned with the first bands coming to trade and reported that raiders who hung around the big river all summer looking to rob or kill those intruders had been disappointed.[18] But the company lacked the manpower or resources to follow up on the opportunity.

After the New Year celebrations of 1815, Jamey Bird set off with a dog train to fetch the hunt of the Southerd Indians. Those were western Cree living among the Piikani who spoke his mother's tongue. When those bands visited the trading houses in the fall or winter, young Jamey practiced speaking to them. As old associates of the Muddy River Indians, they had taught the Piikani the value of taking and trading beaver. During his travels *en derouine* Jamey Bird enjoyed a good relationship with his mother's people whose language he spoke.[19] So the winter traveler returned with 122 marten, a red fox, an otter, three wolverine skins, but only two beaver.

On the nineteenth he and David Johnson were sent to meet Indians who slept nine nights in coming from their winter camps. The forty beaver pelts that he picked up suggests that they were Piikani. Other Muddy River Indians traveled as many as twenty-five nights from winter camps that must have been as far south as the Missouri River.[20] Later in the spring young Bird and his thirteen-year-old brother William traveled overland to the South Branch House to bring news from Mr. Joseph Howse, the only Bay man to have traded on the Pacific slope.

Outside forces were pressuring the magnificent isolation of the Saskatchewan. Capitalism and its grimy hand-maiden, industrialization, reached across the North Atlantic and British traders were pushed to open new markets for manufactures. Over extended, dangerously short of long term capital, and denied access to economical transport routes from the bay, the bully Nor'westers were fighting to keep their bloated organization afloat.

Safely distant from the consequences, a new board of impatient London investors goaded their overseas managers to increase the competitive stress. A new investor in the Hudson's Bay Company was a Scots laird with illusions of humanity. Thomas Douglas, Lord Selkirk, had picked up on Mad Donald Mackay's old strategy of interdicting the Nor'wester's vital supply mainline. When Selkirk planted a colony at the forks of the Red and Assiniboine rivers, the clouds gathering over the northwest darkened.

War and Trade

The relatively comfortable business of the Saskatchewan turned ugly as the rival trading companies came head to head. After 1804 the Nor'westers had eliminated their main Montreal opposition and turned full attention upon the English rivals. New sources of valuable beaver were at a premium. Edmonton House trader James Bird had always known the potential and strategic importance of the distant Missouri River. But he lacked the manpower to send an outfit and remained a bystander to reports of the wealth of beaver there. What Edmonton or Acton received came from the Piikani who hunted there. There were reports of an American expedition that moved up the Missouri River and crossed the mountains to the Columbia. When the Corps of Discovery returned, Captain Lewis had a fatal encounter with a party of Piikani horse raiders. But as far as the Muddy River tribesmen who came to Edmonton were concerned, the death of one of those horse capturers was just bad luck and they did not seem to hold a grudge.[1]

Casting for a new source of beaver the North West Company crossed the mountains in spring 1807 to open trade with the Kutenai and Salish. But David Thompson ran headlong into American opposition. In November 1807 trader Bird copied into the house journal a circular letter that the Nor'wester sent back to Rocky Mountain House. That apparently official document set out United States regulations for the trade of upper Louisiana and the Pacific slope.² What gave it substance was that another American captain with an even larger party was discouraging British traders from going there. An international presence to the south was something that a concerned father brought to the family fireside. Before he was sent to school Jamey saw his father receive peltry taken when the Blood and Falls Indians attacked other American trappers. If those men were foolish enough to take risks like that, an Edmonton trader was not adverse to trading the beaver they lost.³

Bird's North West Company neighbor, James Hughes, also expressed interest in that part of the world, but with little expectation of success. After the end of the war with the Americans in 1814, Hughes hoped that the United States would be forced back to a boundary at a more southern latitude. If that happened, Nor'westers would be free to exploit the Upper Missouri.⁴

Hughes' optimism convinced Mr. Bird that the HBC had to do something "to get some of those Beaver of the Missouri so long desired." But the London board of management was pressing for more intense efforts in beaver-rich Athabasca while the Earl of Selkirk tried to interdict the Montreal mainline. While his lordship tinkered with that misbegotten agricultural colony, the Saskatchewan fur trade would have to make do.

Those pretensions had taken on a forceful bent in 1812 when the earl and his associates recruited and sent out what amounted to a gang of imported Irish toughs. Those brawlers were fully capable of answering the bully tactics of the Nor'westers in kind.⁵ Competition was escalating toward outright violence.

As they smoked by the family fireside, Bird shared his concerns with his sons. The father might have liked to see those young men read, but his library, twenty-one volumes of *Ancient Universal History* or Akenside's *Pleasures of the Imagination* held little to interest boys of a new world. He pounded home the fact that there was more to life than an interest in hunting, dogs, or horses. Their future lay with the company. ⁶

Father was just fourteen when he signed his contract, and hadn't been home since. To him, the governor and committee in London was an almost Olympian tribunal deciding the fate of those who labored in Rupert's Land. From his station high on the Saskatchewan, Bird had watched factors come to the bay with brilliant expectations, and go home in defeat or disgrace. Blunt Mr. Tomison wasn't properly appreciated, while Mr. Colen and Mr. Auld had been too clever for their britches. Frankly, he didn't have much hope for the latest outsider. As long as Lord Selkirk's highlanders remained planted astride the Nor'westers' supply system, it was unlikely that Governor Robert Semple would be able to resolve the difficulties at the forks of the Red River. Surely, interference with the critical pemmican resources of the NWCo was going to be tested on the Assiniboine River.

Jamey Bird was not around on 22 February 1816 when the Muddy River Indians came in because his father had sent him on a more demanding mission.[7] The Nor'westers had responded to the colony interdiction of the vital pemmican manufactory with their usual bully tactics. During the winter of 1815/16, those on the upper Assiniboine River kept the HBC pemmican post at Qu'Appelle under siege.

They also began propagandizing another volatile element. A resident population of freemen and children of the trade was scattered throughout Rupert's Land.[8] Almost as tribal as their kinsmen, those old *voyageurs* and their mixed-blood children would never be welcome in Canadian homes. Some of those fathers were left over after the merger of two rival Montreal firms in 1804. With Indian wives and mixed-blood children, they had been abandoned with few options for maintaining themselves in the country. Some of the freemen along the lower Assiniboine crossed overland to the Missouri River and became associated with the first American trapping parties. Others stayed along the Saskatchewan or rivers and lakes to the north earning their living, as the Indians did, by trapping enough beaver to subsist their families. Caught between cultures, the Métis were now being told that the imported Selkirk colonists meant to steal their homeland, and their only heritage.[9]

During the winter, wild reports and outrageous declarations arced from the Red and Assiniboine to the floating community of the Saskatchewan. In March 1816, William Shaw, the half-breed son of a NWCo partner, appeared at Fort des Prairies. Calling in mixed-bloods from the upper river or from as far downstream as Cumberland House, he appeared to be raising a Métis war party.

James Bird had little confidence in the greenhorn governor that London sent out to take charge of the campaign to reclaim Rupert's Land. The Edmonton master realized that Robert Semple knew little about the actual situation. Bird tried to bring him up to speed with a long, detailed report. To insure that he remained in contact during the winter to offer advice, the experienced officer sent his eighteen-year-old son to the governor. Jamey would be on hand to carry messages between the colony and the Saskatchewan. Crossing the northwest plains in the winter was nothing new, the NWCo winter express had been doing it for years. This winter the usual risk of bumping into opportunistic Indians was intensified by whatever the opposition was stirring up. It was a measure of Bird's dedication that he was willing to risk his son. Likely, it was the young man who carried the several letters that were exchanged between the two officers during the winter. He may have trailed Shaw from Fort des Prairies to find out what he was up to.

In the spring, another of the earl's hired enforcers was sent up the Assiniboine River to the beleaguered Qu'Appelle post to help bring down the boats. A veteran of the recent war with the United States, Pierre Pamburn was urbane, but inexperienced. Pamburn found "a great number of the men commonly called Brules, Metifs or Half breeds viz the bastard sons of Indian concubines – under command of Cuthbert Grant, Thomas McKay, Roderick McKenzie and Peter Pangman [dit] Bostonais, clerks or interpreters of North West Company, with Alexander McDonell in command of the NWCo post."[10] They had harassed the HBC complement all winter.

In early May 1816 the HBC party of twenty-two men embarked in five boats. Jamey Bird, Patrick MacRoney, and the colonist Donald Mackay rode along the riverbank as out guards, but occasionally lost sight of the flotilla. Three days travel from Qu'Appelle, they came down a branch to the river and found their friends prisoners of forty-nine armed and belligerent Nor'westers. Jamey recognized François Deschamps, Beauchemin, Baptiste Marais, and Guardepee, as well as the NWCo clerks, Cuthbert Grant, Alex Mckay, and Roderick McKenzie. When McKenzie demanded Bird's gun, Jamey threatened to kill anyone who tried. But Grant forced the issue and took the gun by force. Bird was returned to the NWCo house at Qu'Appelle as his prisoner.

With a Cree mother and a half-Cree stepmother, Jamey was as much a son of the country as any of the glowering Nor'westers. Claiming now that they were another kind of tribe, they turned on Bird as the tool of distant London investors. Among the bemused local Indians observing the quarrel was Jamey's friend Sissiquoe the Rattlesnake. He later confided to Jamey that white-headed Alex McDonnell had failed to convince the local Indians to join a war party going down the Assiniboine.[11]

After being held as captives for five days, most of the Bay men promised to refrain from taking arms against the North West Company. After all, they were just the hired men of a business operation, not soldiers in a war. They were released, while the suspect, Bird and Pambrun were held until near the end of the month. When the boats prepared to start downstream again, the obdurate young Jamey was forced to accompany the Métis party to Brandon House. When the opportunity arose, he whispered to a half-breed named Wanpiskashes that they had good horses and could slip away to "their native country" on the Saskatchewan. But the Nor'westers owed Wanpiskaskes for the 100 skins he had traded, and he feared that he might not be paid for them ... or worse.

Becoming aware of what Bird was up to, MacDonnell accused him of debauching the half-breed. Threatening to put the troublemaker in irons, he assigned Alex Mckay to guard him. However, Bird had succeeded in making himself an intolerable nuisance. Next morning, after promising not to take up arms against the Nor'westers, he was turned loose without a gun or a good horse.

On his first day on the prairie, Bird found some Indians who took him to the HBC post at Qu'Appelle on 27 June.[12] A week later Cuthbert Grant, who Jamey described as "a Creole," reappeared with several Canadians. They reported that the situation at the forks had been taken care of. After capturing Brandon House the war party went on to the colony where they slaughtered the English governor and twenty-one settlers. If the housemaster, John Richards McKay, knew what was good for him he would turn over the establishment. Still defiant, Bird thought that McKay submitted too easily because Grant was his brother-in-law.

Meanwhile the Edmonton master James Bird Senior brought a boat brigade from the upper Saskatchewan to Norway House on the north end of Lake Winnipeg. Fleeing colonists soon revealed the full extent of the disaster. The governor was dead, but no other company officer was willing to assume responsibility at this critical moment. James Bird would have to do it.[13]

On 3 August, sons of the country from Edmonton and other downstream places came to acting Governor James Bird and declared that they wished to embody themselves into a military force. Under their own officers they stood ready "to arrest the alarming influence which the Canadian Half-Breeds may now acquire by their achievements at Red River." The preoccupied trader thought they were inferior in number to their enemies, but if others were collected from all parts of the country, they could become a powerful check. When Bird advised them to keep their intentions secret, he had no way of knowing the fate of his son.[14]

In September, when acting Governor Bird reported the tragic events from York Factory he added, "The Half-Breeds, sons of your present and former servants, have already volunteered their services and these, when collected, will form a body sufficiently strong to neutralize that of the same cast which has effected so much for the North West Company. If deprived of the aid of Half-breed allies the Canadians will no longer be formidable."[15] Four days later the involuntary inheritor of the government of Rupert's Land left for the interior with an army of several officers and just twenty men in two boats.

The English response came from an unexpected direction. According to the latest news from Swan River, "... Lord Selkirk [had] seized Fort William 20 August last." Four days after passing Norway house the relieved father wrote, "16 October, About 12 AM I met my son, James, who was detained last May a prisoner by Mr. Alexander McDonald because it was reported that he had said that if the North West Company made any attack on the Settlement where he was, that he would himself kill three or four of the Canadian Half-Breeds."[16]

In dealing with heavy responsibilities, the father put aside personal concerns. Two days after the freezing of the Saskatchewan on 5 November, Governor Bird dispatched Jamey and three other men to reinforce Carlton House. The Irishman Francis Heron, and William Ballenden undertook a similar mission to Moose Lake.[17]

By December, the half-breeds who participated in the Qu'Appelle piracy and the attack on the colonists were returning to their Edmonton and Carlton homes. Beginning to realize what they had done, and too few to poise a threat, they were quiet.[18] On the thirteenth, acting Governor Bird sent Heron to feel out the NWCo Nipiwi master John George McTavish. When Heron returned with an invitation to meet and iron out differences, Jamey carried his father's steadfast refusal to negotiate with outlaws. However, Bird expressed hope for the renewal of the friendly relationship that previously existed. With so many blood debts crying for revenge, that was unlikely. The Canadian Batouche, who traded in opposition to George Bird, had lost a son killed at Red River. However, the grieving father blamed the Nor'westers, Hughes, and Haldaine, for involving the boy.[19]

Near the end of the year, the Carlton House master John Peter Pruden sent Jamey and two men to trade with the Indians. Bird met a Lac la Ronge chief on the plains who told him how the Nor'westers had called them to their house last fall. Mr. Frobisher, who they knew as Yellow Head, proposed that they take up arms against the HBC. The prairie travelers also met some "Musceggos" and cemented relationships by resolving a quarrel over two dogs that the NWCo clerk, McLean, had taken from them by force. After nineteen days the Bay men returned to Carlton House on the 15 January 1817.[20]

Ten days later James brought in thirty tents of Southerd Indians who'd stopped well short of Carlton until they saw how the wind was blowing. They reported that a Canadian on the South Branch promised that when the snow was gone Hughes and McLeod would kill the baymen and take possession of Carlton House. When Jamey told his father that the HBC was to be totally excluded from the river, Governor Bird sniffed, "Such are the threats of scoundrels."[21]

On 4 June, Governor Bird, thirteen officers, and sixty-four men in ten boats and two canoes left for Norway House. They arrived on the twenty-first and within a week Jamey, John McLeod, and eight men were driving a large canoe south. Lord Selkirk had arrived at the forks with an army. Jamey was present when the confused hand of British justice tried to muffle the short-lived Métis spasm.[22]

No matter their loyalties, the mixed-blood sons of the country were learning that corporate interests prevailed. Innocent people were being used for selfish purposes. At Qu'Appelle where the Nor'westers singled out Hudson's Bay Company half-breeds for abuse, Jamey's uncle, Bonhomme Montour, was one of the troublemakers. Whatever the larger implications, for James Bird Jr the struggle at the forks was very much a family affair. Kinsmen and countrymen were pitted against each other for the ultimate benefit of strangers. Jamey had passed his childhood and youth in a conglomerate community generally at ease with itself. The tensions that disturbed the shared compound of Edmonton House/Fort Augustus were competitive. When rivalry overreached human decency, he became conscious of his own ambiguous heritage. Bird returned to a clerk's duties with new questions about the standing of sons of the country in relation to the new institutions. That answer came sooner than he expected.

Because Governor Bird was called downstream to a larger responsibility, the young Irish tough, Francis Heron, was put in charge of the Edmonton District for outfit 1817/18. A year later Jamey was also back on the upper river traveling to Big Fish Lake to allow debts to the Thickwoods Cree. After returning to Edmonton on 10 November, three days later he and William Leaske left again to tent with the Indians over the winter. That insured that Heron's fair-trading arrangement with Nor'wester James Hughes was observed.[23] Bird returned at the end of January 1819 with fifty made beaver.

By the first week of May when the new grass was up on the prairies, Bird and several companions left Edmonton. They were driving fifty-five company horses and forty animals belonging to private individuals. They intended to cross the plains to the Red River settlement where livestock was desperately needed. Given the usual Indian interest in horses, that could have been a risky undertaking. As it was the 6 August before the drovers returned to Edmonton, Jamey spent some time in the colony with his father.

For pulling company operations together after Semple's death, London rewarded James Bird's dedication. He was replaced with another greenhorn governor. In the determination to match the Nor'westers step for step, blow for blow, the company sent out amateurs who had to rely on the experience of old hands. Uprooted from the supervision of the Saskatchewan the elder Bird had been pushed into exhausting responsibilities. Now the displaced patriarch warned his son that there would be more upheavals. If a pending merger of interests went through there would be discharges. But Jamey had an alternative. Through his father's intervention with Lord Selkirk, he had been granted a tract of land in the Red River colony near those of his father and old friends. But until matters were resolved, the sensible thing to do was to wait and see how the terms worked out. Jamey returned to the Saskatchewan aware that he could no longer rely on his father's influence. His account on the company's books was not enough to support retirement to the forks at an early age. How would he live? Surely not behind a plow.

As the upper Saskatchewan became more crowded, unproductive hangers-on around the posts were unwelcome. The company had maintained control of the population by strictly adhering to its contracts with imported European or Canadian laborers. Hudson's Bay Company servants were returned home at the expiration of their agreements while the less responsible Canadian partnerships simply set men free in the country. With Indian wives and mixed-blood children to look after, most of those freemen lived with their tribal kinsmen, hunted beaver, and traded for necessaries with their former employers. They were considered more reliable producers of peltry than Indians so traders trusted them with outfits on credit. As returns never quite equaled advances, the reality was that they had exchanged employment for debt bondage.[24]

By 23 September Jamey rode into Carlton House and connected with Heron who was bringing the new outfit to Edmonton. Two months later, Bird and young James McKay were sent to tent with the Red Deer Lake Indians. After coming in to celebrate the New Year, Jamey took George Ward back with him.

Next spring Bird delivered the alarming news that young Blackfeet had killed the black freeman, Joseph Lewis. Although a concerned chief advised Bird to return to the fort, he went back to Red Deer Lake in July. During the next trading season he built and operated an outpost at the White Mud River.[25] After picking up the White Mud outfit in mid-January 1821, he returned to Edmonton next month.

Carried as an Indian interpreter, but actually handling the operation of an outpost, James Bird Jr was nearing the end of his second five-year contract. His responsibility included receiving, distributing, and accounting for the outfit while keeping his Indian customers happy through the discreet combination of firmness, fairness, and sly indulgence. Approaching majority under English law, Bird was already a finished northwest trader. In an English organization short on experienced clerks, he was an asset. But there was no shortage of ambitious young Nor'wester clerks on the upper river.

The exhausted competitors gave up the contest in 1821. Spokesmen meeting in London agreed to merge interests into a new organization. While retaining the name of the Hudson's Bay Company the deed poll required the new organization to make places for most of the North West Company partners. The future of two compliments of workmen was another matter. Two days after Jamey set off with two Indians to trap beaver in the Rocky Mountains, his brother George and Hugh Munroe arrived with the news that the rival trading operations had been combined. The date was 6 April 1821.

The combined manpower on the upper Saskatchewan added up to forty-three English and seventeen Canadians at Edmonton House, eleven English and twenty-seven Canadians at Rocky Mountain House/Acton, four and twenty-one at Dog Rump, three and five at the Pembina River; 131 in all. Until the terms of the new agreement were made known, everyone lived in simmering apprehension. After twelve years serving the company Jamey was on the lowest rung of the new corporate ladder.

Although the Edmonton master, Francis Heron, was an insufferable egocentric, there is nothing in the house journals to suggest that Jamey failed to get along with his father's successor. Until August William Flett and the Blackfoot interpreter, Charles McKay, had summer charge of Acton House. When the old place was merged with Rocky Mountain House, Chief Trader John Rowand gave the charge to the experienced half-breed Nicholas Montour. But worried where he stood in the new concern, the writer Anthony Feisel slipped a critical opinion into the Edmonton journal.

As the new hierarchy formalized on two levels, chief factors and chief traders, Richard Grant replaced Heron until the new chief factor, Colin Robertson, took over. Inevitable staff reductions fell heavily on sons of the country. Sixteen mixed-blood clerks were on the rolls in 1821. Three years later there were only five. In consolidating his new authority, the deputy governor of the Northern Department stifled Chief Factor Bird's attempt to be their champion. The ambitious young clerks who survived would be beholding to George Simpson in the future. The governor also favored the country sons of the Nor'westers, whom he saw as more vigorous than baymen and who had demonstrated a certain lack of scruple.

On 18 October 1821 Grant noted the return of James Bird and James Spence, who may not have been entirely surprised to learn that they were now *freemen*. Saskatchewan Fur Trade servants' accounts show Jamey was in debt for goods worth £5/19/11 supplied to him during the winter 1821/22.[26] At the Red River settlement his father seemed to be settling into the role of an imitation English country squire as old fur traders and retired servants began recreating old Britain out of hides, tallow, and buffalo wool. James Bird Jr didn't want to be part of that. As long as he could fork a pony or follow a dog, Jamey wasn't ready to come in from the cold.

The Blackfoot Barrier

British traders knew the beaver-producing western Cree as Southerd Indians. Since the time before horses some of them had lived amiably with the Piikani and acting as middlemen traders, contributing to the arming of their friends against the encroaching Snakes.[1] As the Gens du Large pushed the Snakes south, there was room left in their wake for other woodland-hunting Cree to experiment in plainsmanship. Finding plentiful buffalo and a dashing life *ahorse*, they metamorphosed under the great arch of the sky into the Plains Cree.[2] Once they had gotten by on charm and retraded goods, but now Cree had to fight for a place among former friends. When retribution loomed, they still fled to the woods.

Recalling when Cree middlemen controlled the trade from the bay, they persisted in calling other Gens du Large "Slaves." That was not a healthy attitude, as the armed Piikani had driven the mounted Snakes back across the Missouri River. As the largest of the three divisions later generalized as Blackfeet, Piikani now dominated the northern tributaries of that river as well as southern branches of the Saskatchewan. Although beaver abounded, their Siksika, Kainaa, and Atsiina neighbors preferred to run buffalo. Those plains-ranging bands disdained stepping down from their ponies to dig rodents out of their dens. If they needed beaver pelts to trade, they took them from others.

Most travelers going south remarked on the lone pine that marked the edge of the parklands and the opening of the northwestern plains. David Thompson made the landmark mythic in his *Narrative* with the story of the distressed father who visited his horror on the tree after his entire family was laid low by smallpox.

Jamey Bird's initial experience among the tribes was among the Cree beaver hunters whose language he spoke. His reception was influenced by mutual interests in the trade. He was still very much a man of his mother's people who now ranged as far south as the Red Deer River. He had known Piikani trading parties that came to the Saskatchewan houses, but most of them preferred to conduct business at Rocky Mountain House.[3] That was a long, trying trip from their usual winter camps along the Bow River or further south on Missouri headwaters, and the Muddy River Indians continued to ask for a more convenient store.

In the flush of the new monopoly, the new lieutenant-governor of the Northern Department saw an opportunity to answer that need. But sending a large expedition up the South Branch as far as the mouth of Bow River to establish a post had an ulterior motive. To increase beaver production, the Bow River expedition would make another attempt at direct trapping and exploit the fabled beaver reserves of the Upper Missouri drainage.

The efficient method of direct trapping that George Simpson meant to introduce had proved successful west of the mountains where tribes had never been conditioned to the old methods of business. Mr. Simpson's plan also ignored the traditional symbiosis of a passive trade.[4] Indians were supposed to do the beaver hunting. That tradition was already degraded by freemen whose tribal relatives were willing to tolerate the intrusion. The green governor also overlooked, or ignored, something older hands remembered vividly. Just before the turn of the century, the Gens du Large had already rejected the concept of direct trapping when Atsiina slaughtered a party of fourteen Iroquois steel trappers.

Beyond that lay a potential violation of the international border. It was four years since the boundary compromise of 1818 set the forty-ninth parallel of latitude as the dividing line between British possessions and United States territory. The attractive beaver resources of the Missouri River were clearly forbidden to British traders.[5]

After being discussed for the past year, plans for an expedition were underway by July 1822. A strongly reinforced brigade was sent up the South Branch with a large assortment of trade goods and supplies. By November they were settling into winter quarters at the mouth of the Bow River on the South Saskatchewan when

Sarcee visitors reported that Peigans had been in contact with Americans who "gave them to understand they intended to Establish a Post at the Bear Paw River [Marias River] above the Belly River where they intend to trade largely and supply the natives at a much lower rate than the European traders."[6] That sounded like the proposals that American leaders had been making for the past sixteen years. Blackfoot hostility had always driven them away. The brigade leaders rationalized that the HBC expedition had mooted that threat.

Because he spent the summer tenting with the Cree, the freeman Jamey Bird escaped participating in the Bow River experiment. He and James Spence returned to Edmonton in October, obtained an outfit, and went off again to hunt and winter around the Eagles Nest plain. After the turn of the year, they moved to the Sturgeon River and Sandy Lake but found poor living on jackfish and carp.

In late February 1823, Governor Simpson arrived at Edmonton expecting to total the success of his first major accomplishment. But initial reports from the Bow confirmed that he had made an expensive blunder. Facing the cold discouragement of thousands of Blackfeet, the expedition piled up a loss that finally totaled £10,000. Although at one time there might have been as many as 6,000 Indians in 1,200 tents, only about 1,100 beaver pelts were traded. Nor was it lost on the disappointed governor that almost half of those came from Peigans who usually brought their returns to existing posts. The expedition managed to get away safely by telling the Indians that a party would come from the Mountain House to build a store among the Atsiina.

Economy was Simpson's response. He traveled to Rocky Mountain House and discharged the former NWCo clerk Nicholas Montour and other old hands. They would have to learn to live as freemen hunters. Closing Acton/Rocky Mountain House left the Muddy River Indians without a store. To trade they had to make a long ride to Edmonton.[7] Dependable old customers like the beaver-hunting Cree and Piikani faced a trying fifteen to twenty-five day winter trip through opportunistic Blackfeet and Bloods always eager to collect a passage toll. Those best beaver hunters had to do it to obtain the ammunition they needed to defend themselves from enemies.

Back at Edmonton on 11 April the governor informed the family men of the floating community that a few would be reassigned to less desirable postings, but many of them no longer had jobs. Next year the ruthless governor could boast that the former compliment of 171 officers and men had been reduced to a lean fifty-three actually on the payroll.[8]

When Bird, Spence, and Turcote returned from Sandy Lake two weeks later, the Orkneyman gave up trying to survive as a freeman. Spence arranged to go down to the colony with the former Acton House master, William Flett. Their families were carried downstream in the boats while Jamey Bird and William Leaske drove their horses overland to the forks. Bird must have reported the Bow disaster to his father. They agreed that beating down the Gens du Large was no way to conduct business.

The amiable relationship with the Muddy River and Southerd Indians began when James Gaddy wintered with them in 1785/86. David Thompson visited the winter camps two years later and Peter Fidler left a detailed journal of his experiences in 1793/94.[9] In 1812, Mr. Bird sent young James Whitway to live with the Piikani, learn their language, and encourage them to hunt beaver. Whitway stayed with the Indians through their summer buffalo hunt and fall beaver sweep.[10] By spring 1823, after the retreat of the Bow River expedition, the responsibility of convincing the Piikani to keep coming to the company shifted to Hugh Munroe.

Munroe came to the upper Saskatchewan eight years ago. He was from distant Montreal where one of his kinsman enjoyed the monopoly on the Assumption sashes that Nor'wester voyageurs wore.[11] Munroe's maternal uncles, the Larocque brothers, had been stalwarts of the North West Company, but Hugh had attracted the attention of HBC's Montreal recruiters.[12] In the 1815/16 list of a hundred and one Saskatchewan officers and servants, Mr. Bird listed him as a young apprentice at a salary of £8 per annum, number seventy, and hoped that he "may become of some value."[13]

Nothing in the house journals or correspondence book that Francis Heron kept from 1816 to 1821 supports Munroe's claim that he was sent to live with the Indians at an earlier time. After serving at Acton House or the Summerberry River outpost through 1819 Munroe was listed in the Edmonton summer compliment for 1820.[14] In November, he came from the unfortunately named Dog Rump with Patrick Small. Starting downstream with the spring boat brigade Munroe was sent back "to live with [the Piikani] and learn their language."[15] After spending the summer 1823 on the Missouri, Hugh returned to Edmonton by 25 November accompanied by thirty-two Indians. They made fifteen camps on the way to Edmonton, but the last nine days of their journey were particularly difficult because jealous Bloods had burned the prairies.

One of Hugh's companions was a Piikani war leader named *Mehkskehme-Sukahs* [Iron Shirt] who had an interesting yarn to relate. Last spring his party was going to war on the Snakes when they bumped into thirty tents of American trappers working well up the Jefferson Fork of the Missouri. During an amiable meeting credentials were exchanged and recommendations given. However, Iron Shirt's party gave up their adventure and returned home to report this new development.

The Americans also saw the light and skedaddled back toward the Yellowstone. News of the encounter activated Bloods who raced to intercept the retreating

Missouri Fur Company on the Yellowstone. According to Iron Shirt, the Bloods killed thirteen trappers and took fifty horses and twenty-eight mules loaded with beaver pelts. By October part of that loot had already been hauled north and traded at Edmonton. Bloods brought in more the following March.[16] Equally vigilant Blackfeet shadowing another party ascending the Missouri River killed four trappers on Smith River.[17] Those vicious developments gave credence to the impressions of the Bow River expedition. The Piikani country was just too dangerous. It took an old western hand operating from the rival Spokane District to prove them wrong.

Nor'westers had imposed direct trapping on the Pacific slope for the past seven years. Those hunting brigades were made up of debt-obligated freemen in parties that were large enough to discourage Indian adventures. Under the terms of the joint occupation compromise of 1818, they were a low cost way of increasing beaver production.

After being set free in the 1822 downsizing, ten former Saskatchewan servants crossed the mountains and appeared at Spokane House. They were in time to link up with the Snake brigade that Mich Bourdon brought from Fort Nez Percés in 1822. Unfortunately, a number of dissidents left his party and Mich had been forced to cache 700 pelts in a hole in the ground before taking the remaining freemen to the Flathead's post.[18] The hunt made later by Mich on the Jefferson Fork of the Upper Missouri was a reason that the unlucky Americans turned back.

After the first of the year Finan McDonald and Mich Bourdon led the Snake brigade that was now reinforced by the men who came over from the Saskatchewan. They hunted as far southeast as "the Croe Indian Cuntre on the rail Spanish river" before turning back.[19] Problems of finding places to make sets prompted the party to separate into smaller bands. Along the most easterly branch of the Salmon River, hostiles killed Bourdon and five men. Leading about forty-five freemen and six engagees across a pass into the Big Hole, Finan lost one of the men who came over from the Saskatchewan. Later a party of Indians was cornered in a bushy ravine. By Finan's reckoning the trappers killed sixty-eight of them. The shock was so great that the Piikani agreed to a peace that allowed the brigade to risk descending the Jefferson Fork. Passing the Three Forks and going as far as the Great Falls of the Missouri, the much-traveled brigade followed the Salish road to the buffalo back to Flathead's Post.[20] Coming down the Jefferson Fork, Finan's hunters were unaware of the fate of the American trappers who had been there in the spring. McDonald scooped up the peltry that the Peigans would have had to carry to Edmonton and left a note with them reporting the loss of his men.

When Finan's letter eventually found its way to Edmonton, it confirmed Munroe's reports that the waters draining from the mountains into the Missouri were "abounding in beaver." In late 1823, traders/trappers wintering with the Peigans included Hugh Munroe, the freeman trapper Primeau, and the Blackfoot interpreter Charles McKay who was to bring in the spring 1824 trade. McKay and Primeau returned to Edmonton on 21 April 1824 to confirm that men from the Columbia District had taken the greater part of the Piikani trade. Worse, to facilitate their access to the conveniently located Flathead Post, the Piikani were working out a peace arrangement with their Salish enemies.

Other freemen were also working along the eastern side of the mountains. They hunted alone or with a partner, always dependent on the indulgence of the Indians. For those risks they were allowed to sell their peltry to the company at the Indian standard of trade. After the failure of the Bow expedition Governor Simpson was still convinced that the best beaver streams were on the American side of the boundary. He tried another tack. The Edmonton House Chief Trader John Rowand would infiltrate obligated freemen. If they ran afoul of Americans, Governor Simpson could always claim that they were beyond his control. However, company accounts show that at least one of them received annual payments for traveling with the Small Robe band of the Peigan.[21]

It was no small thing that the company asked of those trappers. In fall 1822, Rowand reported that the Slave Indians were insisting on being *paid* for the use of their territory and the exploitation of its natural resources. After uncooperative tribes blocked the ambitions of the Bow expedition, the Edmonton journalist mused on the large number of tribal leaders. Every father was the superior head of his family until his sons matured and exerted their own independence. He concluded that "Such people cannot be managed but by people thoroughly acquainted with their nature. A trader must know what advantages may result from a single word rightly timed, from an obliging courage, from a little praise in granting a favor and from softening a refusal with expressions of concern and goodwill, he must ingratiate himself in their favor...."[22] And that was the view of someone safely seated in a secure post. The "confidential servants" he intended to send out had to live with those testy bands.[23]

As more Saskatchewan freemen drifted into the Piikani country, there is no mention of Jamey Bird. Saskatchewan servants' accounts, 1823–28, show that his account ended on 31 May 1823. The balance carried forward to 30 November 1823 was for goods supplied over a year before. About the same time Hugh Monroe was discharged, based on a remark from the previous year; "Does not bear a good character and suspected of being addicted to Liquor and pilfering – will be discharged next season."[24]

Piikani Summer

It may have made no difference to London where beaver pelts came from, but as a corporate entity the Saskatchewan District had to maintain respectable returns. Furs diverted to the Columbia looked like a loss. The *Edmonton Journal* for 1824/25 is missing, but a district report summarizes what took place during that eventful year. The Piikani resented the closing of Rocky Mountain House and continued to petition for a more convenient place to trade. In December 1824 the clerk Henry Fisher was sent to bring them in to trade. He crossed the upper branches of the Battle, Red Deer, and Belly rivers to the Piikani camps on Bears River (the Marias). But camp after camp refused to budge and those who made that long, difficult trip in March 1825 only brought 1,500 to 2,000 beaver.[1] However, four Edmonton freemen were now traveling with the Inuk'sik Piikani. They were Jamey Bird, Hugh Munroe, Morice Piccard, and young Ward.[2]

Before he could perform any marvels of management, Governor Simpson needed to bring the Columbia District into line. In the fall of 1824 he crossed the Rocky Mountains intending to make a dramatic reorganization of the western business. As he passed the Athabaska portage Simpson picked up the Blackfoot interpreter Charles McKay, whose understanding of the Upper Missouri and the Blackfoot language could be useful to a revitalized Snake River trapping brigade.

But the concept of blocking American expansion in the country south of the Columbia River was already mooted. Undeterred by the losses suffered by the Missouri Fur Company, another Yankee party had moved into the killing grounds. After being rebuffed at Smith's River on the Upper Missouri, hunters for the St. Louis-based Ashley-Henry partnership evaded the dangerous Blackfeet by passing through the Crow country. About thirty trappers appeared in the upper Snake country and fanned out across the same area that British trappers had worked unchallenged for eight years. They soon bumped into the Snake brigade.

The western freemen were now being led by Alexander Ross. Although inexperienced in field operations, Ross had been assigned charge at the 1823 meeting of the Northern Council. The duty may have been based on the evaluation of western operations that he had sent in as the appointment intercepted Ross at the Athabasca Portage. The former Astorian and Nor'wester was sent back to Flatheads Post to take the trappers out on a summer hunt.

Leaving Flatheads Post after the first of the year, the brigade worked west along the north side of the Snake valley before turning back toward the unmistakable landmark of the Trois Tetons. Ross failed to grasp that some of his uncooperative trappers were very interested in reconnecting with their fellows who left Mich Bourdon two years before. After some prior exchanges with American trappers, at the end of the summer the dissident freemen returned to the main brigade with seven American mountaineers in tow. Ross immediately reported this unwelcome development before he knew that newcomers meant to attach themselves to the brigade and trailed it back to the Flathead's Post.[3] Whatever followed, the era of the mountain man was beginning.

Simpson and Ross had never met. By 28 October 1824 the governor had the letter from the brigade and expressed strong opinions about the "empty headed man like Ross" and his reports "so full of bombast and marvelous nonsense." Simpson's disgust with Ross had to do with the presumption of the former Astorian in suggesting how to micro-manage field operations. The decision to replace him with Peter Skene Ogden had been made much earlier. The new brigade leader, Peter Skene Ogden, arrived from Spokane just a few hours before Ross returned to Flathead Post on 26 November. In taking the trade at the end of the month, Ross received 4,000 beaver from the Snake freemen, 324 from the Flatheads, and 494 from the Kootenais who were accompanied by ten Peigans. Clearly, production depended on those debt-obligated trappers.

Left at the Flatheads Post, Ross described the 1824/25 Snake River hunting brigade as the most formidable party that has ever set out for the Snakes. He optimistically calculated that they should net 14,100 beaver pelts.[4] The field journals of Peter Skene Ogden and his assistant William Kittson record the misadventures that it encountered.

In his 1824 report to London, the governor did not state his intentions, but he surely wanted to repeat Finan McDonald's success in penetrating the Peigan heartland.[5] There is circumstantial evidence to suggest that Governor Simpson expected Ogden to trap down the Jefferson Fork to the Three Forks of the Missouri. Ogden's daily field notes do not reveal much about the agenda that he was following, but he had the Blackfoot interpreter Charles McKay with him. That changed with the presence of the seven Americans who could observe a border violation. Instead, the brigade worked as far south as the Great Salt Lake.[6]

Ogden took his hunters south into the jointly exploitable, but ever dangerous Snake country. That may have been fortunate as during the winter a force of 200 Peigan warriors, 223 Bloods, and 200 Gros Ventre left the winter camps along the Belly River with the intention of invading the Flathead country. As the outward-bound brigade passed the infamous Hellgate, Ogden had an amiable exchange with some Peigans coming to Flatheads Post to trade. Moving up the Clark's Fork, by the end of January the British trappers were on the Beaverhead River near present Armstead, Montana, where Blackfoot and Bloods horse capturers managed to get away with twenty-six animals. Swinging west Ogden's party recrossed the Continental Divide to the east fork of the Salmon River (the Lemhi). The trappers were fired on in mid-February and on 22 March the assistant brigade leader, William Kittson, had an exciting flight from sixty Blackfeet. On 8 April while working his traps on a tributary of the Snake River, Antoine Benoit was killed. Slipping into trees along the river the killers held a shouted conversation with Kittson. They identified themselves as forty Bloods who were really on their way to attack the Snake Indian camps near the northeast end of the Salt Lake.[7] Benoit was just unlucky.

Although wide-ranging Piikani previously described the Great Salt lake, the Blackfoot interpreter McKay was the first British subject to glimpse that unique feature. Ogden's luck soon ran out when he ran into a brigade of American trappers of the Ashley-Henry partnership who had wintered Willow (Cache) Valley without experiencing Indian trouble. The seven trappers who had been to Flatheads Post rejoined their fellows. The industrial espionage that Jedediah Smith, William Sublette, and five others gleaned at Flatheads Post excited the Ashley-Henry men. In late May a mob of them descended on the British camp. The previously expressed discontent of the Saskatchewan freemen and the price shopping initiative of the

Iroquois who deserted Bourdon came face-to-face with an exploitive Hudson's Bay Company price structure. Almost half of Ogden's freemen were seduced. Dazzled by the attractive prices for beaver that the Americans promised, most of them simply took their packs and left. Their withdrawal cost the Snake brigade twenty-three trappers.

Fearing to lose any more men, Ogden retreated northward, hoping to recover his losses by exploiting the beaver lode of the Upper Missouri. Passing Henry's Fork of the Snake, the British fell in with some Flathead buffalo hunters who were headed for the Big Hole country and tagged along. What they reported about another party of Americans ascending the Yellowstone seemed to confirm previous rumors that the competition intended to establish a post on Maria's River.

Although that was clearly in United States territory Ogden was in a race to sweep up beaver before the door closed.

Seriously reduced in manpower, and disheartened, the Snake brigade ran into the dreaded Blackfeet. Four versions record that electric moment; the Ogden and Kittson field journals, a letter by the interpreter McKay, and what Hugh Munroe recalled years later. Taken together those reconstruct a glimpse of the Inuk'sik Blackfeet and the confidential servants traveling with them.[8]

According to Munroe's recollection, the Inuk'sik band of Piikani accompanied by three fellow travelers had followed up the Beaverhead River and crossed to the Snake Plain. Traveling at night to avoid the hot sun they went as far as the Salt Lake without making hostile contact with the Snakes. By early June they were back at the height of land near Camas Creek in a place that they knew as *Kut-o-yis* (clot of blood). Their travels had yielded about three hundred beaver pelts.

Hearing of white men in the Beaverhead area, Hugh armed himself with a good gun, a double-barrel pistol and a knife and rode ahead on a good horse.

> Suddenly over a hill came a white man riding on a big brown horse and behind him a big Flathead Indian, naked as when he was born, but with bow and arrows. After him rode six more Indians. This white man was a man named Dixon [Kittson]. I had been with him at school in Montreal and recognized him as soon as he came close to me. I was nearly naked and looked like an Indian and he did not know me. He called out in English, "Who are you? It is war or peace?" and he rode on by me.
>
> After him followed these Flathead Indians, charging down on me. Their chief was in the lead. He was naked; a feather was tied to the string about his waist, and he wore a bull's horn war bonnet, one horn of which was painted red, and the other green. He had a bow and arrows, and carried in his hand a

big hatchet which he held up in the air, and as he rode along he was making a prayer. But I did not know whether his prayer was good or bad. I got off my horse and waited, having all my arms ready. I depended most upon my knife. If he made a charge at me I could rip him up. I did not know what to do. I was doubtful. He had yellow hair and a good face. He rode up to me and sprang off his horse, and coming up to me, held out his hand to shake hands with me. I gave him my left hand, for I was holding my pistol and knife in my right. When he took my hand he held it up to heaven and make a prayer. Then all my bad feelings went down. I felt that when my hand was held up to heaven I was safe. He was a Flathead and there were six Indians with him in all, a Nez Percé, a Pend Oreille, a Snake, and others, representing in all seven different tribes. All these six came up and shook my hand, and each held it up to heaven and made a prayer. Then they wanted me to sit down and smoke and make peace. I was a little afraid to do so, but it was all right.[9]

Kittson rode in a wide circle before coming back and dismounting. Recognizing Munroe he exclaimed, "In the name of God, what brings you here?" Munroe explained that his tribesmen were waiting not far off but would not admit any knowledge of the bayman who had been killed three days previously.[10] Hugh led them to the Peigan camp.

Kittson's version is more subdued. "In the afternoon news received of a large Band of Piegans and Blood Indians were coming, Mr. Ogden sent me and McKay to see what they wanted. Soon came up to them and to my great surprise found Mr. Monroe, Picard, and a young man by the name of James Bird, who came to pay a visit. As the natives with them were well inclined to us and the Flatheads I through the orders of Mr. Ogden invited them to our camp."[11]

Hugh later dramatized his lodge yarn for George Bird Grinnell with a prayer to the Father of All, and an appeal to the Chief Rising Head to protect the emissaries. He called on a Gros Ventre named Crow Bull, a Blood chief, and a Blackfoot to "have pity on me and help me." Riding to the Flathead/Snake brigade camp, Munroe steered the main body of those newcomers to a camping place somewhat apart, and saw that guards were stationed to insure that no unfortunate exchanges marred the meeting.

Ogden wrote, "Tuesday 28th ... towards evening about 150 Indians, Peagans and Blood *Indians* arrived accompanied by three Fort des Prairies Freemen, we gave them to Smoke but only allowed the principal men to enter the Camp in Case of Treachery, they expressed a wish of going to the Flat Head Fort this Fall Complaining that the distance to their own Fort was too great & the Stone Indians were at variance with them I traded a few Beaver from them, gave each Chief a piece of tobacco and desired them to return with their beaver from whence they came, & they promised fair."[12]

Munroe claimed a larger role in the trading than would have been possible with men like Ogden, Kittson, or McKay standing by. "Next day I called Peter Ogden and said, 'Put down in a pile all the tobacco and ammunition you have'. They did so putting down a big keg of powder, two big rolls of tobacco and two bags and a half of balls. This was put to one side and the Blackfeet came up. As each man came up he threw down what beaver skins he had, and I measured out the goods, weighing the powder and ball. All night I worked, trading. The white men were well paid for their goods for in the morning there were 240 beaver skins."

Ogden and Kittson reported a trade of 221 skins and the interpreter McKay believed they took in around two hundred.[13] At that time the Spokane standard of trade required ten made beaver for a pound of beads, or two made beaver for a pound of twist tobacco. A common trade gun was worth eighteen made beaver.[14] McKay saw a beaver pelt purchased for six inches of tobacco or fifty grams of beads.[15] Ogden neglected to mention if he sold ammunition, but certainly was taking pelts that would have gone to the Saskatchewan Department. The excuse was week-old rumors that five lodges of American trappers, about thirty men, had been seen descending Henry's Fork.[16]

McKay paid more attention to the three men with the Blackfeet. He knew them at Edmonton. In his letter that found its way to Edmonton with an Indian, the interpreter warned the Carlton House master John Stuart, "these free men that you have wee [with] the Slave Indians they will very likely be against you very soon for the Americans is going to have a Fort at the Bears River in a very short time if not this fall."[17]

Kittson also hinted at distrust in his entry for the twenty-eighth. "Smoking next commenced and ended with day light. Strick watch for the night." Ogden's hospitality disappointed Munroe. "As the Indians traded they got on their horses and rode off, and at last it came to near the end and there were left only myself and a few head men. Then the Ogden party cooked up a lot of food and asked us to help ourselves. They gave me a lot of old clothes. After we had done smoking my old father [Rising Head] jumped up and danced a war dance about me as if I had really counted a coup and defeated this party. They wanted to change my name, but I said 'No, Rising Wolf is my name and Rising Wolf let it remain so long as I walk the plains.' That night I returned to my people."[18]

Ogden also wrote a letter dated 27 June to the HBC gentlemen on the east side:

Blackfoot Indians killing buffalo near the Sweetgrass Hills (circa 1853) by John Mix Stanley. Pacific Railroad Survey. Glenbow Archives NA-1274-14

> ... we have now nearly Three Thousand Beaver, and I have still some hopes of adding another, but really am at a loss where to stir. You need not anticipate another expedition ensuing Year to this Country, for not a freeman will return, and should they, it would be to join the Americans, there is Gentlemen a wide difference in their prices and ours.... I trust you will excuse this scrawl once, if I have not been more particular I trust you will attribute it to my being surrounded by nearly Two hundred Indians and anxiety of mind which I labor under.
>
> P.S. About 40 Piegan Tents appear determined to remain in this quarter, I have done all in my power to send them back, and have been at some expence with them and still hopes of succeeding; while they remain here the Flatheads will do nothing and cause of trouble, their Furs I have refused to trade, but should I see or apprehend any danger of their falling into the American camp I shall secure them.[19]

The letter was given to Picard who finally delivered it to Edmonton House in October.

After the groups parted, Ogden addressed a second letter to the Columbia District, again describing his location as East Fork, Missouri:[20]

> ... we fell on a Peigans Camp who had already trapped two Rivers which had been represented to me as rich, and from the number they had was the case, we also met with 4 of the Saskatchewan Freemen....[21]
>
> The greater part of the Peigans were bent on remaining in this quarter to trade at the Flatheads, but before we parted at some expence I prevailed with the exception of 15 Tents to return back with their Furs to their own Fort, and these fellows who remained I have secured their Furs about 170 Beaver at a most reasonable rate, no good will result from any of them remaining in this quarter.[22]

Ogden added that he planned to go "towards a place called the three Forks of the Missourie said to be rich in Beaver, also the most dangerous on account of Blackfeet indeed I am informed the latter is the cause the Beaver have been allowed to remain in that quarter, if we escape without losing any scalps, all agree in one opinion we will find beaver God grant it!"

In his determination to recoup losses by making an illegal hunt in American territory, Ogden would be risking an international difficulty. Although the gentlemen in London were increasingly sensitive about penetrating United States territory,

Ogden seemed to return to Simpson's initial intentions. But what the Inuksik fellow travelers told the remaining freemen made those trappers apprehensive. In that sense Jamey Bird had some part in deflecting the Snake brigade from trapping the territory of his tribal friends.

After working down from Monida Pass, the Snake brigade turned west into the Big Hole. Taking no chances Ogden meant to send Kittson back to the Flatheads Post with the seventeen packs he had taken.[23] From the wide expanse of the Big Hole the brigade crossed into the Deer Lodge Valley, which Ogden called the Peagan River. Old hands in the brigade knew it as the Arrowstone River, the upper Clark Fork. Piikani trappers were about ten days ahead of the party and had already cleaned out the (Little) Blackfoot River.[24] On 16 August, all of the remaining freemen except seven refused to continue with the brigade and there was nothing Ogden could do to prevent it. On 7 September, as the seriously reduced party turned south through the Big Hole, six trappers and a Flathead chief were ambushed by twenty-seven Kainah and Piikani. Still hoping to link up with a Flathead buffalo hunting party for a try at the Missouri, Ogden pushed eastward. At least the Americans were also suffering. Ogden met Peigans who reported that other raiders had recently arrived at the main camp with fifty-three horses taken from Americans on Bear River.[25]

Back on the headwaters of the Ruby River by the twenty-first, the remaining brigade bumped into two hundred lodges of Bloods, Gros Ventres, and a few Peigans. After a parlay, everyone parted as friends leaving the British to trap Red Rock headwaters before heading west. Finally returning to the Columbia drainage on the twenty-fifth, the brigade worked west along the north side of the Snake Plain.[26]

During the eventful summer 1825, Blackfoot raiding parties had twice visited the Bear Lake and Salt Lake country. In the Green River drainage, Gros Ventres killed a trapper in a night attempt on American horses and later drove off a substantial herd from another American party. But those were just the usual horse capture games, and as long as trappers stayed away from the Three Forks, most adventures were directed against animals rather than men. The panting trapper who barely escaped with his hair didn't see it that way. The campfire yarns of the mountaineers would soon be embroidered with the maxim, "keep a bright eye for the Blackfeet."[27] Whether the fellow travelers with the Piikani participated in those adventures escaped the record.

As Ogden later wrote, "… on the waters of the Missourie as far as I had advanced we were well repaid for our trouble and so far as I can judge from appearances and from report had we gone farther we should have been well repaid, but my cowardly freemen did not dare advance, it was in the vicinity of Maria River a fork of the Missouri from whence we returned."[28] Ogden never understood the geography of the Upper Missouri drainage and he was totally wrong in that description. The misunderstanding is odd as he had the advice of McKay who had been there as well as whatever the three fellow travelers communicated to receptive freemen.

About a thousand beaver traded from freemen went down to the States. The real effect of the meeting with American competitors was more damaging. When Ogden brought the Snake brigade to Fort Nez Percés in late November most of the party were servants and there were few freemen left. Chief Factor John McLoughlin was already reacting to his reports from the mountains. The brigade that he sent into the Klamath country was commanded by that terror of the Peigans, Finan McDonald, seconded by the ever-dangerous Tom McKay. That party was made up of twenty-two relatively temptation-proof, engaged men and only two freemen. The price of doing business in the Snake country had gone up.

Muddy Waters on the Upper Missouri

After the 1824/25 Edmonton Report recognized the 2,400 Peigans attached to the district were the best beaver hunters, Chief Trader John Rowand became concerned that they intended to hunt in American territory.[1] Edmonton Chief Trader John Rowand was concerned because the Piikani planned to hunt in American territory. In March 1825 he sent ten more or less trustworthy freemen when the trading bands returned home. Morice Picard, Hugh Munroe, James Bird, and George Ward were with the Inuk'sik, Jacques Berger and his trapping partner Louis Brunois traveled with the Bloods, while Pierre Berland, Gardipee, Musqua, and Primeau went to other bands. Their example should keep the Piikani producing beaver.

It was not that easy. By midsummer Berland and four half-breeds returned to Edmonton complaining that they had been "tormented night and day," by Peigans and Bloods. Gardipee's opportunism offended his hosts. After delivering 180 beaver the most optimistic thing that Berland could say was that the scattered bands would reassemble sometime in October and come to the old Mountain House.[2] Tracking of Piikani activities during that eventful year suggests that their wandering was not as aimless as Saskatchewan traders thought. The 200 lodges of Piikani and Kainaa that left the

Piikani woman by Karl Bodmer.
Joslyn Art Museum.

Bear River (Maria's River) winter camps moved up the Jefferson Fork hunting beaver with as much dedication as any freemen.

By late June Munroe, Bird, Picard, and Ward were associated with the large camp that met Ogden on the headwaters of Henry's Fork. In the inevitable brushes with Salish the Inuk'sik band usually assumed the role of intermediaries. As forty-five Small Robe lodges intended to go to the Flatheads Post, it appears that the fellow travelers were not all that influential. As Ogden returned across the Big Hole that fall he met a 172 tents of Flatheads headed toward the buffalo country. Their leaders had negotiated some kind of safe conduct with the Bloods. But 200 lodges of Bloods, Gros Ventre, and a few Peigans were still hanging around the Ruby River. The carcasses of 200 slain buffalo suggested that others had already killed their winter meat and headed back to their winter camps.

Because the Peigans were going to the Mountain House, Rowand was obliged to reopen that post. He started from Edmonton with an outfit on 1 October.[3] That was already too late. Picard showed up at Edmonton on the nineteenth reporting that the Peigans found no one there and were following a couple of days travel behind him.[4] Nor did their trade on the twenty-second come up to Picard's prediction of 200 skins. After a less than enthusiastic welcome, the Indians hurried away the next day.

Leaving Patrick Small at Rocky Mountain House, the frustrated Rowand returned to Edmonton to read Ogden's letter and share his feelings with Carlton master John Stuart. In December, Rowand expected the Edmonton trade to total 3,000 beaver, but that included skins taken north of the Saskatchewan.[5] In the past the Muddy River hunters usually brought around 2,000 skins, but would fall far short of that this year. Some of those loses represented the skins that Ogden got last spring or other pelts taken to the Flatheads Post.

When Henry Fisher went to the Bear River winter camps in December he found that "camp after camp refused to come" north. Those who finally relented brought between 1,500 and 2,000 beaver skins to the Mountain House in March.[6] At least that much of the trade of the Muddy River bands was due to the efforts of the "confidential servants."

Sometime during the year, twenty-seven-year-old Jamey Bird married a girl of Tete que Leve's band. A tribally sanctioned marriage demonstrated Bird's commitment to his new friends. According to custom, an older brother confirmed the arrangement that must have taken place at the Belly River after the camps returned from the Beaverhead and Red Rock Country.

Through the winter 1825/26 Munroe and Bird remained with the Indians and in the spring were joined by Jacques Berger and Louis Brunnois. Within a year, Munroe had a serious falling out with their protector, which left Bird as the effective link between the band and the traders. Maintaining the Saskatchewan connection was rewarded by the "gift" of twenty pounds a year; not a fortune, but enough to give him an edge in buying prestige and keep a bride happy.

For an unexplained reason the Indians lingered until the summer was half over before crossing the mountains to hunt. That left them little time to collect furs.[7] Munroe and Bird were still with the Indians when another letter came to the British traders. Jamey knew the author quite intimately. His Uncle Nicholas Montour wrote it near the mouth of the Blackfoot River on 18 April 1826. Montour bragged about the money he had made and expected to make working with the high-paying Americans.[8] Jacques Berger showed up at Edmonton in September to confirm that half the summer had passed before the Piikani crossed the mountains.

A Peigan named *Manecope* (the young man) delivered that torpedo to Edmonton on 7 November. He came north with Munroe who turned in thirty beaver skins at the Mountain House.[9] The band that came to Edmonton was a mixed bag of Gros Ventres, Blackfeet, Bloods, a few Peigans, Sarcees, and even a Kutenai named *Kot-o-kai-yu* (not a bear). According to Hugh's garbled recollection, he traveled with the Small Robes band for three years under the company-financed protection of Tete que Leve. Most of that time was spent across the Missouri River in United States territory, and during a war expedition against the Snakes, Munroe claimed to have seen the Great Salt Lake.[10] That relationship ended this fall.

Upset at finding the price of a gun increased from ten skins to fourteen, Rising Head tried to shoot Hugh as they were leaving. Luckily, the expensive new gun failed to fire, but the furious Indian resorted to his bow. Although his mentor wounded Munroe with an arrow, Hugh knocked him down and escaped. Fearing the quarrel would disrupt an already shaky relationship the Edmonton master loaded two horses with ammunition, tobacco, clothing, and other gifts and sent Hugh after the party. The bribe eased tensions and they smoked together. But Munroe never enjoyed the same relationship with his old sponsor.[11]

It was increasingly apparent that American activities were creating problems. After the Ashley-Henry operation drew away most of the Snake brigade freemen, the first significant returns of the American mountain hunt had been hauled to St. Louis. After squeezing out his partner, William Ashley was already calculating how to get out of an uncomfortably chancy business. The mountaineer Jedediah Smith was sent back with a new outfit, but bogged down along the Platte River trail and failed to resupply the wintering trappers.[12]

Two able clerks wintering in Cache Valley camps were thinking of getting into the skin game. In spring 1826, David E. Jackson and William L. Sublette led some thirty trappers in a sweep down the south side of the Snake Valley as far as the

Brunneau River, crossed to the Boise River and worked back along the north side testing the Salmon River headwaters. They cut behind the reinforced Snake brigade of mostly hired servants that Ogden was leading up the river. After bumping into the American party that Montour was with, Ogden was not willing to risk another encounter with the mountaineers and headed back down the Snake.

Near Henry's Fork of the Snake, Jackson and Sublette met ninety Peigans who had passed the upper Snake Plain at the end of March and carried the letter from Nicholas Montour.[13] By the time the belated Ashley and Smith outfit finally reached the big bend of the Bear River in mid-July 1826, Jackson and Sublette had convinced themselves to risk taking over the operation. Amiable contacts with Piikani had encouraged them.

Two other groups of former freemen were also in circulation. At the 1825 rendezvous, the Iroquois leaders Pierre Tevanitagon and John Gray took small outfits that were clearly intended for trading with Indians. When they returned to the Flathead country those petty traders convinced the Salish to take their peltry to the better-paying Americans.[14] But extending their inroads to the Flatheads cost the Inuk'sik their role as middlemen.

After contracting to take over the mountain business, Jackson and Sublette invaded the Blackfoot heartland. There is no clear indication why the Piikani and other tribesmen tolerated a trapping sweep by the newly-formed partnership. Jackson and Sublette led a trapping party down the Gallatin, across the Three Forks, and back up the Jefferson without incident. Some of their men even went as far north as the mouth of Bear River and traded for several days with bands generalized as Blackfoot.[15] Smith, Jackson, and Sublette counted just under 5,000 beaver pelts; part from the Three Forks hunt and part from trading at Bear River or Henry's Fork.

Jamey Bird was still with the Tete que Leve band and all too aware of his Uncle Nick's success with the Americans. He might have gone to the American depot on Henry's Fork to see for himself. If so, Governor Simpson's plan to exploit beaver sources legally denied to British traders had developed a weak link.

"... nothing but Americans is with every word those fellows utter" was how Rowand heard Munroe's report. In early December 1826, he gave Hugh six horses loaded with trade goods and sent him back to try to keep the Peigans coming to the Mountain House. Munroe was "directed how to act in regard to finding out the truth or falsehood of such stories, which banter much with the feelings whether or no the Americans are established upon lands visited or convenient to the Piegans."[16]

Munroe spent fifty-three days circulating between the winter camps and trying to stir them to make provisions or take beaver. Berger and Brunois were also somewhere in the mountains with their families, sheltering with the Peigans when it was

Mounted warrior with mountain lion skin saddlecloth. Courtesy of Arthur H. Clark & Company.

too cold to trap and undoubtedly thinking about the high Yankjee prices for beaver. By next summer they succumbed and went over to the Americans.

The license that Sublette obtained in St. Louis in 1827 specified that Smith, Jackson, and Sublette could trade at "Horse Prairie, on Clark's river of the Columbia...." Several Iroquois freemen had already exploited connections with the Salish. But favoring the Flatheads created jealousy among the Piikani and within a year the brief harmony that facilitated the Smith, Jackson, and Sublette sweep of fall 1826 was breaking down. Adding to Piikani disenchantment, Jackson led the 1827 spring hunt into the Green River country and only returned as far as the "Camp Defiance" rendezvous at the south end of Bear Lake. That gathering was upset when about a hundred and twenty Blackfeet horse raiders cut off and slaughtered a family of Snakes. When outraged Snakes and Utahs boiled out for revenge, the killers went to ground in a wooded hollow. Sublette and six mountaineers impetuously joined the attack that killed six raiders and wounded others.

Robert Campbell led the Smith, Jackson, and Sublette 1827 fall hunt on the Deer Lodge and Bitterroot rivers. Returning to join the American winter camps in Cache Valley, Campbell's brigade ran into a cold reception from a fortified camp of Blackfeet on the upper Jefferson. In the fight that developed next morning, Flatheads assisted their new friends. Old Pierre Tevanitagon, one of the Iroquois who opened trade with the Flatheads was killed. In the face of another attack, Campbell's trappers decided that it was safer to turn back and winter with the Salish.[17]

Bird and Ward were still traveling with the Inuk'sik when American trappers pushed into the Big Hole. Older contests for buffalo may have had something to do with the breakup of the brief peace between the Salish and the Piikani. Or had jealousy entered when the Salish found an alternative source of supply?

The Snake brigade was also involved in unbalancing the peace. In September 1827 Ogden split off his clerk, Tom McKay, and twelve trappers to hunt along the north side of the Snake Valley. They went into winter camp at the forks of the Salmon and present Lemhi, about as close as they dared without crossing into the Big Hole. Ogden neglected to record what McKay did that winter, but there must have been contacts with freemen or Indians. In later years McKay told long yarns about tricks played on him by the sly Jemmy Jock Bird.[18] In the spring Tom's brigade moved east and rejoined Ogden near the mouth of the Blackfoot River. A few days after the parties were reunited on 8 May 1828, Snakes told them a yarn that still challenges credulity.[19]

That spring the Snake Plain was in uproar as bands quarreled and stole horses from each other. Piikani killed a Flathead chief in the spring. Unidentified ambushers waylaid four Americans leaving the winter camp they had shared with Ogden's

Snake brigade. According to their ingenuous explanation, the Snakes intercepted the killers on Henry's Fork and killed two of them. Half of the American horses were recovered, but the Snakes professed to have cut the packs loose, leaving a small fortune in tradeable beaver to rot on the plain. Unbelievable!

That summer the Indians on the northern plains were also at war, quarreling and stealing horses from each other, neglecting their duties as provision makers. In early August Hugh Munroe and *Parflesh-pasant* came as heralds for a provision-trading band of forty Bloods.[20] They made up for the lack of anything to trade with gossip, repeating that the Peigans had killed a Flathead chief, and four Americans. Given the Blood record, that may have been a lame attempt to fix responsibility for the attack on someone else. The Edmonton journalist could not resist speculating that those killed might have included the disloyal Berger and Brunois.[21] When he found the welcome wanting, Munroe belittled the traders for being cheap. Another principal man, *Stomach-sopetah* of the Buffalo Robes band also stirred up trouble.

Only the Piikani continued hunting beaver. In February 1829, Bird and some Piiknai adherents of Tete que Leve came to the Mountain House in a difficult journey across burned plains.[22] Professing to be starving, Jamey Bird made sure that his companions were properly received. Those forty thirsty "Piedgans" and Falls Indians brought 800 large and 200 small beaver. At the risk of running into hostile Blackfeet, some Cree brought thirty skins. An additional 432 pelts came to Rocky Mountain House with another party. Finally, a gang of forty-eight Peigans delivered 643 skins and the Cree added 166.[23] Those totaled 2,171 made beaver. Worried that Falls Indians might stage a robbery, the Mountain House trader Henry Fisher started a boat to Edmonton loaded with 1,400 skins, large and small.

The Mountain House depended on plains provisions, but Bird reported that the starving Plains Indians were reduced to eating their dogs. To make matters worse, far ranging Crows had killed nine of them and drove away 200 horses. Taking a small trading outfit Bird hurried back promising to take the Piikani across the mountains so they could begin to hunt beaver early in the spring.

That was quite an undertaking for a mere fellow traveler, but Bird was true to his word. Next fall, soon after the Rocky Mountain House outfit arrived on twenty-two loaded horses, the faithful Peigans began to arrive. The initial party of forty was accompanied by four unnamed freemen who said that Bird was herding others along. By 25 October Fisher had 900 beaver and another 242 in early November. Jamey may have stayed in the north as he returned on 7 March 1830 with three Piikani who gave in fox skins, two beaver, and twelve dressed moose hides. About a month after they left, on 11 April Fisher closed the journal that confirmed that our man with the Piikani was producing results.[24]

The Piikani seasonal round moved from customary winter camps on the upper Bow or Marias rivers through summers spent roving and running buffalo. In the five years since he met the Snake brigade, Jamey Bird had lived a double life, oscillating between tribal obligation, self-interest, and service to the HBC. Buffalo were hunted on the east end of the Snake plain and in the Big Hole, but by 1830 they were scarce from the Portneuf River to as far south as the Salt Lake. Disappointed hunters had to settle for tough solitary bulls. As herds decreased, the Salish, Nez Percé, and Pend Oreille hunters had to go farther east. Their incursions upon the Upper Missouri shifted Piikani-Salish relations from horse capture games to a meaner contest for meat. On the upper Yellowstone and Musselshell rivers, Crows were also part of an increasingly dangerous equation.

The northern plains had always known some degree of turmoil as Blackfeet, Bloods, Gros Ventres, Crees, and Stoneys produced little atrocities and major confrontations. In 1824, Beaver Hill Cree and Plain Stone Indians (Assinboine) killed a number of Blackfeet while to the south other Gens du Large fought the River and Mountain Crows. Next October, Blackfeet bragged about a retaliatory raid upon the Beaver Hill Cree that destroyed sixteen tents. Fall 1826 saw a battle with Cree near the South Branch where Blackfeet looted eighty tents. Rumors around Rocky Mountain House in November 1827 held that Stoneys had wiped out fourteen Blackfoot and Peigan lodges. That turned out to be *only* four families of Bloods, but the viciousness was implicit. Next January, trader Rowand noted that hysterical Crees and Slaves fired on a party of Blackfeet and Bloods. Some of those conflicts had to do with controlling the provision trade as protein wars became a deadly part of a plainsman's experience.[25]

Through those tumultuous years, Jamey Bird's association with the Piikani was shifting away from the company to the tribal side of his duality. As mystical and intriguing as the dance of the northern lights, cultural shifts were something that the convention-bound British never managed to explain away. How could it be that one of their own preferred to live with the savages?[26]

In earlier times whites that preferred tribal life were described as "Indian by habit." Although James Bird Jr developed an affinity for the Piikani, his annual appearances at the posts, and the promises he made to the traders, showed ongoing attention to duty. As a self-interested mobile trader, his association with responsible tribal leaders led him to a larger sense of duty, of community, of love. That went along with being a dedicated husband and a father.

The ten-year-old shock of downsizing spoiled Bird's mountain idyll. After the 1821 merger and layoffs several disappointed British clerks went to St. Louis where they found an obliging American front man. Returning to the skin game as the Columbia Fur Company, Kenneth McKenzie, William Laidlaw, and James Kipp opened business at the Mandan villages on the Missouri. They intended to exploit the Assiniboine trade from south of the line and became so successful that the American Fur Company was obliged to buy them out.

That deal made Kenneth McKenzie field superintendent of the Upper Missouri Outfit with his headquarters at the mouth of the Yellowstone River. Before long he was attracting mountaineers who were dissatisfied with the prices that the Smith, Jackson, and Sublette monopoly charged at the annual rendezvous. One of the first to come to Fort Union was the former Saskatchewan freeman, Jacques Berger. His profession of influence among the Peigans convinced McKenzie to risk advancing a small outfit and four men to help him drag it upriver on the ice.

Berger and his apprehensive companions took forty days to get the sleds up the frozen rivers. At the head of the Badger Creek branch of Marias River they were intercepted by seventeen Piikani from the camp of *Onestenatoue* (he who eats veal). Recognizing Berger, an old warrior named Petty Woman took him under his wing.[27] During the next twenty-two days, Berger circulated the Sun River winter camps, dispensing liquor and making promises about the prices being offered at Fort Union. By the end of March 1831 he convinced ninety-two men and thirty-two women to follow him there.[28]

Our man with the Inuk'sik could not have been entirely unaware of that development. But Jamey Bird was curiously reticent in the letter that he dated "James Bird Jr., Mountain House, 10 March 1831 to John Rowand, Esq., chief factor."

> Received your kind letter and was very thankful of your trouble in writting me those few line. I was sorry of not working Beavor this summer, the enemy was so many for us that we got afraid and rict [risked] only that. There are about Six hundred Horses died in the Spring [1830] – that the poor Indians was carrying on their backs, that it was Impossible for them to cross the Mountains this last Summer but now they have a few Horses again, now this Summer we will try and make up for the last Summer lost. If it is in my power I will try to get the Indians work well this Summer. I think about going to Edmonton House next Fall and If I get the Indians work well I hope you will give the Wages that I had this Summers past, there is Donald McDonald he has Five pounds to pay me for a Horse that I sould him – If I had seen you myself I had plenty to inform. Sir, the Indians are calling for you Sir and would wish to See yourself. I would wish Sir If so good Sir to take the trouble of this Bill, whither

to take the value of my account or the worth of it from York in Cloth or Shirts, Blankets, large. I hope to have plenty of Beavor the next fall.

I remain Sir

Your Humble Servant s/ James Bird Junr.[29]

That letter reached Edmonton on 10 May, just a few days before Berger and the Piikani delegation arrived at Fort Union. Their visit was so enjoyable that the reeling chiefs invited the Upper Missouri Outfit to come to their country. That was all the approval that McKenzie needed. He assigned forty-four men and a fifty-ton keelboat to James Kipp.

Reaching the mouth of the Marias about the beginning of October, the traders found themselves surrounded by five hundred Peigan lodges clamoring to trade. Determined to secure the outfit before opening trade, Kipp told those bands to go away and not return until that work was completed. He wisely induced three unnamed principal tribesmen to remain to discourage annoying stragglers. They also made handy hostages.

That place was still building when Jamey Bird wrote another letter to the Mountain fort.

> Dear Sir Fisher Bears River 31 October 1831
>
> I take the pleasure of writting you these lines to let you that I am well. I am gone to join the American Company. Its what I wished for this long time to have revenge on the Hudsons Bay Company, which I will have, you thought Money was too good for me and goods. And for your being so bad [to my] woman and Children you was afraid to give them any thing Good to eat, and myself You cant say that I was in debt to you, for three Years Wages I got no pay, and for my Horses that I sold and take care of yourself that you dont come two my on this business and take care.

The remainder of the letter, including the signature of the writer, seems to have been torn off, perhaps in the anger of an outraged reader. But on the back Jamey had added, "My compliments to Donald McDonald, Give my horses to the horne."[30]

A Taste of Corporate Comeuppance

Jamey wasted no time in appropriating the marginal man's prerogative to act as power broker. Many chiefs had their say in council so it is too much to suggest that Bird single-handedly turned the Peigan trade over to the Upper Missouri Outfit of the American Fur Company. But the fellow traveler was a forceful speaker in those councils, condemning the company for thirty years of neglect, blaming other Americans for price increases, and praising the liquid generosity of the Fort Union trader. Having a store in their backyard was something they had been begging for since they began trading. If that upset the Bloods, let them step down from their ponies and dig for beaver.

In December, Kipp finally started the bung on a keg of pure alcohol that he diluted into two hundred gallons of "Blackfoot whiskey." The prices he paid were in some cases three or four hundred percent above those usually given by the British. Over three days the reeling Piikani turned in 6,450 pounds of beaver.[1] In exchange they received 160 guns and ammunition aplenty that was bad news for the western tribes. By February 1832, armed parties were already in the mountains, confronting the Snake brigade on the Beaverhead and vowing to extinguish the Flatheads.

When a Peigan warned Kipp that the dangerous Kainaa were coming in force, he stocked up on firewood and ice (to melt for water) and prepared the Upper Missouri Outfit for a siege. After an eleven-day standoff, Kipp blew up a snaggy tree to demonstrate the power of his cannon. Two Bloods who were tricked into coming in attributed their unfriendly behaviour to the instigation of British traders. That gave the Americans an excuse to dismiss the unpleasantries.

The 1831/32 Mountain House journal is missing. Too bad, as it might have revealed something about the exchanges that Henry Fisher had with the Bloods when they went north to their winter camps. A new day had dawned for the Gens du Large when they told him that the Americans gave sixty balls and powder *for a buffalo robe*.[2] The herds had become a commodity.

The standoff was resolved by Kipp's agreement to accept 3,000 buffalo robes.[3] During the Bow River expedition, the company had recognized that robes could be a tool to placate the plains tribes. The success of Fort Union was founded on a trade in Assiniboine- and Crow-prepared robes that found a market in the eastern states. Kipp had the advantage of being able to float a heavy cargo downstream.

The Kainaa converted the infusion of surplus capital into munitions. They hurried to catch up with a Peigan invasion of the Flatheads, brushing aside the Snake brigade that was now conducted by John Work. Other traders and trappers saw the Blackfeet on a path of determined genocide. On 18 May the attack fell on a Salish camp about twenty miles down the east fork of the Salmon River.[4] Determined resistance killed sixteen attackers, but there was little doubt that a new intensity of tribal warfare was impacting the central mountains.

Misguided glory failed to foresee what the initiation of the buffalo robe trade would mean. In placating the Kainaa, the Upper Missouri Outfit began the elimination of the great herds. The key to that inevitability was that the Americans could cheaply float heavy cargoes all the way to St. Louis and New Orleans.

After a tense winter, Kipp could not find anyone willing to stay in the new post. When an express pirogue pulled out, Jamey Bird and nine of his tribesmen were aboard. Picking up the flamboyant architect of the upper river expansion, Kenneth McKenzie, at Fort Union they continued down the river to Fort Tecumseh. That place near present Pierre, South Dakota, had been the re-shipping depot of Upper Missouri River returns. Traveling in the fast dugout the party pulled in to shore on 27 April 1832.

There was more than a touch of the showman in McKenzie, but his reason for bringing Bird and his associates so far down river is unclear. Perhaps it had to do with the anticipated arrival of the American Fur Company principal, Pierre Chouteau Jr. and the United States Indian agent for the Upper Missouri? Agent John F. A. Sanford should be interested in the grandiose, but scurrilous, treaty that

McKenzie had concocted last fall. During an intoxicated St. Andrew's Day celebration, the trader had concluded a peace between the Blackfeet and Assiniboine. The only negative technicality was that there were no Blackfeet present. McKenzie signed on their behalf. Now he delivered nine of them to attest the authenticity and had their half-breed intermediary nicely in his pocket.[5]

The expansion of the Pax American Fur Company may explain why Bird and his friends were taken to the Teton Sioux camp on 1 May. During the month they spent at Fort Tecumseh, Bird and his companions visited the "Sawons" (Soulier Noir or Blackfeet) and met their Chief *Mah-to-een-nah-pa* (the white bear that goes out). The western delegation also smoked with *Wan-ee-ton* of the Susseton band. Those councils were for show as nothing seems to have developed from them.[6]

It is possible that Jamey had encountered McKenzie during the previous visits to the Red River settlement. The Scot had been a young clerk then, not long in the country. What they shared was the humiliation of having been shoved aside by the new corporation. McKenzie had collected on the debt by planting opposition all along the river. That spring he rubbed salt into the wound when the Upper Missouri Outfit hired Bird at the rather munificent salary of $1,200 a year. The contract was probably made while Pierre Chouteau was around to approve it.[7] Entries in the surviving Fort Union Journal did not begin until October, but the post Account Book confirmed the deal on 1 January 1833. The amount paid to Bird was far more than the $200 to $250 that most men of the Upper Missouri Outfit received. It was closer to a bribe than an engagement, but as the beaver obtained from the Peigans was expected to bring $43,000, Bird was worth it.

This was the landmark year on the river when the steamer *Yellowstone* climbed to Fort Tecumseh and for the first time went all the way to Fort Union. The Peigan delegates returned to Fort Union in time to observe Francis Chardon, Baptist Defonde, and the iron-handed former Smith, Jackson and Sublette brigade leader Samuel Tullock preparing an outfit. They meant to establish Fort Cass for the Crow trade.

Bird and his Piikani entourage wasted no time in going back upriver, so the Indians who remained at Fort Union were Bloods. The visiting artist, George Catlin, painted portraits of the notable Bulls Back Fat and the famous warrior Eagle Ribs. Contrary to his reputation, the later had skipped the murderous western campaign against the Salish to monitor a rapidly changing commercial situation.

While sitting for their portraits they clarified Catlin's understanding of tribal divisions with an up-to-date tribal census. There were 500 lodges of the Blackfoot "band" and 450 of Bloods. Five hundred lodges of "Pe-a-gans" combined with 250 of "Small Robes" were still the largest entity. Adding to the total Gens du Large population there were 430 tents of Grosventres des Prairies and 220 lodges of "Circees."

Also worthy of enumeration were 250 tents of Cotounes. Although they spoke a different language and practiced their own customs, the western-dwelling Kutenai hunted, ate, fought, and intermarried with the Blackfeet, "living in a state of confederacy and friendship with them."[8] Catlin was gifted to an outsider's glimpse of an increasingly complex tribal world.

This year matters were moving fast on the upper river. After Kipp left the mouth of the Marias jealous Assiniboine moved in and burned the place. They rightfully feared having potential enemies so conveniently armed and munitioned. News of the vandalism came downstream in time for McKenzie to outfit David Dawson Mitchell with $30,000 in trade goods and materials for rebuilding.

That outfit traveled up the river in tandem with Catlin's returning portrait subjects. But Mitchell's inept boatmen allowed the keelboat to broach, swamp, and sink. The scene of outrage over their lost presents staged by the disappointed Bloods could not be ignored. Leaving the frustrated Indians, Mitchell hurried back to Fort Union and put together another outfit.[9]

Meantime, Henry Fisher's report of Bird's defection shocked Chief Trader John Rowand. That old hand had survived the NWCo and gained an appointment as chief factor in 1821. Despite the disappointment of the Bow River expedition, Rowand enjoyed the confidence of Governor Simpson who appreciated his "fiery disposition and as bold as a Lion." Rowand had a reputation to live up to on 26 May when preparations began on the upper Saskatchewan to counter Bird's influence. The Edmonton trader intended to personally confront the Peigans. He would straighten out those ingrates "who have lately gone to the American Fort established about the mouth of medicine river below the great Falls of the Missouri."[10] When the chief factor left on 5 June he was backed up by George McDougal, Henry Fisher, fourteen well-armed men, and a boy.

According to the second-hand description of the Edmonton journalist, Patrick Small Jr, they went for "the purpose of ascertaining the cause of the Piegans having left off trading with us as usual, and in order to get them back to their old station, from which it is supposed they have been drawn away by the persuasions of James Bird who has deserted the service;"[11] After meeting a band of fifteen Sarcees at the Platte Bone River on 27 June, Rowand continued to the Blackfoot camps that were located in the vicinity of the Sweetgrass Hills. Although that was north of the Missouri, it was in American territory.

Small recorded that Rowand's party:

... saw the Piegans headed by their chiefs and endeavors made to get them back to their old station and it is supposed they will do so – though the

> Americans, whom they met near the sweet grass hills, will on the other hand try to stop them from coming in order to make as much as they can while in that quarter – James Bird, we understand, made an attempt to visit Mr. Rowand at his Camp, but his manner of doing so with arms accompanied by several men and Indians singing, appearing to all present more like a show of contempt than that of respect, caused Mr. Rowand to step out of his tent to ask the reason, but on his being perceived by James Bird, who could not foresee what was to happen, and Knowing that Gentleman had every right to be vexed with his shameful conduct in leaving his employers to join the Americans, made him wheel round his horse to leave his perilous situation as he thought, yet in the act his animal came in contact with a tree, the shock was so severe that Bird was thrown off and received by the fall a cut in the head, however the fright was so great he felt nothing, mounted his horse and left the field with all speed he could muster. During this time Mr. Rowand was surrounded by Indians who were endeavoring to appease his anger and stop him from shooting, which they supposed were his intentions – Every precaution had been taken for the safety of the party, and we are happy to learn that during the whole month nothing of serious consequence had been met with.[12]

Syntax and structure aside, that was only one side of a complex story. In the face of prices he could not hope to match, and that most fragile of mercantile advantages, customer loyalty, Rowand resorted to intimidation.

The news of Bird's defection spread like ripples on a pond. Governor Simpson hated troublemakers with the righteous indignation of a corporate man who could not be comfortable with anyone he couldn't control. Once again, he was in danger of being exposed over border violations and the illegal extraction of commodities. In August the governor mentioned to London that John Work, the latest conductor of the Snake brigade, like Ogden eight years ago, dated his 24 January and 3 February 1832 letters from "Beaverhead, Small fork of the Missouri." Smoothly gliding past a potential embarrassment, Simpson feared that Work had not exercised good judgement in selecting hunting grounds in American territory. Then he shifted the blame upon the western superintendent, Chief Factor John McLoughlin.[13]

In describing the Peigans as the company's best customers, Simpson pointed out that Rocky Mountain House was only maintained for their accommodation:

> ... and in order to stimulate them to industry it has been usual with us of late to send a confidential servant or two with them on their hunting excursions

with such supplies as they are most likely to stand in need of. It has likewise been usual with us to keep in pay among them a half breed son of Mr. Bird who was brought up at the Honble Company's establishments, and was for many years a Clerk in the service, but who relinquished his position some years ago and assumed the habits and character of an Indian, connecting himself with the tribe by marriage/or rather marriages as he has some half score of wives/, and being a perfect Indian in nature and a brave determined blood thirsty fellow, he has acquired some influence among them and now ranks as one of their chiefs.[14]

The confidential servant who Simpson familiarly called Jamie Jock had been getting a present of twenty pounds a year (about one hundred dollars) for his faithful service. Last year Rowand sent him off "with a large, well equipped band to return in the fall, but AMFCo established a post, sent coursers to find him through the Blackfoot country, and he took every Piegan over whom he had influence to visit them, with 3 or 4000 beaver."[15]

Another company servant, only identified as Tourin, also traveled with the Indians. He returned claiming that Bird tried to rob him of his outfit or attempted to seduce him into the American service. While he was in the American camp, Tourin saw several old servants including one named Bercier (Berger) who had been supposed dead. The excessive liberality of the AMFCo had unhinged the minds of those Indians and created a feeling of prejudice against the HBC.

But Governor Simpson was also beginning to realize that it would be costly dispelling those illusions.[16] Over the past nine years Saskatchewan returns had shown reasonable growth. In the last twelve months that suddenly turned into a loss.[17] A lot depended on what Rowand would accomplish, but as late as December Simpson was still worried about his safety, and still in the dark about the dramatic encounter with Bird.[18]

The Upper Missouri Outfit post at the mouth of the Marias was rebuilt a few miles upstream and named Fort McKenzie. Recollections of David Mitchell's management of the Fort McKenzie trade during the winter 1832/33 are sparse. Bad luck with the sunken keelboat had upset the Bloods. It was not exactly a demonstration of confidence that Mitchell lived on the boat until the fort was secure. The hasty replacement of the trading outfit showed how far the traders were willing to go to placate them and the depth of the new company's pocket.

The shift to the robe trade opened the store to anyone who had a hide to sell. When the bands arrived to trade Mitchell timidly limited the customers to fifty-four principal men. But the familiar practice of recognizing trading chiefs no longer applied, and any favoritism might set up deadly jealousies between leading tribesmen. As the former recognition and prestige networks were replaced by self-interest and social dispersal, the value of an influence broker like Bird was mooted. A product of the old beaver trade, he was now drifting into unfamiliar territory.

An experienced trader, James Edward Harriot, was sent to the new post that Chief Factor Rowand established on the Bow River to counteract the Americans. Harriot had been the only clerk of the Bow River expedition to get anywhere near the Missouri. After failing to override the influence of the mixed-blood Henry Fisher, Harriot admitted on 6 January 1833 that, "Mr. Fisher is the only person perfectly acquainted with the Piegans." Between 15 and 20 October Fisher drew in forty tents. But those were "the only Indians who had not visited the American Fort this season." Even that was suspect as they brought a piddling eighty beaver pelts and were still treated most liberally.[19]

A visiting Piikani told Harriot that all the Indians in that quarter had disposed of their beaver to the Americans and were camping with them. But they planned to visit the HBC in the course of the winter. He made that statement despite the fact that five hundred tents of Bloods, Blackfeet, and Sarcees camped in sight of Peigan Post. They refused to pitch away toward the Saskatchewan and their potentially troublesome presence was nothing to encourage the Peigans.[20]

Harriot would have taken comfort had he known that things were not all that rosy for his American opponent. One of the Indians whose portrait was painted at Fort Union by Catlin was the extravagantly costumed Blood, *Petohdekis*, who was also known as Eagle Ribs. While the artist worked he recounted his war record noting the number of men he had killed. At Fort Union *Petohdekis* observed packing of an AMFCo supply train that would meet and reoutfit an AMFCo hunting brigade in the Crow country. In a previous attempt to invade the Three Forks from the Yellowstone River the trappers had lost so many horses that they had to turn back. Before *Petohdekis* left Fort Union, McKenzie may have given him a letter to deliver to the brigade leader, William Henry Vanderburg. The warrior was cautioned to display a white flag when he approached the nervous trappers.

That information surely interested the bands that gathered for the annual sun dance.[21] During that ceremonial Blackfoot elders, perhaps influenced by Jamey Bird, decided to adopt a more conciliatory attitude toward American trappers. Young warriors could concentrate their energies on the Snakes and Flatheads. But the spring invasion of the Flathead country had been a fiasco and that was not an attractive proposition. Beyond the direct losses in the attack, an appalling consequence almost destroyed a relatively innocent party of Gros Ventres. Returning from a visit to the southwest, those wanderers tried to slip past the Pierre's Hole trappers' rendezvous.

Camp of the Atsiina previously victimized at Pierre's Hole in 1832. Courtesy of Arthur H. Clark & Company.

Discovered and cornered, they had been severely mauled by militant trappers. To complete the disaster, the battered survivors were later attacked by the Crows and lost many captives.

After the rendezvous, Vanderburg's AMFCo brigade trailed the rival Rocky Mountain Fur Company through the Big Hole and up the (Little) Blackfoot River. But an even more competitive party of Piikani trappers working ahead cleaned out the beaver ponds. By 14 October, Vanderburg was fumbling around on the Madison Fork when he bumped into *Petohdekis* and a considerable war party. In what was either an accidental encounter, or an adroit ambush, Vanderburg and another trapper were killed.[22] Later, in another fight with the AMFCo brigade, Eagle Ribs had another close encounter of the nearly fatal kind with the leather-tough trapper Jim Bridger.

Petohdekis had some exciting adventures to relate when he arrived at the new Fort McKenzie that winter. He showed Mitchell a brace of pistols that the trader recognized as Vanderburg's. The news of the killing came down the Missouri after the turn of the year and gave Pierre Chouteau Jr cause to reconsider the wisdom of sending trappers into dangerous Indian country. It was only a passing thought.

By November, peacemaker McKenzies' high-handed initiatives were also beginning to backfire. When he went down the river to arrange the striking of medals like those the British gave their loyal Indians, the king of the Missouri found that the bung was being plugged. In the interest of tranquility, the United States had prohibited the importation of liquor into the Indian country. The ingenuous trader's answer was to build a still of his own in the country. Corn grown along the river from the Iowas to the Mandans would be refined into something more profitable.[23]

After thirty-six years of working in a trade centered on beaver pelts, Jamey Bird had delivered the last bonanza to the Americans.[24] On his trip downstream with Kipp and McKenzie he saw the Upper Missouri Outfit accepting buffalo robes all along the river. Their new-fangled steamboat could ship those heavy packs at a profit. There was no way that Hudson's Bay Company boats on the Saskatchewan could compete in that business. The future on the northern plains had passed to the Yankees.

No one could have realized at the time, and it would take years for the reality of that momentous change to sink in. Buffalo were now a commodity. From now on the robe trade would give all the Gens du Large access to wealth and power. But it would be a business directed against their staff of life. How would that fit into the great scheme of Napi the Old Man?[25] But for the moment Bird's beaver trapping Inuk'sik friends still had the leverage to play off competitors against each other.

Mr. Bird was expensive. After 1 January 1833 the Fort Union Account Book noted that his $1,200 salary would end that summer. It was up to the Upper Missouri Outfit traders to exploit the opportunity that he had delivered. What to do with the payoff? There were no banks in the Indian country. During the summer Bird, his Piikani wife Sally, and their children left the Upper Missouri. The family went to the Red River settlement to deposit the cash with his father and put their oldest child in school.

Over the years, the exploits of his errant son and namesake certainly interested former Chief Factor Bird. The aging trader must have enjoyed how his son played rival interests against each other. Although the former chief factor held several important offices in the colony, including collector of customs, he had a habit of going outside the restrictive rules of the company and dealing directly with American suppliers. It was a small way of showing how little he owed to a damned London sugar clerk.

George Simpson, the "little emperor," was surrounded by the usual toadies or those who recognized what they had to do and kowtowed. Not all that many in Rupert's Land liked George Simpson. He was the perfect corporate man before that became an embarrassment. As the tool of a distant, insensitive London management, Simpson had early on shown a lack of appreciation of the floating community of the old fur trade. He broke up their cozy connections on the excuse of efficiency. His brags about astonishing feats of travel that were accomplished by the strong arms of real *voyageurs*. Simpson just rode along. Cute gestures at Scottishness never concealed the narrow soul of an anglicized accountant. No matter, in twelve years Governor George Simpson had made himself the unchallenged suzerain of a commercial empire monopolizing a third of the continent.

Business could not be inhibited by imperialist obligations. Something of Simpson's mind had been revealed in his recent meeting with William A. Aikin, superintendent of the Fond du Lac operations of the American Fur Company. At Fort Garry on 21 March 1833 they agreed to suspend competition eastward from Pembina as far as Lake Superior. The mutual benefit was the elimination of petty traders who plagued both operations. For the payment of £300 a year, the AMFCo agreed to abandon its posts for five years and allow the HBC to exploit a monopoly of the Indian trade.[26]

After fixing prices for the east, Simpson addressed western problems. Too many competitors had frustrated his idea of exploiting the jointly occupied Oregon Country. John Work's recent experience with the Blackfoot invasion indicated that it was time to close down the Snake trapping brigade. From now on, the Columbia Department would have to settle for a share of whatever McLoughlin could extract from the mountaineer's annual rendezvous. Plans were already underway to use the reclaimed Nicholas Montour as a stalking horse for that risky adventure.[27]

A prior attack of apoplexy and lingering illness caused the governor to reschedule the annual meeting of the Council of the Northern Department from Norway House to the Red River. Only Simpson, J. D. Cameron, Alex Christie, and the old Oregon hand James McMillan were present at the meetings held between 1 and 8 June 1833. Paragraph twenty-eight of those minutes addressed the arrangements for the Saskatchewan District where Simpson's favorite lion, Rowand retained the charge with Richard Grant and William Glen Rae as his clerks. J. E. Harriott would continue to operate the new Peigan post. The 500 pieces (packs of trade goods) for the Saskatchewan outfit required ten boats. In addition to peltry the department was expected to produce 600 bags of pemmican. Those orders dated on 7 June contained an interesting addition to the general rule of discouraging the trapping of cub beaver. Traps were not to be issued, "except for sale to Piegan Indians."[28]

After extensive readings in HBC records for his book *Les Métis Canadien*, Marcel Giraud felt qualified to comment on the company view of a new arrangement: "The Metis son of Chief Factor Bird was a case in point. Simpson first engaged him because of his greater influence with the Piegan, with whom he virtually identified himself, and he had commissioned him, with rich presents, a regular salary, and advantageous prices for his furs, to sustain the fidelity of the Indians to the Company."[29]

Everything worked well to begin with. But in 1832 Bird gave in to the offers of the American Fur Company and persuaded the Peigan to frequent the post, Fort Union, which had just been established at the junction of the Missouri and Yellowstone rivers.[30] Some years later he again changed his alliance and undertook to lead them back to the company they had temporarily abandoned.[31] Simpson then entrusted to him the task of entering American territory and, there, carrying on commercial operations on behalf of the Hudson's Bay Company, but without formal mandate, so that it need not officially take any responsibility.[32] Unfortunately, Giraud's analysis was too pat.

Returning to the Red River settlement after seven years in the mountains must have been a cultural shock for the wild Birds. Most of Jamey's older brothers were married and settled on their river lots with growing families. His younger sisters found good husbands among the sons of the fur trade. The patriarch of the family held important offices in the administration of the colony. After trials of flood, fire, and insects, the community seemed solidly established.

But social complacency had been turned on its ear when Governor Simpson brought out a young English wife. He gave the old squaw men to understand that a new propriety prevailed. To emphasize the point that there were so few qualified to socialize with a flower of English gentility, the governor removed his lady and her sniffy pretensions to the newly built Lower Fort Garry. But the transplant wilted.

Mourning the death of their baby, Francis Simpson longed to escape the dreary place. A dark mood also discoloured her husband's evaluation of officers in his character book. Illness had left him weak and sensible of his mortality. At that low point Simpson was finally obliged to deal with the problem of James Bird Jr.

Although Simpson knew Bird through Rowand's negative correspondence, there is no indication that they had previously met. But face-to-face, instead of crushing a traitorous half-breed, George Simpson preferred to cook a new deal. The contract between Governor Simpson and James Bird Jr was signed in June 1833.[33]

Bird was rehired at a clerk's salary of £100 (about $450) per annum. As Jamey Jock and Sally headed back to the Missouri, the Simpsons were being paddled toward civilization.

A Company Man Again

Returning north John Rowand's party encountered thirty-three Kutenai Indians at the traditional meeting place on the Oldman River. The baymen took the opportunity to exchange tired horses for fresh, throwing in tobacco and ammunition to boot. Munitions were fortunate as the Kutenai soon had to fight the Siksika and Kainaa. Seven of the western Indians were killed, but they accounted for eight attackers and wounded another twenty.[1]

Although the situation on the southern marches was far from resolved, Rowand left Fisher and nine men to build a more convenient post for the Peigans on the south branch of the Bow River.[2] As soon as Rowand reached Edmonton he started the bagpipe player Colin Fraser and five men with an outfit to Fisher. The packers found Siksika camped near a prominent peak known as The Nose. Kainaa and Piikani persisted in hanging around the Sweetgrass Hills allowing that there were Assiniboine, Cree, and Crow camps hovering not far away in the Bear Paws. Assiniboine arson had not discouraged the American traders from rebuilding a few miles above the mouth of the Marias River.[3]

Taking over the operation of the Peigan Post from Fisher, John Edward Harriot recognized that "the Indians are in a most dreadful state of malice amongst themselves and that *War* will soon break out throughout the Plains tribes, owing

Piikani camp near Fort McKenzie. Courtesy of Arthur H. Clark & Company.

to the envious mind of their chiefs."⁴ In January 1833, the Blackfoot fellow-traveler Hugh Munroe brought word to Edmonton that the Bloods were coming to trade but were not expected to bring much "unless that of giving us trouble." Putting on a bold face, Rowand saluted them with the cannon and presented handsome gifts. Failure of Piikani to appear at the post built for them could not be entirely attributed to the unusual depth of snow south of the Bow River.

Disappointed in expectations for the Peigan post, Harriot fell back to Mountain House in mid-February, but planned to return to in the spring. The most encouraging news was that James Bird "was now at Breast [Heart] River with another half-breed and wishes much to return to this quarter." But nothing more on that rumor had developed when the boat brigade left Edmonton on 20 May. After what had been a bad year, Rowand took down very few southern beaver.

On the bright, sunny morning of 14 August 1833, Jamey Jock Bird and several Indians looked down from the bluffs overlooking the poorly sited Fort McKenzie. His companion who came with him from the Red River settlement was a Saulteur (Ojibwa) who wore a European coat over a breechcloth and mitasses (leggings). At the end of a long and dangerous ride, the new arrivals did not come in immediately. After noticing the riders silhouetted on the skyline, trader David Dawson Mitchell was in no hurry to greet them.⁵ Mitchell explained to his guest that the man on the bluff was a former employee of the Upper Missouri Outfit who was well acquainted with the Peigan.⁶

Fort McKenzie was entertaining an illustrious traveler. Come so far to study the Blackfeet, the amateur scientist Alexander Phillip Maximilian, Prince zu Wied, was interested in anyone who could facilitate that purpose. To capture their images, the prince had brought along a contracted artist named Karl Bodmer.

When Bird finally rode down to the fort, the prince saw a dark-complexioned half-breed with ringlets of curly hair. After delivering letters from Kenneth McKenzie, the plainsman said that he was no longer in the service of that company and intended to hunt and trap on his own.⁷ Maximilian recognized an Atsina with Bird as *Niatohsa* (the little Frenchman) who had been at the mouth of the Judith River when the keelboat party passed nine days before.⁸

Maximilian should have been pleased to connect with someone who lived with the Indians, spoke their language perfectly, and promised to be a useful source of ethnographic data. But he had already picked up Mitchell's bias. The half-breed was immediately put down as a bad, deceitful, and potentially dangerous man. Maximilian was a former soldier with strong opinions about proper discipline. He concluded that Indians were often silly, childish, and ungrateful. Did he have second thoughts in the cool of evening when Indian men brought girls to barter for whiskey.[9]

At noon the temperature was a pleasant seventy-one degrees. It was not to escape the sun that Bird rode over to the lodge of old *Ninoch-kieiu* (Bear Chief) whose leather tipi had been set up in the shade of trees at a distance from the fort. Considering Bear Chief to be the most respectable Indian leader, Mitchell had set him up in a gaudy new uniform. That recognition amplified a growing tension. Two days previously Bloods "accidently" killed an unlucky *engagé* before running off four horses. The placative Mitchell was willing to pass it off as a regrettable accident, but Bear Chief beat the killer out of the fort with the butt of his gun and threatened to shoot him on sight if he dared return. With drunken Indians staggering around the compound, Mitchell turned off the spout. After being refused whiskey four times, the offended Bear Chief not only threatened to take his people away, but had the brass to demand the return of the beaver already traded.

Next day, shots from across the river announced the arrival of Little Robe's horde (the Inuk'sik). As individuals came to trade, Jamey was pleased to see old friends as well as his wife's kinsmen. That evening the Europeans visited the fifteen to twenty tents pitched around the fort. The honor of an invitation into a Blood lodge soured when they learned that their host had struck one of the traders last year.[10]

Mitchell's habit of overlooking incidents like that led to a tolerance of insults that no self-respecting Indian leader would have endured. The situation escalated on the sixteenth while the trader and his guest were riding in the hills behind the fort. An excited *engagé* galloped up with the news that Bear Chief's nephew had been murdered by the Bloods. When Bear Chief brought this latest outrage to Mitchell, the trader, relying on the advice of a "sensible old Indian," he told him that the killing was a family matter and not a tribal affair.

It was not unusual for a bereaved family to give the body to the traders for burial. The post interpreter Pierre Berger drew the duty of dressing, painting, and ornamenting the remains. The grave was large enough to accommodate the body of a younger brother of the deceased, as well as that of a dead infant said to be Mitchell's child by an Indian woman.[11] As a perverse eulogy, another of Bear Chief's brothers told the weeping relatives that the dead man was gone to the Sand Hills. It was now their duty to kill at least two Bloods to revenge him. After the burial of his relative, Jamey Jock moved his lodge into the grove of trees.

Despite those distractions Bird provided Maximilian with descriptions of the country at the head of Maria's River. That was about 150 miles away, an easy ten-day journey by his estimate. He introduced the handsome *Mikotsotskina* (the Red Horn) who claimed to have killed more white men than even the terrible *Petohpekis*. Riding on a panther skin saddle pad lined with red cloth, the Red Horn was the model for the artist Bodmer's drawing of the perfect Indian horseman.[12]

There were the usual brags about war experiences. In a recent encounter, the White Buffalo had captured a Flathead bow. At the other extreme, Bear Chief's brother had taken an arrow in the shoulder, and another under the jaw that came out below the corner of his mouth. As proof of their honor, those livid scars were not unlike the dueling scars that a former German university scholar might have admired.

Bird's Saulteur companion fascinated Maximilian. To the scientist's way of thinking, the curiously dressed Ojibwa represented an example of a once-noble savage spoiled by contact with Europeans. Although his conglomerate costume spoiled the authenticity of his medicine, he had a corner on the trade in "kutaneh-roots" which were highly prized by the other Indians.[13]

Previous communication with Fort Union must have warned Mitchell that Mr. Bird was returning in the interest of the Hudson's Bay Company. Bird's announcement of a trip to the falls of the Missouri, and farther, was seen as a plot to lead the Indians away. The German wrote, "We may see distinctly, that Bird is stirring up the Indians, he is quite certainly a spy of the Hudson's Bay Company and has been entrusted with the spoiling of the business of the American Fur Company with the Indians. An Indian woman from the fort came yesterday and said that she had been told, that the Indians will ask for the beavers the two-fold price and should this not be given, so they will kill all the whites. Even if such gossip is without foundation, it is indicating the evil frame of mind among the Indians."[14]

Mitchell had already agreed with the ever innovative Berger and an expatriate Kutenai named *Homach-Ksachkum* in a scheme to extend trade across the mountains. The plan provided Mitchell with an excuse to refuse Bird's offer to buy a horse on the grounds that most of the available animals were needed for that expedition. After withdrawing in a pout, the half-breed later sent notes asking for whiskey. That was also refused. Maximilian wrote, "The state of mind of this dangerous man is very bad for the American Fur Company and his influence among the Indians is rather great."

Mitchell tried to offset Bird's influence by seeing his young clerk, Alexander Culbertson, wed (according to the custom of the country) to a Peigan kinswoman of the White Buffalo. As guardian of the family honor the White Buffalo had once shot his own sister for having an affair with a man not her husband. Understandably, the new union took on a certain gravity that cost Culbertson about a hundred dollars in goods for the bridal exchange. The gifts included a rifle and the promise of a horse. The marriage was on the twenty-seventh, about the time that rumors began circu-

The fight at Fort McKenzie 28 August 1833 by Karl Bodmer. Courtesy of Arthur H. Clark & Company.

lating that the Indians intended to double their asking price for beaver.[15] Marital diversions aside, Mitchell's indecision allowed resentments to build up between individuals and expand to include their tribes.

It was something of a relief when the day ended in another clear, warm evening. The moonlight defining the cottonwoods reflected in the placid river. The breeze that developed slipped under the rolled-up lodge covers cooling those glowing leather cones where the Indians drank late into the night. Given their great sense of humor, there must have been ribald comments about what Culbertson and his bride were doing.

Bird woke at the first shot.

Behind the echoes of that startling barrage he heard whoops and terrified shrieks. Guessing that an enemy might be waiting outside, instead of rushing out of the lodge door, he snatched his gun and rolled out between the poles. Bear Chief's camp was in an uproar. As attackers in the bushes fired into the Piikani lodges, more daring warriors darted forward to slash the leather tents and shoot into families cowering in the paralysis of complete surprise. Thirty or so Piikani men tried to cover the women and children streaming toward the fort. Their flight to the fort was marked with the bodies of four slain Piikani women, several children, and many wounded. After a glance at the warriors crowded on the overlooking bluffs, Jamey ran for his life.

Someone in the fort had the presence of mind to open the gates. Rushing past Mitchell and Berger, the Piikani climbed to the roofs of the buildings and joined fort employees who were returning fire and calling for more ammunition. Bird guessed there might be as many as six hundred painted Assiniboine and Crees on the roiling plane.

Leaping in front of the gate with a drawn bow, an attacker shouted at Mitchell and Berger to stand aside so he could get a fair shot. Realizing that the attack was directed against the Piikani, Mitchell tried to get his men to stop shooting. But their blood was up and ten or twelve continued taking shots at tempting targets. That was more than a veteran of the Napoleonic Wars could resist. Loading his fowling piece with ball Maximilian began firing. As they began receiving counter-fire, the attackers pulled back about three hundred paces giving cowering stragglers a chance to slip into the fort.[16]

The courtyard was full of wounded howling in pain, terrified women and children, and twenty stampeding horses. In the cloud of roiling dust, a dog, a horse, and an *engagé* were struck by arrows arching over the palisades. Wounded were slumped against the walls or were dragged about by despairing friends. The handsome young *Natah-Otann* seemed to be dying from severe wounds. Bleeding from a terrible head wound the White Buffalo was singing his death song. In the midst of the confusion, old *Otsequa-Stomik* stoically endured having a ball cut out of his knee. The balsam and linen bandages that Mitchell passed out were not much more effective than the singing, rattling, and display of amulets of Piikani healers.

In an ironic aside, old *Kutenapi* the beaver hunter asked Mitchell for a copy of the treaty that he had signed with the company. He wanted it to protect him from being shot.[17] Missing the sarcasm, Maximilian later recorded that Bear Chief thought Bodmer's portrait had insured his survival.

After the several groups of attackers fell back to the bluffs overlooking the flat, the fort gates were opened and the Piikani sidled out to assess the damage. Shot by the *engagé* Loretto, an Assiniboine had fallen within sixty-eight paces of the pickets, too close to be recovered by his fellows. After the scalp was ripped off, the body was blasted with guns, beaten with clubs and pelted with stones until it was nearly unrecognizable. Maximilian, who hoped to obtain the skull as a specimen, noticed that the women concentrated their fury on the private parts.

Keening Piikani carried their wounded back to the shredded tents in a camp that was now littered with dead dogs and horses. Down by the river, Old *Haisikat* found the body of his grown daughter who had been accidentally shot by the excited *engagé* Deschamp.

While gallopers raced to the main Blackfoot camp about eight miles away, Bear Chief and *Hotokaneheh* turned on Mitchell for failing to help them. They raged that firing the cannon in the bastion would have driven the attackers away. Mitchell was finally goaded into ordering his best hunters and riflemen to saddle and ride to the heights where one hundred and fifty to two hundred Blackfeet reinforcements were exchanging fire with the Assiniboine and Cree. On the rolling hills, groups of three to twenty painted and beautifully bedecked warriors raced around on lathered ponies, whooping and singing war songs. What more could a visiting anthropologist have asked?

By one o'clock the temperature registered eighty-four degrees as Mitchell and his sweat-soaked cavalry returned on wounded horses. The half-Cree Deschamp had redeemed his error by killing or wounding several enemies. Driven as far as Maria's River the attackers managed to hold position in the trees. During the night they slipped away toward the Bear's Paw Mountains and the exhausted Blackfeet lacked the will to pursue.[18]

That night most of the great Blackfoot chiefs stayed in the fort: *Tatsika-Stomik*, *Penukah-Zenin*, *Kutenapi*, and the Siksika leader *Ihkas-Kinne* (the Bent Horn). Leaving in a cold rage, Bird told several of them that they should stop trading with the pusillanimous Americans. He promised they would have tobacco if they went back to their old friends in the north. Maximilian realistically mused that "it would be highly important to the Company to deprive this dangerous, influential Half-breed of the power of injuring them."[19] Undeterred by the recent battle, the expedition to the Kutenai got underway the next day. If Berger had any illusions about repeating his success of bringing in the Peigans, Bloods spoiled them by intercepting the party and killing one of the packers.

Chief Trader Harriot had left Edmonton on 1 August with twenty servants. They rode 210 miles to the head of the Bow River "to await according to instructions, Mr. J. J. Bird Junr and those of the Piegan tribe who have for some time past been trading with our opponents the Americans, which Indians [Bird] while at Red River last spring promised Governor Simpson he would bring to Mr. Harriot at the appointed place. Colin Fraser with Mr. Munroe and four men who were sent in spring to pass the summer with the Piegans were back to this place on 24 July in good time to accompany Mr. Harriot and did so."[20] The camps Fraser traveled with would not hunt beaver. They stayed out on the plain playing with the buffalo, and going back and forth to the American establishment. The war party that crossed the mountains last summer boasted of having killed forty-four Flatheads and two white men. Returning with a great number of horses, they felt too rich to do anything useful. That summer, tensions continued to build as far south as Chief Mountain where Cree killed two unwary Peigans.

Jamie Jock Bird finally came to the Peigan post on 19 September. "Mr. James Bird whom Governor Simpson engaged at Red River in June last for the purpose of bringing the Piegans to trade at this post arrived with four of that tribe. He informs me – beaver killed by Piegans during last summer were traded to the Americans before he reached their camp on 14 August."[21] So it was finally revealed that Bird had visited those camps before he went to Fort McKenzie.

Near Chief Mountain, Bird had overtaken four Piikani who accompanied him to the post and delivered twenty beaver. Their tribesmen still on the Missouri intended to go to the mountains for beaver, but Bird would need an outfit to keep them in line. After that was settled with Harriot, Bird rode away on the twenty-third. He was accompanied by Colin Fraser and three trustworthy baymen to insure his performance.[22]

Riding south, they learned of the attack on Mitchell's expedition to the Kutenai. Bird advised his companions that it was unsafe for them to go on, but he and his Saulteur companion would risk it. If they hadn't heard from him in eight days, they should go back to the post. As it turned out Fraser stretched that to twelve anxious days before returning to Peigan Post.

Bird wrote Harriot from Badger River on 23 October 1833 that the Piikani had no skins to trade and were now calling for a post at the Chief Mountain. "... if the H.B. Company want the Piegans much they will have to build at Chief Mountain the next summer they think its too far to go to the Bow River." Although Piikani feared the Bloods and Cree, the attractions of the American fort were too seductive to resist. "I had all the Indians under way coming to Bow River and the Americans got word and sent presents to the Piegans and stopped their way." With seventy lodges under his influence at present Bird hoped to attract more by telling the "Child" (a Piikani chief) that buffalo were plentiful toward the north.

Bird's firsthand account continued, "Had a long travel of it, about my 20th day I got the Piegans across the Mountains right to the Read's River 40 lodges of them. I got there myself alone. I had the Bungee and a Piegan with one [me] in my travels and a misfortune happen to me. I got both my men killed and the greatest part of the Companies property taken, all the Rum lost I got off safe myself and all the horses of the Company except one cart horse, the little brown horse he was taken." Bird later bought the animal back from a Peigan war party.

> I can't understand how they were killed I know they were killed on the night but how I can't say tho I got off safe We had got in the track of Indian lodges fresh so I started off ahead an hour before the sun set expecting the lodges close and told the two Indians to come on as fast as possible, but however it happened that the lodges were a little farther on than I expected, however I passed the night alone when I saw the night come and no lodges I turned back, by this [time] it was dark I started back thinking to find my 2 men no sign of them that night so I had to pass that night alone myself alone, Snow and rain, only the coat on my back I had a bad night of it so the next morning I went on thro the track of the lodges not knowing of this misfortune of my two men being killed I got to the lodges about 8 o'clock of the morning and I sent my brother back to meet them he came back late in the evening and no sign of the 2 Indians however that night passed on so the next morning I started off myself in search of them there I found one of them with his scalp taken off this was the Piegan and two horses of the Company and the remains of the property, the Bungee I don't know what became of him I believe the rascal killed the Piegan and he got killed after, a war party of Piegans met him with the scalp, and the property that he had taken, he himself killed and his scalp taken and my getting myself in a scrape about killing the Piegan, one story passes on so. I got news again a war party of Piegans killed them by

mistake on the night, thought it was the enemy until the next morning, they knew the Piegans scalp.

That was a bad thing on my side, the rascal. I am sending my two men on to the fort to let you know what's going on in the plains in my part of the country I am sending Jack Yorston to the Fort because I can't make anything out of him, and this Chief along with them, a great man of the kind. I hope Dear Sir you will let me know for the best by this man, very few Beavor, I am dry, I remain, Sir Your humble Servant J. Bird.[23]

In return for the two or three pieces of trade goods that had been advanced to him, Bird only brought back two beaver pelts. Still hopeful, Harriot sent him off again, this time making sure that the confidential agent was accompanied by ten men including Fraser, Munroe, and another half-breed interpreter. They hoped to trade with the Peigans camped at Badger River, or about the Chief Mountain.

The report that Edmonton Chief Rowand penned at the beginning of the year confirmed that Harriot had done all he could to support Bird. Despite the failure, he would be outfitted again next summer. Rowand was so discouraged that he even suggested taking the trade of the Flatheads on the Columbia, as the western Indians had wished ... before the Americans got to them.[24]

Rowand might have taken heart that there were few restrictions on HBC rum.[25] His American opponents were now hampered by a prohibition of the liquor trade. When downstream authorities began confiscating liquor in the holds of the river steamers, Kenneth Mckenzie imported a still to Fort Union. But there were too many observant competitors in the country. In late 1833, both Nathaniel J. Wyeth and Sublette and Campbell reported the distilling operation to the government. McKenzie lamely explained that the still really belonged to the Red River settler, John P. Bourke. He had asked the trader to haul it to a place where he could pick it up. As long as the equipment was just laying around, he might as well see if it worked.

That explanation was too fine for anyone to believe. For what he had done, Mckenzie was ordered out of the country during the next outfit. After an enforced vacation in Europe, he returned to find that the beaver-skin game had turned into the gross buffalo-robe trade. The disposed king of the Missouri decided to retire.[26]

Next year the Astor interests sold the Western Department of the American Fur Company to Ramsay Crooks and Pierre Chouteau Jr. Instead of grinding Sublette and Campbell into dust as McKenzie expected, the new directors agreed to "the partition of Poland." Under that compromise, Sublette and Campbell would be free of opposition in the mountains for a year, so the Rocky Mountain Fur Company could earn enough to clear its debt to them.[27]

Even Governor Simpson was softening. In the annual report he wrote at York Factory in July 1834, he admitted that the Saskatchewan returns were down £2,000 from those of last year. That was due to the proximity of Americans and the tribes being drawn to the banks of the Missouri by higher prices, "which have rendered all the personal influence of their old traders in the Saskatchewan to little avail; and notwithstanding all Jemmy Jock's exertions to bring the Piegans back to us, our trade with that tribe did not exceed 500 B and taking the expenses incurred collecting them into account at a cost exceeding double their value in the London market, with the danger to which lives & property were exposed, in watching this losing trade, by the occupation of Piegan Post, in the midst of the plain was very great, we have therefore determined on abandoning that post and of re-establishing the Rocky Mountain House this season."[28]

When The Old Head brought his Piikani band to the HBC outpost on 5 December, he said that Bird was following with seventy lodges. Hostilities between the Peigans and Crows had forced the Bloods and Blackfeet to leave the south because "they can no longer stand their ground." Fifteen days later Bird confirmed that a fight with Bloods had taken place on Burnt River in which three Peigan camps had been routed. Some of the warriors with him were so apprehensive that they dared not allow themselves the treat of a good drink.[29]

Marginal Man on a Closing Frontier

In the declining years of the mountain beaver hunt, skin gamesmanship became increasingly convoluted. A couple of years after Bird's Uncle Nicholas Montour went over to the Americans, the Columbia Department was obliged to rehire him. Montour and another old hand, François Rivet, traveled with the Salish much as Jemmy Jock did with the Piikani. It is possible that those kinsmen had opportunities to meet on the buffalo ranges.

As competition tightened, the HBC outfitted the clerk Francis Ermatinger to stay close to the buffalo hunters and sent Montour back to his old post among the Kutenai. After surviving the attack on Vanderburg, the sometime trapper Warren Ferris showed up in the Flathead country proposing to front an HBC outfit at the next American rendezvous. Although the Green River country was technically west of the continental divide in jointly occupied territory, the baymen feared the temper of the mountaineers. After making sure that the venture was secured by Montour's life savings held on company books, the Colvile District master bought into the scheme. After Montour showed the way, Tom McKay and John McLean were more confident in taking outfits to the mountain fair.

In order to celebrate New Year's 1835 at Edmonton, Jemmy Jock (as Simpson familiarly identified him) accompanied

Harriot from Rocky Mountain House. If the confidential servant's operators were softened by the warm glow in their bellies, they might have recognized that Bird had done his best.[1] With little hope of seeing any Indians other than war parties, the Mountain House trader had only received 120 beaver since last spring. Alexander Culbertson, the American trader at Fort McKenzie, did better in shipping 1,500 pounds of beaver. And the Upper Missouri Outfit made up the difference by sending down the hides of 9,000 buffalo.

Rowand reported that James Bird passed the previous summer about the plains with the Peigans. Unfortunately six Americans were also with them supplying ammunition, tobacco, &tc. The &tc was disquieting. When Jemmy Jock reappeared at the Mountain House in September, he told Harriot that "the few of our Peagans who had kept Staunch to us ever since the Americans had been upon their lands were waiting at a certain place along the Rocky Mountains in expectation of seeing some of us cast up...." Rowand continued, "... but the Blood Indians being encampt between the Piegan camps and the Fort, Mr. Harriot thought it most advisable to send Mr. Small accompanied by Bird & five men to endeavor to bring them to the Rocky Mountain House, and they did so but none of the Indians who were first dragged to the Americans by Bird made their appearance except two, his brothers-in-law, who took care to pay a visit to the American fort with what they had, so came empty handed to us, Bird is off again with another supply of trading articles to trade whatever he can get."[2]

Rowand did not expect much in the way of returns. Heavy trapping across the mountains had destroyed all of the beaver and Piikani hunters were finding few animals in their traps. With Americans giving the trapping Indians every encouragement, Bird's position was increasingly tenuous. Our man with the Inuik'sik complained that the competition was so generous that the tribesmen were no longer satisfied with "*us, half-breeds.*"[3]

Bird and some of his associates were thinking of going to the Red River settlement when their contracts expired. Other rovers, also talking about retirement, lacked the funds to buy land in the colony. From those depressing observations it might be supposed that Governor Simpson's ten-year-old plan of "denuding" the Snake country in order to keep Americans away had succeeded. By now trappers in the central mountains were complaining that beaver were scarce and many disillusioned mountain men were also thinking of retiring. When they did, it was to the western Oregon country, the same place where discharged company servants were also settling.

The British trade was suffering and the frustrated correspondence of Hudson's Bay Company officers, who had a stake in profits, usually fixed resentment on Bird.

However, there is the recollection of a less biased son of the country giving another view of how the myth around Bird was developing at Edmonton or in the Red River community. Traveling with the York Factory express Andrew D. Pamburn passed Edmonton that spring. Pamburn was the mixed-blood son of the officer captured with Jemmy Jock during the Red River troubles. Raised west of the mountains, he was being sent to the Red River for education. In a later recollection Pamburn wrote,

> On those plains roamed, the most notorious treacherous, cruel and therefore the most dreaded man. His name was James Bird alias Jimmie Joke, was educated in England, and a large finely built man, very fair for a half breed and his beautiful raven hair, hung down in ringlets from his shoulders. He was undoubtedly the finest specimen of a man I ever saw. Disagreeing with the Hudson's Bay Company, left, and joined his Cree relations, then one tribe and another. Those were Cree, Blackfoot, Sioux, and Assiniboine. He boasted families in each. His stay with one tribe depended on his whims, imaginary injuries or a desire to revenge supposed injuries. If Cree, he would join the Blackfeet, if Blackfeet the Sioux, and so on, and whichever tribe he headed was always victorious. I do not know that he did much of the fighting himself, but he planned and the warriors executed.[4]

That yarn was undoubtedly coloured by bits that Pamburn picked up at the settlement where he taught for a while after finishing school. Like most reminiscences, it combined fact and fiction.

The 1836 meeting of the Council of the Northern Department reconfirmed company dependence on James Bird Jr. "Resolved 85. That the engagements of the undermentioned Clerks and Postmasters be renewed for the term of 3 years from the date and salaries affixed to their names respectively, Viz... Henry Fisher from 1st June 1836 at £100 per annum; John J. Bird, Clerk, from 1st June 1836 at £100 per annum."[5] Had the council been aware of Bird's latest exploit, they might have reconsidered. The motto of the Hudson's Bay Company, pro pelle cutem, was sometimes interpreted to mean, a skin for a skin. Somehow that became twisted into a private vendetta of near operatic dimension.

Iroquois experience in the skin games stretched back over two hundred years to the trade in New France. Participation in the American Revolution finally split the League of Six Iroquois nations and many of those traditional beaver hunters relocated in Canada. By the end of the eighteenth century, young Iroquois hunters and their families were being brought into the greater northwest as contracted steel trappers. Perhaps Montreal recruiters hoped that the technicality of their "Indianness" would lessen the violation of the trader/hunter symbiosis.

But western tribes immediately recognized Iroquois as greedy destroyers of their resources, and despised them. That was emphatically driven home in 1802 when Atsiina on the South Branch slaughtered fourteen Iroquois trappers.[6] Iroquois preceded David Thompson across the northern Rockies. Having concocted a phoney permission from the Piikani to allow them to hunt in the mountains, Thompson soon called for more. Hunting families were brought west in 1816 and over the next decade worked out a tenuous accommodation with the resident tribes.

Alexander Ross's biased rants about the Iroquois had some merit. Peter Skene Ogden was appalled when Old Pierre Tevanigon and the troublesome John Grey saw a better opportunity and went over to the Americans. Old Pierre still had property in Canada when the Blackfeet killed him in 1827. His death gave others like Thyery Godin pause to reconsider. From his dealings with Americans, Godin had accumulated enough savings to be able to retire. But Blackfoot raiders picked him off before he could escape the mountains and his son Antoine inherited a blood feud.

In 1832 Antoine Godin was employed by the inept New England entrepreneur Nathaniel J. Wyeth. As their party rode away from the Pierre's Hole rendezvous, they bumped into a band of Gros Ventres returning from the southwest. Those travelers were unaware of the recent battle between the Salish and Blackfeet. When the unsuspecting leader came forward with a white flag, Godin and a Flathead chief rode out to meet him. Antoine immobilized him and the Flathead revenged his slain tribesmen. Their rash act precipitated the infamous battle of Pierre's Hole.[7]

Returning east Wyeth saw the HBC's Frank Ermatinger traveling with the hunting Indians to claim a beaver skin as soon as it was taken. In 1834 Wyeth ordered the construction of a trading post in the bottoms where the Portneuf joins Henry's Fork. That was near a favorite Shoshone winter camp. But a permanent trading post planted right in the middle of the Shoshone and Salish ranges, and Blackfoot beating ground, put residents and raiders in jeopardy. It also drew Salish and Piikani with beaver to trade away from company posts.

Antoine Godin was listed in the Fort Hall account books, but after two years the place was a sagging monument to the iceman's faltering mercantile vision. Wyeth offered to divide the trade with the HBC Columbia Department, leaving the western parts to the company and taking the interior for himself. But that was refused because the Fort Vancouver management still believed that investments founded on ice making would melt with the next untraded outfit.

In late spring 1836 the Portneuf River bottoms were already getting hot when Wyeth's sweltering storekeepers were surprised by the appearance of several Indians across the river. From long distance, they signed for a trader. It was up to the post interpreter Antoine Godin to go out and negotiate. While they were speaking a warrior slipped behind Godin and blew him into eternity. Stepping over the body, Jemmy Jock, the terror of the Snake plains, coolly took the scalp and carved the initials, "N. J. W." in the bloody forehead.[8]

Although it has the smell of a good yarn, the description came from someone who was unlikely to have invented it. The Quaker naturalist John Kirk Townsend came west with Wyeth and was still wandering around the Blue Mountains with an Indian companion and a packhorse to carry his "nick-knackeries" on 1 September when the bayman John McLeod returned from the rendezvous, accompanied by the missionaries Spaulding, Whitman, Gray, and their wives. McLeod repeated the details that he recently heard at Fort Hall. Given that saintly crowd it is unlikely that McLeod enlarged on the truth.

Although Townsend recorded the incident as an act of personal revenge, it dramatically ended the thirty-year-old vendetta between Gros Ventre and the Iroquois. But Bird's motivation is less clear. Usually a traveler with the placative Inuk'sik, he had no incentive to go out of his way to collect an Atsiina blood debt. Although what happened may have been spontaneous, the mutilation suggests something more deliberate, more ... political. Was the gory mutilation meant to scare off Americans?

Fort Hall was an unwelcome inconvenience, but it is unlikely that company officers would have resorted to such extreme intimidation. The comment that Rowand made early next year made seems to deny it. "... he took a band of them [Piegans] to an American Establishment on Snake River and got one of their men killed, it is evident that whatever influence he many have over the Indians to stop the evil, he had not to bring them back to the Company's interest."[9]

The killing at Fort Hall entered the mythology of the mountain hunt as a gross example of random violence. In 1837 The Company simply bought the place. When the New Englander went back to the ice trade, all he had was the satisfaction of leaving a stone rolled into his competitors garden.

After thirty years of unrelenting violence, most of the transmontane Iroquois had been killed off. Others survived by integrating with the Salish. Lately they had taken to sending delegates to St. Louis in search of Catholic missionaries to offset Protestants who threatened to "save" the Flatheads.

Whether it was Protestant broadcloth or Catholic black robes, imported religion was a threat to the Piikani way of life. The religious education of Jemmy Jock had started with whatever Anglican views his father imparted to the family. That must have been formalized during the boy's brief education in the York Factory school. Since then, he had spent more time listening to the drumming and singing in Indian camps than he ever had sitting in a pew.

In spring 1837 Jemmy Jock returned to the Beaverhead Country with the Inuk'sik. At least two hundred lodges were set up in two camps near the famous beaver rock landmark. They were warned that Salish buffalo hunters were approaching through the Big Hole. Five unlucky Piikani horse raiders had been killed and a woman made prisoner. Two Inuk'sik and a curious Kutenai woman set off to ransom her.[10]

The Salish were accompanied by the HBC traveling store. This year Ermatinger had the secular agent of the American Board of Commissioners for Foreign Missions in tow. William Henry Gray hoped to reach the mountaineer's rendezvous in time to join an east-bound party. Although appalled by the dances over the Blackfoot scalps that went on for several days, Gray stiffened his ambition to extend the missionary word. His associates, Marcus Whitman had claimed the Walla Wallas, and Henry Spaulding was with the Nez Percé. Gray hoped to work among the Flatheads, whom the first Methodist mission had bypassed. That not only fulfilled a great missionary opportunity but also blocked potential popish intrusion. Gray was on his way east to raise the funds.

The pragmatic company saw no profit in tribal warfare. In unspoken intercorporate competition between the Saskatchewan and Columbia HBC, the Colvile District now had Nicholas Montour with the Kutenai and Francis Ermatinger trying to keep the Flatheads away from the Americans. Bird, "Our man with the Piegans," was keeping harmony in the great meeting ground of the Big Hole.

The buffalo hunters and traders were camped on the east fork of the Salmon River when the Little Robes band came into camp. Anxious to encourage a permanent peace, the principal men and chiefs were willing to overlook the killing of the horse capturers. After the first delegation laid groundwork, "the half-breed" Jemmy Jock rode over to the Salish camp. While his exchanges with Ermatinger were none of Gray's concern, Bird took the time to expound on tribal relationships. As Gray wrote, Bird explained that "the Black Feet tribe is in five bands, three of which speak the same language, viz., the Squashins [Siksika], Bloods and Pagans. The Fall Indians [Atsiina] are with them a portion of the season. They have a dialect different. The Cercees are a band that unite with them occasionally; their language is different. He thinks we [missionaries] might travel safely with all these bands, and that there ought to be two with the Squashins, two with the Bloods, two with the Pagans, two with the Falls, and one with the Cercees."[11] Obviously, Gray had a lot to sort out before he started saving souls.

The Inuk'sik fellow traveler left early on 10 June to head off others coming from the Beaverhead who might attack the Flatheads. "He says he will do all in his power to stop them from coming to join those already here." Gray had surely heard of Bird's involvement in the killing at Fort Hall last summer when John McLeod brought the news to Fort Vancouver in September. That gory incident was still being retold during Gray's visit in February. What overrode the missionary's abhorrence was the killer's interest in bringing religion to the Blackfeet.

Bird seemed receptive to the idea of introducing Protestant missionaries among the Blackfeet. He suggested that the best approaches to them were from Fort McKenzie or the South Branch. That was a new field of endeavour that New England missionary societies supporting the western call would not ignore.

Going on to the Green River rendezvous Gray continued east in company with another Salish/Iroquois delegation seeking Catholic priests. At Ash Hollow on what was already becoming known as The Oregon Trail, the party was intercepted by Sioux. During a standoff the attackers gave Gray and two other white men the choice of separating from the doomed Iroquois, or dying with them. For saving his own skin, Gray lost the respect of anyone in the mountains. No warrior, or mountain man, would forgive his cowardice, which pretty well doomed Protestant expectations.

Jemmy Jock's first brush with onrushing Christianity was soon followed by what Christians might have called the wrath of God. A deadly little enemy was chuffing up the Missouri River on the AMFCo steamer, *St. Peters*. The trader at Fort Clark noted the death of a local Mandan on 14 July. It was smallpox. In less than two months, eight hundred Mandan, Hidatsa, and Arikara were gone. At Fort Union the desperate trader Edwin T. Denig resorted to the direct inoculation of live smallpox matter, but his efforts failed to prevent the reduction of one thousand Assiniboine lodges to four hundred, and most of those thinned in number.[12]

The death machine climbed no higher. But keelboats loaded with the outfit had to go on to Fort Mckenzie. After Alexander Harvey saw one of his boatmen, a Blackfoot passenger, and a Mettise fall ill, he stopped at the mouth of Judith River. Harvey was no humanitarian, but he wrote asking Alex Culbertson what he should do. Culbertson responded that although he did not think it wise to proceed, the Blackfeet were assembled in anticipation of the fall trade. They threatened to bring the keelboat on by force.

As it spread quickly among the fort personnel the disease killed twenty-six of the Indian or Méttise wives of the traders. Culbertson was infected but only one white died. After taking five leisurely days to complete their trading, the Indians

Piikani Warrior (note fingers cut off in mourning). Washington State Historical Society Sohon Collection.

departed in apparent health. As summer waned, the traders thought it was odd that no one returned.

In the fall Culbertson went out to see what had become of his customers. Stench from the cottonwoods near the Three Forks led him to a silent camp. Hundreds of rotting bodies were scattered among flapping lodges and abandoned gear. Two old women who survived had probably acquired immunity after the 1781/82 epidemic. Now they keened plaintively for fallen families and dead friends.

Breaking up into small bands, the Indians tried to flee into the mountains or out on the insulating prairies. But their deadly little conqueror rode faster than any horseman. Nothing could fully describe the months of torment, suffering, and despite that the Blackfeet endured until the awful thing finally burned itself out.

His admirer Andrew Pamburn promoted a statement that Jemmy Jock Bird brought Indians to be inoculated, but there is no supporting evidence. Jamey reappeared on the Saskatchewan on 31 December 1838. During *La Quignolee* festivities at Edmonton, the unforgiving Rowand took time to write to a York Factory correspondent. "Master Bird has at last made his appearance at R Mountain House after an absence of nearly two years, he arrived with nothing, he got about 60 Beaver, of that number he gave forty, to our people across the Mountains and twenty to his old friends the Americans for supplies for himself which he told Mr. Harriot he could not do without. In his absence he got the small pox which has marked his face well, he also had the misfortune of losing one of his Piegan wives by that same disease, however it is nothing for him as he got another for a horse which cost him a small trifle, besides this he has a tent full of them for sale."[13]

The beaver trade also expired with those fallen hunters. World fashion was turning to hats made from elegant silk. Although beaver fibre was less necessary for the felting process, the old habit of trapping did not immediately evaporate. But the bonanza was over and the hell-roaring adventure of the mountain hunt had slipped from under their moccasins. Mountaineers and tribesmen would have to find alternative careers. That summer two Catholic priests passed Edmonton House on their way to Fort Vancouver. They were called to minister to former mountain hunters who were settling as farmers and herders in the Willamette Valley.[14]

Many of Jemmy Jock's Piikani friends had gone to the Sand Hills. The robe trade was tipping the balance of terror back toward the other Gens du Large. Our man with the Inuk'sik had reached the end of his career as a confidential servant. Unable to bring himself to forgive Bird's disappointing performance as a secret agent, Rowand was soon under orders to break it off.[15] It was time for a marginal man to come in from the cold.

After pulling north of the international boundary that he had ignored for the past eighteen years, Bird Chief wrote to Governor Simpson on 6 July 1840 requesting a statement of his account with the HBC. Six months later the governor responded that, "from 1 June '40 ... there is a balance of £408.14.7 at your credit in the Company and by that statement you will observe that you have been credited with £100 salary per annum for the years 1833/34, 4/5, 5/6, 6/7, 7/8, 8/9 and £100 for the year 9/40 being as follows: £43.3s.0d credit for furs £56.17s.0d gratuity for Sundry services."[16]

In the Shadow of the Cross

Was Old Man sending the people greater spirit power? Soul-mindful Iroquois and curious Salish had taken to sending petitions to St. Louis for a "black robe." In 1840 Father Pierre-Jean de Smet, Society of Jesus, rode to the Snake Country scouting for a place where St. Louis Jesuits might plant missions. Traveling past the Beaverhead with his Flathead hosts, Father de Smet met a few Blackfeet who were polite and seemed receptive. Likely they were Inuk'sik or Piikani whose connection to the Salish was a marginal man known as Wolf Child.[1] Before floating away on the Yellowstone River, de Smet promised to return next year and build a mission.

At that time Jemmy Jock Bird was in the north and missed meeting the *black robe*. But he heard the particulars when Piikani friends came to the Mountain House to trade. Bird's views on religion recalled the Church of England teachings he knew briefly in his youth. Starting with whatever his father instilled in the family, those beliefs had been formalized during the brief stay at the York Factory school. In the thirty years since, he spent more time listening to drumming and singing in Indian camps than in a pew. When he met the expectant missionary, William Henry Grey Bird encouraged a Protestant effort among the Blackfeet. But outlining

Rocky Mountain House by Paul Kane. National Archives of Canada.

the best way to make a connection may have just been an expert plainsman's advice on a technical matter.

Before returning to the Saskatchewan Bird heard of the Iroquois visits to St. Louis. Two months before he arrived, two Catholic priests had passed Edmonton on their way to the Willamette. The company assisted their passage to the Columbia Department where they were sent to minister to retired freemen settled in the Willamette Valley. When the priests passed in 1838, Hugh Monroe and his Cree wife Sinouahake had three children aged seven to four baptized. At the same time, J. E. Harriot confirmed his marriage to Rowand's daughter Nancy.[2] If the fur trade community took such matters seriously, then the Catholics had stolen a march. Christianity was closing in.

The Catholic challenge at Edmonton was soon answered. The Reverend Robert Terrill Rundle, a twenty-nine-year-old Wesleyan missionary, arrived in October 1840 as the company chaplain.[3] He soon displayed disquieting indications that he saw a much broader mission to the Indians. Fresh from the certainties of indoctrinated Cornish parishes and a recent seminary education, Rundle saw his proselytizing as a self-righteous obligation to enlighten the heathen. No matter, the introduction of Christianity to upper river and mountain tribes had as much to do with maintaining company control as it did with charity.

At the beginning of the year 1841, the chaplain requested Bird's services as his Indian interpreter. Given his opinion of Bird, Chief Factor Rowand felt obliged to pen a letter to Governor Simpson concerning this unfortunate turn of events. More concerned about salary than salvation, Rowand admitted that Bird spoke Cree and Blackfoot as well as the Indians themselves, but his services would not come cheaply. He would probably "not agree for less than what he gets from the Company, with a Clerk's allowance for tea, sugar, flour."[4]

Setting out from Edmonton in a dog cariole, the enthusiastic preacher carried his Methodist message to Rocky Mountain House. As a courtesy to those benighted traders he brought the latest news from the winter express. By 22 February, Jemmy Jock was shocked to learn that his brother John had been shot by the governor's cousin. The party of mixed-bloods called to the scene of the crime on the plains toward St. Paul, returned to the Red River settlement with the bodies. They reported that after the killings, an apparently demented Thomas Simpson had committed suicide. By Indian concepts of justice, prompt reaction was proper. But the question of what really happened gave company men sensitive to the governor's feelings, and scandalized settlers, an excuse to try to pin Simpson's death on revengeful half-breeds.

At the end of the month, Blackfeet and oddly apprehensive Bloods arrived after a six-day journey from their big winter camp on the Bow River to the Mountain House. Those trying customers were eclipsed by the Peigans who presented a beautiful white horse to trader Harriot. When the coast was clear, Rocky Mountain Cree, Strongwoods Cree, and Strongwoods Stoneys also slipped in to trade while cautious Sarsi lingered nearby. Just like old times.

At Rocky Mountain House on 28 March, the Methodist baptized another of the Munroe's daughters and eight other children. Four of those were from the family of Jamey and Sally Bird. Edward, the oldest boy, had been born on 1 September 1830, but was too young to leave at the Red River settlement when his parents visited three years later. During that visit Jamey and his sits-beside-wife Sally were treated very well by Jamey's half sister Letitia and her husband Charles McKay. No surprise then that the Birds named the daughter who was born in July 1834 Letitia. Another daughter born in May 1836 was Maria, after the McKay's eldest daughter.

The Reverend Rundle found a problem with the boy who had been born on 9 January 1837. To the embarrassment of imported morality, there was another wife. Although that was in keeping with time-honored Piikani practice, the second wife offended Rundle. Using the Cree syllabics devised by his Norway House associate James Evans, Rundle disguised the existence of the mother of the four-year-old child who was baptized Charles Bird. According to the Cree characters, her name was *Se-no-pa* (*sinopaa*) which meant kit-fox in Blackfoot.[5]

In condemning multiple wives as a proof of pagan degeneracy, the Reverend Rundle failed to realize that was a way of caring for extra women who had no other support. If Rundle expected to achieve moral supremacy, he was dead wrong. What did the codified beliefs of ancient desert tribes offer that was better than the Indian way?

Interpreter Bird dutifully assisted Rundle's visits to the Cree and Assiniboine camps. But when they traveled to the Blackfoot winter lodges on the Bow River something offended the half-breed and his attitude took an inexplicable turn. After an inconsequential difference, Bird refused to continue translating the missionary's words. The bewildered Rundle thought that Bird was reacting to how he had handled the matter, but it is possible that Jamey balked for another reason. Rundle saw Sally as the tool to use in forcing his views upon the family.

It was difficult for Jamey to suffer a young greenhorn. Fresh from seminary, Rundle spoke in all seriousness about the decalogue, the thunders of Mount Sinai, Philip the Eunuch, and the joy of Xtianity, hallelujah, hallelujah, men.[6] When he launched into a parable about the Pascal Lamb, Jamey Bird had difficulty describing an animal most Indians had never seen. Worse, the young preacher lacked the sense to avoid insulting someone as vital to his mission as the sensitive interpreter. Deciding that he would determine who Bird spoke to, Rundle *ordered* him to perform his duties. If the preacher considered him a mere hireling then he could do his own speaking. Jemmy Jock simply walked out, leaving the red-faced preacher forlornly singing a hymn to the bemused congregation.[7]

Rundle failed to grasp that the English religious beliefs and social standards that he meant to impose were incomprehensible on the upper Saskatchewan. Beyond learning a few words in the Cree language, Rundle admitted very little about the validity of the Indian way. He rejected their misguided pagan beliefs out of hand. After living with the Piikani for so many years, Jamey had absorbed enough of their beliefs to know true men when he met them. More than just nodding to a Sunday sermon, Piikani community standards stressed honesty, generosity, and attention to duty. Bird earned the respect of the Piikani in the same way as their young men, by demonstrating responsibility, initiative, and generosity. He helped defend the community. Now intruders like Gray, Rundle, or de Smet were trying to overturn the spiritual foundations of his friends.

The "extraordinary express from England" that passed Rocky Mountain House early in the year announced the elevation of the governor to British knighthood. Sir George Simpson was coming to claim the disputed Oregon Country for British Empire and cap it with a spectacular journey "around the world." The great man would not be the only traveler on the northern plains. In spring 1841, Bird knew that a party of Red River colonists was also coming on their way to the Pacific coast.

When Chief Factor Rowand left Carlton House to ride overland to the Red River settlement and meet Sir George, Jemmy Jock Bird rode part of the way with him. The plainsman was concerned about the safety of his relatives who had to pass through the dangerous Blackfoot country. Rowand and Bird intercepted the emigrant cart party in the vicinity of the saline lakes north of Qu'Appelle. The plainsman was pleased to find his sisters, Letty, Chloe, and Charlotte, traveling with their husbands. The Flett family had one of the murdered John Bird's children with them. The conductor of the party was sister Elizabeth's husband, James Sinclair. Their younger brother, Nicholas Garry Bird, was in the party as well as old friends, James Spence, old John Tait, and the three Flett brothers. In fact, most of the twenty-three heads of families or their wives were relatives or former acquaintances from the old floating community of the Saskatchewan.[8]

Company Conductor Sinclair had been engaged in a scheme to colonize north of the Columbia. Half-breeds and Métis were being shifted to new homes in the west in order to encourage a boundary drawn down that river. Over a hundred accepted the proposal. They had found that it was more and more difficult for the country-born to hold positions in the company.[9]

Everyone's favorite sister, Letty, was an accomplished camp cook who treated the plainsmen to her bannock. After touching base with his brother, John Richards McKay at the Qu'Appele post, her husband Charley had a new appreciation of the western Indian situation. If the party needed safe-conduct through undependable tribes, Jemmy Jock was their best reliance.

The cart brigade was trailing along the north side of the Saskatchewan when they were overtaken by Governor Simpson's horseback entourage. This was Simpson's first meeting with Bird since 1833 when they agreed that he would rejoin the company. That deal had been suspect, if not illegal, and Bird had done his best to keep the Peigan beaver hunters coming north. Simpson had no one to blame except himself for Bird's disappointing performance over the past seven years. But it was not in the great man to forgive. There was no mention of their meeting or Bird's service in Simpson's largely ghost-written book.[10] During the hunter's breakfast Sir George shared with the cart party, he affected the image of a great man on horseback. But between the beaver hat and doeskin breeches there was still a Tom Thumb in Mr. Barnum's clothes.

Continuing ahead to Edmonton Simpson wrote warning the superintendent of the Methodist mission to beware of the untrustworthy Bird. He also left definite orders for the emigrants to cross the Athabasca portage, build boats, and continue by water down the Columbia. But the upper river was a perilous stretch of water where experienced boatmen sometimes died. Families had recently perished at Death Rapids. Bird's presence, and his connections with the tribes, hardened the colonist's resolve to proceed by land. From the head of the Bow River they would cross the mountains on long established Indian trails.

Abandoning the last Red River carts in the vicinity of the closed Peigan post led to some hilarious lessons in packing horses and oxen. Jamey rode along as the twenty-two families headed into the mountains. When they were well on their way he turned back. Simpson's book later accused him of abandoning the party.

Louis Piche was one of the servants who assisted the governor's party through the mountains. Whatever he overheard around the campfires led him to go to the Red River and confer with Bishop Provencher. As a consequence, Father Jean-Baptiste Thibault performed his first mass at Edmonton on 11 June 1842, and Father Joseph Bourassa was soon ministering to the Métis and Indians at Lac Ste. Annes. Protestant and Catholic missions were now head-to-head on the upper Saskatchewan.

When Conductor Sinclair returned from the Columbia with the spring express, he brought letters to Rundle from a Methodist counterpart in Oregon. Jason Lee, the missionary who chose to bypass the Flatheads, described the contest between Catholics and true believers for the souls of the retired trappers and Indians in the Willamette Valley.

In mid-August 1843 the sky was clouded by smoke from prairie fires when the Reverend Rundle went to the Cree camp on the Red Deer River. After frost killed the buffalo grass, fires cleansed weeds and helped those hoof-compacted pastures reseed. That autumn the plains were burned as far south as the Red Deer River and hungry Mountain House entertained small hope of seeing buffalo.

In that dismal situation the Catholic Piche and his son were killed in a gambling quarrel with other "half-castes." Drunkenness was often an excuse for political surgery, but there is no indication that the killings were premeditated.[11] Four days later when Rundle baptized Nancy and Mary Bird he identified their father as an English half-caste.[12] That brought the total of Bird children who had been baptized according to the tenets of the Methodist Church to five.

Although Jamey does not seem be acting as Rundle's interpreter, in late October they traveled together between the Red Deer and Bow. Bird's large lodge was the leather chapel where Rundle preached to Indians seeking the spirit power of another world, another heaven, another hell. After losing so many to disease or war, those dazed survivors were susceptible to the pronouncements of pre-Victorian religion.

To the south the Jesuit Black Robes were making inroads among Bird's Inuk'sik friends.[13] As soon as St. Mary's mission was planted in the lower end of the Bitterroot Valley, Father Nicholas Point began traveling with the Salish buffalo hunters. His intermediary was another kind of marginal man. The mixed Piikani/Kutenai Wolf Child had married a Salish woman and divided his time between their people. Baptized Nicolas by the priests, he tried to broker their beliefs, crying into the darkness beyond the light of the camps to those watching in the night, to come, to come.

In autumn 1845, Father de Smet outflanked the Blackfoot heartland by passing through the Kutenai country. To the discomfort of the resident Protestant Rundle, the Black Robe arrived at the Mountain House on 4 October. Next morning de Smet said mass in the great hall while the Methodist meeting was being conducted in the Indian House.

After enduring most of Rundle's discourse on the 147th Psalm "the Power of God and Providence in Nature," Bird retreated to his lodge leaving the two men of God to argue religion late into the night. Rundle admitted that his constitution was unequal to the enthusiasm of his vigorous opponent and begged off, going to bed with a pain in his head.

During October, the competitive sectarians blasted Indians and Métis with pious barrages. Trader Harriot tried to allow equal facilities and time for both versions. De Smet had taken immediate hold by resolving the two-year-old Piche killings. Dutifully suffering through Rundle's prayer sessions that were conducted in Cree, Bird brought up the subject of the destitute children of a slain chief. In response, the Methodist loaned him a hymn book to study.

Expecting this to be his last Sabbath at Rocky Mountain House for some time, Rundle instructed the congregation to "work out your own salvation." They took it to heart as only a few returned for the evening prayers in Cree.[14] Before leaving, the Reverend loaded Bird with the Apostles' Creed, the Lord's Prayer, and the evening hymn, all translated into Cree. Just as the first Piikani began arriving to trade, Rundle pulled out muttering, "Popery, Popery, Alas for the pure light of Protestant Xty."[15]

Father de Smet may have won the Rocky Mountain House religious debates but he had yet to find an inroad to the Blackfeet. On the thirtieth he wrote, "My greatest perplexity is to find a good and faithful interpreter; the only one now at the fort [Bird] is a suspicious and dangerous man: all his employers speak ill of him – he makes fine promises. In the alternative ... I accept his services."[16]

Bird learned the fate of old friends. Crows attacked the smallpox weakened Inuk'sik. "Fifty families, the entire band of the Little Robe, were lately massacred, and 160 women and children have been led into captivity." Hadn't Black Robes traveled with the Salish buffalo hunt for several years, what had their God done to prevent that?

After picking All Hallows' Eve as the time to depart, the Black Robe wrote:

> ... my interpreter did not long leave me in doubt of his true character ... he became sullen and peevish, always choosing to halt in those places where the poor beasts of burden could find nothing to eat.... The farther we penetrated into the desert, the more and more sulky he became. It was impossible to draw from him a single pleasant word and his incoherent mutterings and allusions became subjects of serious apprehension. Thus passed ten sorrowful days; my last two nights had been nights of anxiety and watching; when fortunately I encountered a Canadian with his family, upon whom I prevailed to remain with me for some time. The following day my interpreter disappeared.[17]

Rowand must have had that news when he sent a belated warning to de Smet on 3 December. "Beware, my good sir, of your interpreter Bird. He hates everything

Father de Smet crossing the Rocky Mountains by H. J. Warre. National Archives of Canada.

Meeting with Père de Smet in the Rocky Mountains

In the Shadow of the Cross

connected with the French or Canadians." The Edmonton chief explained that Munroe did well enough in the trade shop but he could not be recommended to interpret the complexities of what the priest had to say to the natives.

Arriving at Edmonton on New Year's Eve, de Smet skipped the celebrations to pen painfully-acquired advice to other workers in the vineyard. "... beware of placing your dependence upon a morose half-breed, especially if he has been for some time a resident among the savages; for such men usually possess all the faults of the white man joined to the cunning of the Indian...."[18]

If Jamey meant to inhibit the missionaries, he had held the line at Rocky Mountain House, confining Rundle's proselytizing to the Cree and Stoneys, and blocking de Smet's end run against the Blackfeet. In the spring, the militant Black Robe returned across the mountains and launched a frontal attack from St. Mary's mission. That summer, Fathers de Smet and Nicholas Point penetrated the Peigan world with the guidance of the aging Wolf Child. The dozen surviving lodges of Small Robes had joined the Flathead and Nez Percé buffalo hunters. During the fall hunt they gave the Crows some of their own medicine and danced proudly with the scalps.[19]

Fort McKenzie had been replaced by another post called Fort Lewis. When the Indians went there to trade, the two Black Robes spent about six weeks baptizing several hundred children and adults. Father de Smet left on the departing boat, but Father Point spent the winter 1846/47 with the bands and tribes camped in the vicinity of the fort. By the following spring he had visited twenty-five or thirty camp leaders and chiefs of the Gros Ventre, Peigan, Bloods, and Blackfeet proper and recorded 667 baptisms in their camps or at the American fort.[20]

On 25 March 1846 Sally Bird gave birth to a daughter. Two months later, with the baby snuggled in the moss of a cradle board bumping at Sally's knee, the family was back in favorite old haunts along the Highwood River. The Sly Shooting River was an old battlefield, but nowadays hostile contests for buffalo were concentrated farther south, on the Yellowstone or on the Musselshell. It was a surprise on the sixteenth when a party of western Indians was discovered and attacked by twenty-eight young Piikani who killed two Flatheads in the resulting melee.

Next morning at sunrise Bird rode out with twenty singing warriors to visit the battlefield. They walked into a Pend d'Oreille, Kutenai, and Salish ambush that cut down the Piikani leader *Mikistuki*, a warrior named *Sakpu* (Sinew Piece), and two young married men. During a six-hour fight four more westerners were killed, but the Piikani were forced to yield the field.

Jemmy Jock was surprised to find himself in harm's way so late in the war games. Dating the incident calls into question the reliability of tribal legend and later lodge stories. Fifty years later, the robe trader turned journalist, James Willard Schultz, picked up a yarn from that same period. In 1935 Schultz devised a quest yarn "The Theft of the Sacred Otter Bow Case" to thrill the young readers of *Boy's Life*. According to Schultz, after returning from a horse raid to the distant southwest, Piikani horse capturers spent the winter 1846/47 on the Musselshell River. When they went to Fort Benton to trade robes they carried with them an otter skin bow case that was seen as a symbol of tribal security. Slipping into the camp, Cutthroat (Assiniboine) raiders carried the important object away. Bird's brother-in-law, Mad Wolf, induced him and six others to follow the raiders to their camp on the lower Milk River and reclaim the bow-case. Nine lives were lost before the sacred object was recovered and offered at the 1847 sun dance.[21] Given Bird's presence in the north, the time line that Schultz gave is wrong.[22]

Pursuing missionary labors north of Edmonton in March 1846 the Reverend Rundle was relieved that de Smet returned across the mountains. During the rest of the summer Methodist activities were confined to the Edmonton vicinity, so it was fall before Rundle went up to Rocky Mountain House to devote his energies to the nearby Assiniboine camp. On 23 October the Bird and Monroe families reappeared. After listening to prayers given in Cree and Stoney, Bird was put to work interpreting Rundle's discourse for the Blackfeet; subject, "Last Day."[23]

Next spring the missionary trailed south across the Battle, Red Deer, and Bow rivers to a branch of the Steep Rock River notable as a place where Bird's son had been lost at some past time. At the end of May, Jamey met the chaplain in the beautiful country along the High Wood River. A chief in the Piikani camp displayed a picture and a "thing about popery" given to him by the Jesuits on the Missouri. But another leader, the Bull's Head, hosted a well-attended prayer meeting in his enlarged tent. The smaller evening meeting was conducted in Bird's spacious lodge.

On 1 June the camp meeting had grown to twenty-five tents of Peigans and a like number of Cree and Stoneys. Six days later, when Rundle baptized Bird's daughter Catharine, the large tent was crowded with a hundred Indians. Next week when twice that number attended, Hugh Munroe had to stay outside and interpret for those who could crowd into the tent. Bird was getting sulky again, but Rundle had finally learned to use discretion in dealing with him, and avoided an uproar.

At the end of the month they were tenting in the mountains near the head of the Bow River. The long mirror of Lake Sakahigan (Minnewanka) near the old Bow Fort was a place holding poignant memories for the Birds. The daughter they had buried there was one of the girls whom Rundle previously baptized. The chaplain remembered how she lay in her father's arms too weak to sit up for prayers. When she died in the mountains there was no suitable place for a grave and the little body had been brought to the side of the lake. That chance image of a doting father and sorrowing family did not quite fit the myth of the renegade.

In early July when Sally approached the chaplain about baptism, she was put off. "Yesterday Sally asked about baptism & today she was spoken to. The other woman has been living in incest with her father & brother!" Rundle also spoke with Mr. Bird, but the consequences of that were not recorded. However Rundle made no more references to the Bird family and returned to Edmonton on the twentieth.[24]

A year later at Rocky Mountain House, Sally approached Rundle again. Throughout the winter the irrepressible, perambulating artist Paul Kane had been making life difficult for the chaplain. Not many came to evening prayers, "only Mr. Birds 3 daughters." They came to morning prayers on 26 April and Sally returned with them for the evening service. "Afterwards Sally spoke about baptism. She wished to be baptized but one or two things in the way. Other woman still there. Not married." Despite that insulting refusal, the Bird children continued to come to prayers for the next three days and Sally returned on the twenty-ninth. At the forenoon service next day Rundle noted in Cree syllabics a Bird whose name was written as *Ichukoo*.[25] Next day Jemmy Jock rode off with Kane leaving his family to move above. However, Sally and Mary Bird showed up at Edmonton in early June and dutifully attended services. Sally's desire for Christianity seemed to be sincere.

It had been two years since the boat brigade returned from Norway House with gossip that the missionary there, Rundle's superintendent James Evans, had sexually abused a girl and was recalled to England.[26] When Rundle proposed that Bird leave his daughters at Edmonton for additional instruction, Jamey became upset and stopped attending services.

In November 1847 Jamey's nephew, William Bird, and his daughter Mary, were suspected of some unspecified indiscretion. That might have suggested the deterioration of morality as they were asked to leave the Edmonton mission. Or was it the paranoia of a religious zealot?

Rundle's peace of mind was upset by the reappearance of the irrepressible Paul Kane. The Irish artist had been west of the mountains painting Indians. He returned on 5 December to pass the rest of the winter at Edmonton where his hard drinking, bohemian attitude, and exaggerated yarns tried Harriot's susceptibility to alcohol and Rundle's tolerance of sin.

After the famous Christmas dinner at Edmonton House that featured mouffle (moose nose), Kane amused himself by going to Fort Pitt with the wedding party of Rowand's son.[27] While the artist was away, Bird arrived with four Assiniboine Indians. He was still cool to Rundle, but they made up their differences. When Jamey departed on 27 January, he carried the preacher's testament to study.

If his drinking wasn't bad enough, the worldly Kane could not resist needling the narrow-minded missionary. In the disputes that followed, Rundle and Harriot had their first quarrel in eight years. After refusing to speak to each other for some time, they made a chilly truce, but Rundle continued to lament, "O that Rum, that Rum."[28]

Blackfeet were expected to come to Mountain House. On 12 April 1848, Rundle, Kane, and several others set out for Rocky Mountain House. After a nine-day trip they found Jemmy Jock looking after the house and surviving on a lean diet of snared rabbit. Although Kane "always found him trustworthy and hospitable" after a Saturday night carouse, Bird failed to call the Stoneys (Assiniboine) from their tents for Easter Day prayers. By the twenty-sixth, the only people attending the Reverend Rundle's services were the three Bird daughters and a few Stoneys. Yet when Sally came to the preacher asking about baptism, Rundle continued to find "one or two things in the way."[29] Bird apparently refused to put the second wife aside.

On 1 May, Kane, Mr. Clare, Hugh Munroe's son, and Bird left for *below*. Ever the raconteur, Kane penned a dramatic version of the trip to Edmonton. After forcing the march to reach a food cache that Bird knew about, they found that a fat wolverine had beaten them to it. The trapped animal had spoiled what he could not ingest. Taking most of the horses Kane and Bird raced for Edmonton leaving a trail of exhausted animals.[30]

Feeling very much "alone with God," Rundle followed on 20 May. He was crippled, unhealthy, and showing signs of paranoia when he questioned if Bird had properly translated his words last year. Weakness made him a bit more understanding in early June when he allowed the banished Mary and William Bird to attend services. Exactly a month later, the Reverend Robert Rundle left Edmonton in a rickety wooden boat steered by an Indian and a boy. He would never return.[31]

Religion, faith, and belief were secondary to Jemmy Jock's obligation to protect and support his family. While contesting missionaries wrestled with their doubts and abstract frustrations, disparaging rival dogma, a family man still had to hunt or trade to feed his family. Bird had to make what he could of a world that was changing. After God's heralds drifted off in a purposeful haze of belief, Old Man still prevailed in the world of the Gens du Large.

Under the Long Knives

Beyond past petty trading and the distractions of religious proselytizing around Rocky Mountain House and Edmonton, Jemmy Jock Bird was just another squaw man who had to subsist a large family. The older children left at the Red River settlement twenty years ago were grown and living lives of their own, but the survivors of those born later were still with the family.[1]

The small services that Bird continued to perform for the company were not enough to support so many and his savings still held on the ledgers of the HBC were evaporating. As he began the second half of the century, James Bird Jr was fifty, old by the rigorous demands of life in the open and still following the main chance.

His arrangement with the Hudson's Bay Company had been based on the beaver trade. That old business was beginning to falter on the northern plains as the attractive new market for buffalo robes commanded the attention of the Gens du Large. In the twenty years since he helped the Upper Missouri Outfit of the American Fur Company shift to that business, countless boatloads of heavy hides had been floated down the easy water-road of the Missouri River.

Although the border inhibited British access to the Piikani, those traditional beaver hunters still brought their small furs to British traders. To retain their loyalty and counter the large number of buffalo hides being traded at Fort Benton, the company was also obliged to accept robes. Some could be shipped to Montreal as warm wraps to keep British officers and their "muffins" cozy on winter sleigh rides. Those were better accepted at Fort Carlton or the South Branch, but Edmonton traders could not refuse hunters who carried them so far. But there were too many laborious portages to reach the bay and the Saskatchewan traders could not compete.

Complaining about the outfit that York Factory sent up in 1840, Rowand grumbled, "If robes are not worth taking at the rate of 2/6 in goods, we may abandon those Indians and let the Americans have all their own way."[2] Twelve years later the company was receiving ten thousand robes and that rose to twelve thousand in the next year. Of the 11,345 robes traded in 1855/56, about half came from the Saskatchewan.[3] And that was nothing to what the Americans were buying.

Three thousand robes were traded when the Upper Missouri business began in 1831. Three years later it increased to nine thousand.[4] Ten thousand hides were received in 1838 and the number doubled three years later. It has not been determined how many Pierre Chouteau and Company shipped after ten years but their main competitor, Harvey, Primeau and Company shipped 16,409.[5] The impact upon the herds of increased hunting doubled when cows carrying calves were killed.[6] The Fort Benton journalist was a man who lived by the buffalo robe trade. But he could see a problem developing and was appalled by the improvidence of the tribes. "The Indians who went out after meat also returned today well supplied. They killed ... one hundred and seventy six cows – If this aint Slughtering buffalo by the whole sale you can take my hat –"[7]

Complete head and tail robes were worth twelve dollars in St. Louis. Split robes sewed together brought five dollars.[8] Tribespeople trading a robe at Fort Benton might receive twenty-five loads of powder and ball, a yard and a half of calico, three knives, or a gallon kettle. For three robes, an Indian could get a two and one-half point blanket. Ten bought a trade gun. Trade shops were also stocked with an irresistible collection of bells, mirrors, beads, shawls, handkerchiefs, and twenty-one kinds of men's coats.[9] The pictures an Indian artist drew for Father Point show that liquor was being traded.[10]

Through those years the standard of trade was a prime robe taken from a cow or heifer during the winter when the fleece was fullest, the same time as they were carrying calves. It usually took women two or three days bending over the skin pegged down on the ground to chip off flesh. Then it had to be softened; hard work for something that at a post might bring as little as a cup of sugar, a pound of tobacco, or a cup of coffee beans. Doing that work required more hands and may have been the reason that the number of wives in a buffalo hunter's lodge was increasing.

In order to support his family Jemmy Jock Bird returned to the Upper Missouri. During the years when he rode with the Piikani their ranges stretched beyond the upper most branches of the Missouri to as far as the Snake River Valley, Bear Lake, the Spanish country sometimes. Now those who adventured to those old marches returned with unbelievable tales of a river of wagons flowing west each summer. Thousands were going to Oregon or California. Entrepreneurs along the trail bought worn-out cattle and drove those thin plodders north into the Big Hole or Bitterroot Valley. They fattened on the grass that once fed buffalo.

Great changes roiled beyond the horizon, but the world of Jemmy Jock Bird was a cartload of children, some nearly grown. After they bumped across the line in his cart, Jemmy Jock began going around to the band camps collecting robes for the American traders.[11] Fort Benton was now central, its development linked to a string of problems that began when the revenge-seeking traders Alex Harvey and François Chardon crammed 150 lead balls into a cannon. They blew away the next band of Piikani to appear at the gate of Fort McKenzie, which ended doing business there. But the downstream retreat at the mouth of the Judith River was too far from the customers. Returning to a more convenient place the traders built Fort Lewis and took in 21,000 robes in the first year. Not long after Father Nicolas Point departed in spring 1847, a second Fort Lewis was dismantled and moved to a better location six miles above the mouth of the Teton River. In recognition of the "great compromiser" it was initially called Fort Clay. In the giddy enthusiasm of Christmas Eve 1850 it was renamed Fort Benton to honor the proponent of western expansion.[12]

Acquiring robes from old friends, or sometimes former enemies, Bird hauled them south to Alexander Culbertson. Bird had known Culbertson since he came in fall 1833. Alex wasted no time in marrying a Piikani woman of the family of *Tomeksik-Siksinam* (the White Buffalo), and a few years later also married into the Bloods.[13] They shared ability in several tribal languages and the robe trader was usually ready to share a drink with a thirsty plainsman.

A few old friends were camped about sixteen miles from Fort Benton. Ten year ago the Inuk'sik were still recovering from the smallpox epidemic when a sudden Crow attack destroyed the manhood of fifty lodges. Two hundred women and children were taken captive. The twelve surviving lodges had thrown in with Flathead and Nez Percé buffalo hunters, but found their hosts quarrelsome. In summer 1848, the surviving Small Robes were encountered on the south side of the Missouri. Six years later the Inuk'sik had recovered to thirty or so tents that were still friendless in an unforgiving world.

Culbertson's second at Fort Benton, Malcolm Clark, considered the Inuk'sik to be just another Peigan band, and a visiting artist found little to admire in the lodges of the "Little Rogues." In 1854 the trader David Dawson disparaged the "few lousey Pagans from Little Robes band" who lived on Pablo's Island and dressed what robes they could.[14] Their days of glory were over.

With so many of his tribal friends gone to the Sand Hills, Bird's worldview was limited to the traders hanging around Fort Benton. That changed in 1853 with the appearance of a large party of strangers. As representatives of national interest and territorial politics, they were surveying for an iron road across the buffalo plains. That intrusion began two years before when the inept former Fort McKenzie trader and present United States Superintendent of Indians at St. Louis, David D. Mitchell, called a great tribal council at Fort Laramie. Mitchell asked his former associate, Culbertson to bring in the Upper Missouri tribes. The trader reported that it was impossible to locate those scattered bands in the time allowed. That had implications because the Fort Laramie Treaty set the western boundary of the Crow country. That arbitrary boundary along the upper Yellowstone and Musselshell rivers initiated the definition of the Blackfoot world.[15]

As masters of the Upper Missouri, the Piikani had never been concerned with boundaries. They ranged as far south as their sense of superiority took them, to the Big Hole, the Snake Country, or Bear Lake. Their annual encounters with western tribes or Crows were contests for protein or horses. Before the easy availability of arms and munitions those were just dangerous games. But in September 1853 the United States Blackfoot agent Alfred J. Vaughan reported that it was increasingly difficult to maintain order. War, liquor, smallpox, measles, cholera, and other erosions were shattering. As bands split into smaller, less controllable bodies, leadership, political alliances, hunting strategies, and even marriage patterns were being altered.

The Fort Laramie Treaty began to bring the plains tribes to heel. Encouraged by what appeared to be progress Congress appropriated $150,000 for the exploration of three potential railway routes to the Pacific. The survey of the northern route was assigned to an ambitious young West Point engineer, Isaac Ingles Stevens, who headed west from Minnesota in June 1853. He also carried appointments as territorial governor of Washington and superintendent of its Indians.

When the Stevens party arrived at Fort Benton, the leader relied on Culbertson as a functionary. Letters were sent to the scattered bands inviting them to come and meet Stevens. One of those envoys was the expedition artist, John Mix Stanley, who was escorted by the Piikani leader Little Dog. Delegated to travel to the sun dance encampment in the Cypress Hills, Stanley hauled along an early daguerreotype outfit. The ability to capture the sun and turn the horizon upside down astonished the Indians. Unfortunately, all that survived of that remarkable photographic opportunity was Stanley's drawings.[16]

The thirty chiefs who met Stevens at Fort Benton on 21 September 1853 expressed a commendable desire for peace. Their control of heedless young warriors was stiffened by six hundred dollars in presents, theirs to distribute. Promising to return and conclude a treaty next year, Stevens hurried on after the other elements of the railroad survey. When he crossed Cadottes Pass on the twenty-fourth the new governor proclaimed Washington Territory and went on to Olympia to assume office.

The son of the governor of Wisconsin was left at Fort Benton to make weather observations, examine the country, and promote another treaty meeting. In a letter from Fort Benton dated 28 December 1853 James Doty reported that their Peigan connection, Little Dog, had been wounded during a Cree and Assiniboine attack on his camp. Although the chiefs agreed to restrict intertribal warfare, what seemed like hundreds of Blackfeet were passing the fort on their way to attack the Flatheads, Snakes, or Crows.

Faced with the dismal reality that the Indians were not adhering to their promises, Doty needed to find a good interpreter. He must have met Bird after the governor left as he wrote, "The only man I can at present recommend is Mr. Bird. He is a half-breed, English and Blackfoot: is an elderly man, respectable and intelligent, and the best interpreter in the country. He may not wish the situation of interpreter at the agency but can no doubt be engaged for a council."[17]

In his visit to the Piikani camps on Maria's River, Doty was beginning to realize that the United States had inherited two hundred lodges and six hundred warriors; as many as eighteen hundred Piikani. Another ninety Peigan lodges, around two hundred and seventy warriors or five hundred souls, lived north of the line and traded with the British. In addition there were 290 lodges of Blackfeet, and 270 lodges of Bloods who would have to be included in treaty negotiations, as well as various Gros Ventre, Cree, Stoney, and Sarcee. Negotiating a treaty promised to be a complex undertaking.

Those free-ranging bands foresaw an end to horse capture gamesmanship. During the next year and through most of 1855 perhaps as many as five hundred rustlers raced to exploit their neighbor's herds. The Fort Benton journalist recorded the passage of forty-eight outward bound or returning war parties. So far, Governor Steven's peace agreement was an illusion.

Matters in the north were also tense. On 10 February 1854, the Rocky Mountain House journalist noted the departure of the sent Munroe's son, Piscan, and seven men. Joseph Brazeau, a former Missouri River trader who came over to the HBC, sent them to the Blackfoot camps for provisions, but they came close to getting their heads broken.[18] Violent exchanges became so bad that the Piikani sent a delegation north to Edmonton seeking an accommodation with the Cree. That was why the famous Cree leader *Maskepetoon* (Broken Arm) planned to attend the treaty meeting.

David Dawson, the keeper of the Fort Benton journal, also recorded glimpses of the ordinary service of extraordinary characters. Culbertson returned from a trip to the Milk River plains in his carriage in time to welcome the Peigan Little Dog. In mid-October 1854, Louis Rivet, the beaver trapper who helped James Kipp build the first Peigan post twenty-three years before, started to the Gros Ventre camp with a wagonload of supplies. Hugh Munroe took two wagons and three men to the Blood camp in the wooded bottoms of the Teton River.

"Old man Burd [sic]" went from band to band, collecting conditioned buffalo robes for the American company.[19] Appearing at Fort Benton on 9 November the Peigan Chief Little Grey convinced Bird to bring two wagons to his camp. The robe trader returned in less than two weeks with a good haul. He took out another outfit on 1 December, but that expectation was frustrated when the camp he meant to service turned its hides over to another trader. After enjoying the year-end festivities at the fort, Jemmy Jock took his family on a winter hunt. Before the end of the month they returned with a good supply of meat.

About the same time, the shopkeeper Michel Champagne's attempt to reach the Peigan camps on Milk River was blocked by the swollen Teton River. Going in his stead, Bird managed to cross the flooding Maria's River to a provision cache. When he returned with a wagonload of meat on 1 February, Jemmy Jock reported good prospects for future trade.[20]

Lame Bull was emerging as a considerable Piikani leader. Someone bearing the honorable name Tete que Leve was recognized as *aapatohsipikani* (north Peigan). In mid-June, Bird's son and two Indians reported that the north Peigan camp would arrive in a few days with beaver to trade.[21] Those experienced shoppers planted themselves between the rival trading houses and let competition set the price. When Mr. Bird's took in forty beaver pelts it was just like old times.

A month later the post canon roared and the flag was hoisted to greet the return of Governor Stevens. He came after completing a treaty with the Salish and their western associates accompanied by a large delegation of Flatheads and Nez Percé. But they would have to bide time until the scattered Blackfeet were assembled.

By August the Americans had their hands full keeping tribesmen from each other's throats. Some incautious Pend Oreille made the mistake of turning their ponies into the herd of over a hundred animals. Two astute Blackfeet with a good eye for horseflesh expertly cut out four of their animals and headed north.

About to introduce a critical new territorial concept Stevens realized that he had to demonstrate the government's authority. After Little Dog failed to overtake the rustlers, Doty and the tailor/trapper Thomas Jackson (Hugh Munroe's son-in-law) raced away. Riding at the stiff pace of fifty miles a day they reached the Bow River, 200 miles from Fort Benton, only a couple of hours after the troublemakers.

Ignoring outlying lodges, the two men rode another ten miles to the upper camp where Lame Bull and "Mr. James Bird came out to meet me." Surprised to find someone he understood to be an American trader so far north in British territory, Doty "immediately secured the services of Mr. Bird as interpreter." When the principal chiefs assembled, Jemmy Jock explained that their invitation to council was in jeopardy because their young men had insulted the United States. Doty turned three recovered horses over to Little Dog and rode on with Bird.[22] The determined young man and bemused old trader rode another seventy miles to the Elk Fork of the Saskatchewan and reclaimed the last animal.[23]

The bands were in no hurry to hear their fate. By mid-September the Piikani had moved as far south as Milk River. When Jackson and Bird trailed in later they reported seeing a small party of Bloods, but failed to locate the main camp. Reluctant to come under the shadow of authority that was creeping across the brown hills, Lame Bull's camp held at Maria's River until 3 October. The snap of autumn was already in the air when news arrived that the supply boats carrying the "gifts" to be distributed at the treaty could only get as far as the Judith River. The water was too low. The government party had to travel a hundred miles east to the redesignated treaty grounds and the Indian delegations had to follow.

The council was held on the left bank of the Missouri just below the mouth of the Judith on a wide, level plain that had a grove of tall, now naked cottonwoods. A large leather Indian tent was set up as the headquarters with the camp of the hundred, mostly German, boatmen a bit removed.

Secretary Doty assisted the impatient commissioners, Isaac I. Stevens and Alfred Cumming, with Thomas Adams and A. J. Vaughan as the recorders. There were a number of interpreters; those for the Blackfeet being Alexander Culbertson, Benjamin Deroche, and James Bird.[24] Jemmy Jock was pleased by the opportunity to earn a little government money. He would speak for the Piikani or Cree, as required, while Culbertson interpreted for the Bloods. That should limit misunderstandings. Of course, a minor functionary had little prior information of what the commissioners intended to propose.

Blackfoot Treaty Council at the Judith River 1855 by Gustav Sohon.
Washington State Historical Society Sohon Collection

After a day of smoking and discussion, the commissioners hosted the gentlemen of the party, a few chiefs, and the interpreters at a feast that included racks of buffalo hump ribs, pancakes floated in melted sugar, and coffee. The guests snipped off bites of backstrap with their belt knives or gnawed on hump ribs as the grease ran down their arms. The convivial gathering included the former mountain men William Craig, Delaware Jim, and Ben Kiser who came as interpreters for their western friends. Those practiced raconteurs entertained the diners with tall yarns.

Nearly out-of-date mountain men were their own press agents. Most trapping adventures included either a fight with a grizzly bear or some adventure involving Bug's Boys (Blackfeet). Craig's yarns got better by the yard as he repeated the stories about Jemmy Jock that Tom McKay liked to plant on gullible visitors. There was the one where the devilish Bird liked to leave warnings posted along trails. Or how he used English from the darkness to distracted horse guards while his Indians ran off the stock.[25] The killing of Godin was darker. But hadn't those been times when a little mayhem, or an occasional killing, were the spice of life. There is no record of the renegade's response; whatever Jemmy Jock knew about the background of those events stayed in his discreet silence.

Finally, there was an image. During his years in the mountains, Jemmy Jock encountered most of the artists who came to document the early west. George Catlin, Karl Bodmer, Paul Kane, and John Mix Stanley left invaluable collections of western landscapes and Indian portraits. It is through the eyes and talent of those field artists that we can still visualize that lost world. They had known Bird, profited from what he told them, but neglected to take his image. Stanley even had an early camera. Now the modest draftsman with the railway survey, Gustav Sohon, made the only likeness.[26] In his drawing, Sohan outlined a rather broad-faced, low-browed, mature man with a prominent Indian nose, firmly set mouth, and a steady gaze. He wore long ringlets, but only a trace of thin beard or sideburns. Young for his fifty-seven years, Mr. Bird was well fitted out in a coat and soft collar shirt.

Doty was an uncritical admirer and Governor Stevens did not question the reliability of the sometime British double agent. Freewheeling Americans had an easier acceptance of skin gamesmanship. Generally, the Americans, whom Jemmy Jock had injured over the years, held a better opinion of him than the sniffy British who profited from the risks he had taken, but could not forgive his failures. Alex Culbertson found no fault in Bird's interpretation.

The work to be done had already been laid out in Washington. In trying to guide the treaty, commissioners from long-distance United States Commissioner of Indian Affairs George Manypenny hoped that the government would be able to "gradually reclaim the Indians from nomadic life" by encouraging them to settle and learn to "obtain their substance by agriculture and other pursuits of civilized life."[27]

Commissioner Cummings came from St. Louis as head of the Central Indian Superintendency. As a former sutler during the Mexican war he had little firsthand experience of the Blackfeet, but a good understanding of the potential for fraudulent behavior by his countrymen. As far as he was concerned Indian farming was just a way to rechannel government funds into the pockets of opportunists. Disdaining to participate in the revelry Cumming kept apart on the keelboat which gave the Stevens faction ammunition to disparage him.

The empire-visualizing Stevens was dazzled by the potential for agriculture. Most of the previous year had been spent concluding treaties with the western tribes that ceded their ranges and "extinguished" their title to huge chunks of Washington Territory. The fishing families around Puget Sound had agreed to give up their homes at the mouths of salmon streams and live on designated reservations. But by time that Stevens arrived at Fort Benton, his agreements with the wider-ranging tribes of the plateau country had flamed into an Indian war. That conflict eventually seared most of the Pacific Northwest, but Stevens was oblivious of the escalating disaster when he came to the Judith.

The commissioners were jealous of their authority and official responsibilities. Stuck in a contentious relationship they found few matters that they could agree upon.[28] "In the squabbling between Governor Stevens and Commissioner Cumming at the Judith council, Culbertson was accused by Stevens of being too friendly with Cumming. Feeling wronged by Stevens' accusation he refused to continue as a Blackfoot interpreter. Bird had to take his place at the council."[29]

As William Farr recently pointed out, the treaty only considered land cessions in a general way. What the commissioners hoped to accomplish was a peace treaty to end the old, ancient actually, contests for buffalo. After the tribes of the northern plains obtained horses there had been contests between those who ranged the Saskatchewan drainage and those of the Upper Missouri River. Adding to those territorial contests, tribes from the headwaters of the Columbia River also crossed the Rocky Mountains on annual hunts. The opportunities for what is now described as "cultural expression" were risky and rewarding.

It was thirty years since the American entrepreneur William H. Ashley described those attitudes. "In waging war upon us, they are not instigated by considerations of that nature [intrusive hunting]; they delight in war, because their other pursuits afford not sufficient employment for their vigorous minds, and because they like all other men are fond of fame, and war is the only means by which they can acquire it."[30]

Old hands like Craig or Bird accepted those encounters as part of being mountain men. Tribal contests for meat and horses became deadlier as more effective arms and supplies of munitions were readily available. There were getting to be too many strangers in the west and the war gamesmanship had to stop. The government intended to set off two vast hunting territories, one specifically reserved for the associated Blackfeet and the other a southern buffalo commons where all tribes could hunt without fear of having to fight for that privilege.[31]

In the announcement of the division of the buffalo country the Salish and Nez Percé recognized a threat to their accustomed road to the buffalo. Kalispel (Pend Oreille) leaders Alexander and Big Canoe objected to any restriction of that ancient prerogative. Recalling his father's stories of contests around the Three Buttes (Sweetgrass Hills) Alexander said, "Which of these chiefs [pointing to the Blackfeet] says we are not to go there?" Ignoring that challenge Little Dog added that he feared the bad attitude of the northern Peigans. They had refused Doty's invitation to come to the meeting.[32] But if the western tribes persisted, they were still welcome to use the northern approaches ... and take their chances.

Commissioner Cumming admitted that the territory under consideration was Blackfoot according to the Fort Laramie Treaty, but it would be a generous gesture if they were willing to set apart a common hunting ground. He explained, "The object is not to prevent social intercourse between the tribes. It is only to preserve their hunting grounds distinctly apart." Stevens undercut Cumming's argument by interjecting that the Flatheads had other food sources, including salmon and farming, while the Gens du Large were entirely dependent on buffalo. What Bird thought was that two men who came with the intention of imposing "permanent relations of peace and amnity" were unable to get along with each other.

The recorded minutes were kept palatable for congressional readers and later edited into a perfect version. Those were complex concepts. How the interpreters Bird, Craig, and Kiser, two half-breeds and a squaw man, managed to translate that to their listeners in three different languages is another matter. Just understanding the English was hard enough for buckskins shifting between tongues.

Speaking near the end of the meeting, Lame Bull expressed reluctance at having to come to *any* agreement. "It is not our plan that these things are going on. I understand that what the White Chiefs told us to do, we were to do both sides. It is not us who speak, It is the White Chiefs." He resented that the western Indian observers had been doing all the talking to insure they would continue to have access to the buffalo grounds. In the end he said, "we intend to do whatever the Government tells us; we shall take care to try to do it."[33]

Stevens adjourned the council. Through the sharp autumn night, fires burned in the lodges and the Indians talked. According to older protocols the delegations met apart to consider developments "in the bushes." Because interpreters had to be present to confirm questions about what had been said and what had been heard, those generally benighted wanderers among the tribes had opportunities to end a century of conflict on the northern plains.

The tribes struggled with a new concept of legally defined territorial rights. In the past, traders usually negotiated just enough land for a business house and adjoining kitchen garden. Missionaries lusted after intangible souls. But there was one man present who understood what was happening. After retreating for several generations, Delaware Jim's people had finally lost it all. He understood what the wagon trains rolling into Oregon and California really meant for the tribes. But what could an inarticulate frontiersman express about that awful inevitability.

As a man of two worlds Jemmy Jock Bird understood the skin games, but had only limited ideas about legalized property rights. As long as the tribes were not being asked to "cede" anything beyond the mutual use of the southern part of the buffalo range, he saw no problem. As a step in protein gerrymandering, the buffalo commons set apart a hunting ground where tribes could come without fear of competition, exploitation, or reprisal. They did not realize what it would mean to allow the construction of roads, the stretching of telegraph lines, and the location of military posts, agencies, missions, farms, mills, stations, and schools.

Next morning there were no more objections to specific parts of the treaty, the Blackfeet accepted the Crow boundary as their eastern border and the buffalo common became the southern line. Accepting those territorial limits also reemphasized the international boundary. Seminomadic hunting people had never paid much attention to that abstraction, but from now on those south of the Medicine Line would begin thinking of themselves as *aamsskaapipikani* (south Peigans) and those to the north as *aapatohsipikani* (north Peigans). It was only a little step from that to becoming American Indians or the children of the queen.

White Man's World

While James Bird Jr participated in the protein peace process, his relatives living in the Red River settlement were feeling spasms of resentment over the company's lock on Rupert's Land. Fourteen years ago, Jemmy Jock's married sisters and his brother Nicholas left the community. But when they arrived in the disputed Oregon country they found that the promises made to them by the company were false. Turning their backs on the Puget Sound agricultural colony north of the Columbia River they became Americans ... and sued.[1]

Later the freedom of individuals to trade around the Red River became an issue. In the ensuing flood of letters, petitions, and eventual riot, Bird's former brother-in-law, James Sinclair, was a leader, and his brother, William Bird a participant.[2] Old James Bird complained that his sons, Phillip, Henry, and Frederick were drawn into the dispute that challenged the company lock on the community.[3] All in all, the Red River settlement was not an attractive option to a plainsman thinking of leaving the Indian country.

Afterwards Sinclair gallivanted off to the California gold rush and refocused his attention on Oregon. During the summer 1854, he led another party of immigrants across the northern plains. The group included Jemmy Jock's English stepsister, Emily Lowman, and her husband

Roderick Sutherland. Their large herd of sheep were killed by hungry dogs at Fort Pitt. Two younger half brothers, Philip and Arthur Bird, carried a less than complimentary letter about themselves that the old chief wrote to his favorite daughter Letty. Passage across the northern plains was still risky as Blackfeet and Cree were brawling around Edmonton and the country as far south as the Bow was in uproar. Jemmy Jock wasn't around to smooth the way and Siksika welcomed the Bird brothers by shooting their ox and stealing a horse.

The Fort Benton journalist mentioned that *Mr. Burd* started north with two wagons in November so he missed connecting with the immigrants. But other exchanges brought him tidbits about his family and their difficulties. Sometime after the peace council, Jemmy Jock learned that his father's health was failing. Last February the fur trade patriarch had resigned his seat on the Council of Assiniboia. After his eldest son, George Bird, died on the twenty-eighth, the grieving father drew up his own will. The deaths of his brothers David and George made James Jr the eldest son. The question was whether English laws of primogeniture applied to a primitive?

That autumn the Fort Union bourgeois Edwin Denig visited the Red River settlement. He was seeking a place where he could retire without generating too much comment about his two Indian wives and half-breed children. The advice from someone who had worked through that problem was welcome, and in return Denig favored Mr. Bird by carrying a letter to his son. Eventually the trail-worn document arrived at Fort Benton.

The imposition of federal politics distracted the buffalo hunters, and the robe trade at Fort Benton was slow for the rest of 1855. Old habits prevailed and Jemmy Jock seemed to prefer operating across the line. Treaties or no, the time was still in the future before Brother Jonathan would dare to come and "whoop-up" that vast country. From the old winter camps along the Highwood River, the northern Piikani could look south toward the loom of Chief Mountain or down the valleys of Milk River to the purple shadow of the Sweetgrass Hills. If there was a "Medicine Line" dividing the ranges of the buffalo and the buffalo people, it was in the conniving minds of distant politicians and frustrated imperialists.[4]

Wintering with his friends, Jemmy Jock didn't return until the next year. On 18 January 1856 he came from the Belly River with Lame Bull and three lodges *aapatohsipikani* (north Peigans). They found the pitiful Little Robes still hanging around Fort Benton although the post journalist considered them an unproductive nuisance.

That spring Fort Benton sucked in over 5,200 robes and the opposition post Fort Campbell took even more. The lots brought in by individual Indians were usually under a hundred while trading chiefs for bands delivered larger loads. But most returns were collected by individual traders with wagons who circulated between the camps. Dried tongues were another valuable by-product of what was turning into wholesale slaughter. Real meat was being left on the prairie to rot.

Although he may have puzzled out the letter from his father, Bird did not return to the Missouri from a second circuit until 20 April. Seventeen days later the Bird family went off with the squawman James Chambers who had been called up from Fort Union to assist in getting over a thousand packs of robes downstream.[5] Instead, he and the fort interpreter Baptiste Champagne were assigned to drive a herd of eighty-nine horses and some colts to Fort Union. The Bird family trailed along because twenty-six of those animals represented their savings on the hoof.

Traveling on the north side they crossed Maria's River and passed the Bear Paws. There was still a spark of daring in fifty-six-year-old Jemmy Jock. Riding along in the dust of the herd he bantered with Chambers about the merits of the latter's fine black horse. Bird just had to try him out and Chambers neglected to mention that the spoiled animal was untrustworthy. The aging plainsman was almost killed during the bucking fit.

They passed the Atsiina camp near Eagle Creek safely, but lost fourteen horses to rustlers at Milk River on the twenty-sixth. The insulted drovers set out on the trail of what turned out to be Siksika or Kainaa thieves and soon recovered a beautiful cream-coloured mare. Chambers turned the animal over to Bird and rode another fifteen miles before giving up the chase. Apparently, the pacification process was not fully accepted by tribes north of the Medicine Line.

Next day, Dawson's boat came in view on the river. The drovers put the ailing Baptiste Champagne and his wife on board and took off Bird's young son to take his place in getting the herd across Riviere du Tremble. When they reached Fort Union on 26 May, Chambers considered it the hardest trip he had ever made.[6]

Although the Bird family was primed to go on to the Assiniboine River, they may have waited for six weeks. On 13 July, trader Denig took his last payment from Pierre Chouteau Jr and Company. By mid-September the Denigs were resettled on the White Horse Plain west of the forks, and James Bird Jr was with his father.[7] That was none too soon. The old fur trader died on 18 October 1856.

Those who remained of the Bird family were gratified that the great men of the community carried the coffin to Saint James Church. The patriarch was lowered into a grave in the shady churchyard. Ten of the patriarch's eighteen children were still living; four in distant Oregon. Attracted by better opportunities, and escape from the stifling authority of the company, seven sisters or brothers and one stepsister became American citizens. As the world beyond the forks accelerated, some of its best were drawn west by a series of gold rushes and business opportunities.

But when the will was read, the cost of the English wife became apparent. The younger members of the second family received the major portion of the funds invested in United Empire bonds. Mary Lowman had enough to keep her in style, and her son, Curtis James Bird, received £2,000 and possession of lot 101. Her daughter Elisa Margaret received a bequest of £1,100 and there was a £600 dowry for the sickly, unmarried daughter Mary. The mixed-blood children of Elizabeth Montour; Letty, Joseph, William, and Henry received bequests of £100. But James Bird Jr, Levi, Thomas, and the useless boys who went to Oregon were not included.[8]

Jemmy Jock had been on his own for many years, but it would have meant something to have been recognized. Although not included in his father's estate, he was heir to the old trader's thirty-year commitment to the Indian trade. Operating on the northern plains, the son had realized the father's ambition to trade to the Muddy River Indians. The Boundary Compromise of 1818 drew a line in the dust that Governor Simpson never managed to penetrate, but that Medicine Line never inhibited Jemmy Jock.

In retirement, old Bird had continued to offend the governor. The retired chief factor conducted his private business across the border until he was manoeuvered back into line with the appointment of a collector of customs for Assiniboia. That was the same time his son was engaged in the illegal extraction of peltry from United States territory. Jemmy Jock's value as a "confidential servant" increased from £20 to £100. Fired or rehired according to the swings of business, his life was manipulated to answer corporate needs. While the prospects of other mixed-bloods declined, Bird shouldered a place for himself with a hand that Governor Simpson had never managed to trump.

Company managers could not have missed that Jemmy Jock Bird came to the Red River settlement after helping the United States confirm its relationship with the western tribes that still passed back and forth across the border. In addition to installing an official presence at Fort Benton there had been surveys for a transcontinental railway. American activities led a Canadian official to declare in September 1856 "that it was Canada's destiny to extend to the Pacific and that it was imperative that a railway be built across the Hudson's Bay Company territory to British Columbia. The Hudson's Bay Company must step aside."[9]

As a matter of fact, the "Little Emperor" was also thinking of selling off, if a buyer could be found. The last years had not been kind to the declining George Simpson who continued to suffer not quite debilitating little strokes. His old supporter on the London committee died in 1852, his wife the next year. Two of his

Red River Settlement by Paul Kane.
National Archives of Canada.

White Man's World

trusted field lieutenants, Peter Skene Ogden and John Rowand, rode the last trail in 1854. So, he treated the passing of old Bird lightly without understanding what that life meant; the human need for independence. In June he wrote, "Here [near Norway House], as at Red River, it is vain to conceal from ourselves the fact that we are in a certain degree overawed and dictated to by the numerical superiority of those we are supposed to govern: ..."[10]

James Bird Jr, Sarah, and their family finally settled on the Selkirk grant that he had been awarded almost forty years before. River lot number sixty-three was located on the east bank of Red River about twelve miles below the forks. His neighbors on lots sixty and sixty-one were James and John Irving.[11] On lot sixty-five Jean Baptiste Derosiers was a son of the country about the same age as Jamey. Across the river, John Tait lived on lot sixty-two and Thomas Setter on the adjoining lot sixty-four. In a neighborhood of former fur traders, the Birds were not out of place.

The Red River community was an aging mix of transplanted highlanders, Swiss immigrants and assorted old mercenaries. Retired fur traders, Company servants, and former North West Company *engagés* were still the dominant element. Those of British descent thought of themselves as half-breeds while the French preferred the term *Métis*. Raised around the trading posts and often reassigned, few mixed-bloods ever spent very much time with the people of their Indian mothers. Jemmy Jock was unusual for having been an "Indian by habit" for over thirty years.

By mid-century both sides of the Red River from Upper Fort Garry to the Lower Fort were well settled. Keeping with older Canadian tradition the narrow lots were only two chains wide at the river bank, but extended back into the plain as far as the holder felt necessary in order to crop hay or engross usable timber. Although there was a wide, straight road across the prairie, the small log houses depended on the looping river, and connected to each other by meandering footpaths. Some houses, like his father's large White Cottage, were plastered with mud and whitened with lime. For the most part, appearances were not a large concern to families raised at wilderness trading posts.

Lacking a market for more extensive crops, most families cropped just enough wheat, barley, potatoes, and summer vegetables for subsistence. Turning the heavy sod or finding a piece of potato with an eye in it was not a very demanding agriculture. According to tribal custom digging roots was woman's work so Sally worked the garden and picked up horticultural advice from neighbor women. Many were Indians like herself more accustomed to digging roots than planting them.

Sally finally gained Christian legitimacy. During the years when she attended the preaching of the Reverend Rundle, he had refused to baptize her. Now the difficulty of the other wife was left behind and Sally could be accepted into the Church of England. She and James were married at St. Paul's Anglican Church on Christmas Day 1857. Six months later she was baptized there with the name Sarah.

Determined to build a new life, the prairie wanderers put the children in school. Five of the six children born in the mountains accompanied their parents to the settlement. Twelve-year-old Thomas and his seven-year-old brother Philip were baptized at St. Paul's church on 24 April 1859. That was in keeping with the previous baptisms in the mountains and was not forced by social pressure. As authentic Christians the family was in good standing with the church and respectable in an increasingly gentrified society.

The imposition of social order began over twenty years before when Governor Simpson and his cronies put off Indian mistresses and country wives in favor of imported British brides. The great man intended to raise the level of propriety to a place in keeping with his personal expectations, but that had not worked out quite as expected. The Birds had confronted the Simpsons just when that arrangement was beginning to crumble. But Chief Factor Bird succumbed to Simpson's example, and to the amusement of other old traders, married the English schoolteacher Mrs. Lowman. At the reading of his father's will, Jemmy Jock had a very personal lesson in the real cost of social climbing.

He was still part of endless prairie time, a buffalo runner, whose marginality challenged the growing consciousness of race and belief that was beginning to infect the community. As strangers came into the Anglicized settlement Bird saw his kinsmen and his Catholic friends relegated to lesser roles as a convenient labor pool in a company town run by outsiders.[12] The prairie provision factory offered an escape of sorts. Undoubtedly, a young man like Charles, who was already experienced as a plainsman, went off with the buffalo hunt. He could have accompanied the Red River hunt that went south beyond Pembina or joined the White Horse Palin band that traveled to the southwest. The pemmican factory was taking around three thousand buffalo a year. Or there were opportunities for adventure in the cart brigades going to St. Paul.

The northern plains were big enough to tolerate two levels of discovery: the practical, and the perfect. Practical men had been going about for two centuries uninhibited by the lack of maps, guide books, or world appreciation. The perfectionists came as explorers like Lewis and Clark, John Charles Fremont, Isaac I. Stevens, or Captain John Palliser, usually wearing a uniform and planning to write a book. The relentless march of progress was filling in the blank spaces, surveying and plaiting.

British North America depended on the impressions of a series of gentleman adventurers; Robert M. Ballatyne's description of the fur traders, the Earl of Southesk, Viscount Milton, W. B. Cheadle, and Captain William Butler's sniffy impressions of the northern plainsmen. Sons of the country like Piscan Munroe, the Favels, and the McKays kept those inexperienced gentlemen from embarrassment in the field and were rewarded by mention as quaint footnotes to the vanishing wilderness.

Within a year of the Bird's retirement, two exploring expeditions arrived at the forks of the Red and Assiniboine rivers. The mission was to perform surveys similar to whatever Isaac Stevens had done south of the line. British Royal Engineer Captain John Palliser arrived late in the evening of 11 July 1857, and by the next afternoon he was milking the retired John Edward Harriot about the west. After an initial circuit to Pembina, Turtle Mountain, Fort Ellice, and Fort Carlton, Palliser left for St. Paul. He was riding one of Robert Tait's horses, but apparently made no effort to question the experienced plainsman living just across the river.[13] Returning in the spring, Palliser spent nine days in the settlement before heading for Fort Ellice and the Rocky Mountains.

The Canadian Red River expedition from Toronto arrived at Lower Fort Garry on 5 September. While commenting on the commodious and comfortable residence of Mrs. Bird not far from the Stone Church (St. Andrew's), Henry Youle Hind noted that the middle settlement's St. Paul's Church perched on the edge of the endless prairie. Of the 6,523 inhabitants in the settlement, he estimated that about 816 were half-breeds or natives. In the last thirteen years their number had only increased by 245; proof that the wild place was becoming civilized.[14]

Hind brought along the photographer Humphrey Lloyd Hime. After returning from an extensive tour of the prairies, in October 1858 Hime took a charming photo of a plains-Cree half-breed named Letitia who might have been the girl Rundle baptized in the Rocky Mountains. But Hime lacked the good sense to take an image of her father.[15]

Oregon boundary disputes of the last decade taught Great Britain and the company hard lessons about the politics of colonization. Assiniboia had cause to be concerned about the exploding population of neighboring Minnesota.[16] In his August 1857 letter, Governor Simpson expressed company concern that the small numbers in the Red River settlement might be overwhelmed. In October the War Office sent 120 officers and men of the Canadian Rifles. But imperial concerns were secondary to business. Next year when steamers began running on the upper Red River, those aging baymen, Sir George and "Bear" Ellice paid a visit to St. Paul. Recognizing that a rail and river connection to the settlement might be more economic than the old access through the bay, they considered forming a bank in association with American capitalists.[17] The Selkirk colonists were now aging highlanders, a few tottering discharged soldiers, and a few remaining Swiss. The starch had finally gone out of the Irish toughs. Few saw much promise in a landlocked community. Disputes about the control that the company could exercise over the private business of individuals had been mostly resolved by the Sayer trial. That was a rare time when the community had banded together to challenge the company lock on enterprise and finally proved that the monopoly was unenforceable. Three years later, after staging a grand display to entertain the Prince of Wales, Governor Sir George Simpson died. His passing on 7 September 1860 symbolized the retreat of the old commercial empire of Rupert's Land.

The discovery of gold on the Fraser River in distant British Columbia had excited American businessmen. Ready to cash in on the bonanza, the "Fraser River Convention" met to consider ways of promoting St. Paul as the Mississippi River trailhead to the new gold fields. They were looking for the most direct route to the gold fields. Jemmy Jock Bird was as unmindful of the abstract border as the great vees of geese following the middle continental flyway. He traveled to St. Paul with the petty traders who drove carts five hundred miles to obtain merchandise. While men with official sanction were defining western geography, Jemmy Jock Bird scooped them by giving an interview.

Between 10 and 14 July 1858, he gave an interview to a young lawyer from New York. James Wickes Taylor immediately published his interview with a retired Indian.[18] James Bird Jr understood plains geography. He described the Bears River (Maria's) Pass, Chief Mountain Pass, Bad Back Fat Pass, Medicine Rock Pass, or Crow's Lodge (Crowsnest) Pass, all of which he knew from direct experience. According to Bird,

> From St. Paul, let a good strong party go straight across the plain to the upper head of Cypress Mountain – then rather northwest, west more than north, about eight days travel – then enter the mountains, and, with moderate traveling, reach the Columbia River. Medicine Rock pass comes out on Tobacco Plains, near the border.... Medicine Rock must be the best, for the Kootenais prefer it – travel it in winter. They carry packs on their backs, with snow shoes and kill buffalo on the eastern plains. Then, when they have made their provisions they go back on the Crows Lodge route ... Medicine Rock or Kootanais Pass have been passed by me in one day's ride on horseback.... I estimate the distance as about 70 miles – 3 or 4 days journey on foot.[19]

In a time before wire services, newspapers lifted stories from each other so Bird's views were soon reprinted in the *New York Herald* and *New York Journal of Commerce*.

In addition to anticipating the reports of the Palliser or Canadian exploring expeditions, Jamey's information influenced the Minnesota rush to the Fraser mines.[20]

The gold fever that infected the community drew Bird into the business of outfitting miners. He was influenced by the enthusiasm of a Kentucky adventurer with the euphonious name, Timoleon M. Love. After rushing to the Fraser River mines, Love returned to winter at Edmonton where he worked for Chief Factor William Christy as a carpenter. Coming back at the Red River settlement in the spring 1861, Love went to Minnesota to obtain supplies. As he rode back on the Red River steamer *Pioneer*, the prospective outfitter became acquainted with a fellow passenger. The scientifically minded Mr. Lewis Henry Morgan was not entirely convinced about Love's reasons for leaving the California mines, and mistrusted his statements about the Indians of California, Oregon, and Puget Sound. But he responded to the mention of someone who knew about the tribes of the northern plains.

Unfortunately, Denig, the transplanted squawman and sometime scholar of the Indians of the Upper Missouri, had expired at Headingly three years ago. His amateur descriptions of savage folk were already being sucked into the budding field of scientific anthropology. In August 1861 Morgan, the thinker credited with the invention of American ethnology, stepped off the *Pioneer*. Given the return schedule of the boat, he only had a couple of days in which to locate and interview a living example of miscegenation.

The pioneer ethnologist hoped to find the origin of the North American tribes. The clue might be in how they designated their lines of kinship and consanguinity. Or what they wore to bed. At St. Paul, Métis cart traders told Morgan that Mr. Bird of the Red River spoke several Indian languages and knew a good deal about the habits of many western tribes. On the boat, Morgan became acquainted with Joseph James Hargrave, the son of the former factor at York, and nephew of the present factor at Fort Garry. But Uncle William MacTavish was disinclined to interrupt his Sunday dinner to put the scientist in touch with a disreputable half-breed living twelve miles downstream.

The fuming scientist walked three miles to the house of the local functionary, Robert Tait, who forwarded him to the house of John Tait. As luck would have it, Mr. Bird was visiting from across the river. Over supper Morgan explained the purpose of his visit which was favorably received. Crossing to Bird's house on the east bank, Mr. Morgan was introduced to Sally. During a warm evening they worked out a complete schedule of Peigan relationships.

Jamey named the bands or clans of the Pe-kan-ne (Piikani) whose name for themselves meant rich people. Those bands were the Ah-pe'ki-e or Skunk tribe, Ih-po'se-ma or Web Fat tribe, Ka-ka'po-ya or Inside Fat tribe, Mo-ta'to-sis or Conjurers,

Ka-ta'ge-ma-ne or Starving, Ka-ti'ya-ye-mie or Blood, and E-po'to-pis-taxe or Half Dried Meat tribe. Apparently the Inuk'sik were no longer considered a body worth mention.[21]

Morgan was told that according to Piikani custom a man could not marry a woman of his own tribe but the children of the marriage belonged to the tribe of the father.[22] When the questioning turned to his other wives, Jemmy Jock explained that a man who married the eldest sister was entitled to marry all the other girls of that family as they came of age, about fourteen or fifteen. But he had to be a good man and use them well. Like many other original people, Pekane had no terms for nephew, niece, or cousin. A brother's or sister's children were your children, and brothers and sisters to each other. However, there were words for uncles and aunts.[23]

At the nearby home of the Assiniboine, Iron Woman, Morgan collected additional data. It was past midnight when the scientist finally paddled back across the river. The night was warm and a brilliant aurora borealis danced in the sky. Jemmy Jock sat for a while in the dark watching the lights reflected in the water. He had spent most of his life trying to explain the strange ways of the traders to his tribal friends. It seemed odd to interpret Reds to a white man.

What had taken place that evening reminded him that he was always in the middle, always between someone or something. After the company changed, he went off with the Muddy River Indians. It had been good hunting with friends and having his own lodge to return to, and the welcome of a responsive young wife. But the thin thread of twenty pounds a year still tied him to the Edmonton traders. The company men never respected him until they realized his value to the competition. They thought of him as just another commodity to be bought or sold. He got out of the damned hide trade before the good memories were completely spoiled. That world became meaner when beaver skins and buffalo robes were converted into guns, and powder, and whiskey. Now his old friends were drowning in the blood of slaughtered buffalo, taking tongues or hides and each other's lives for no good reason.

His children were learning to live in the world that took all that away from him. Sally fitted into this place better than he did. Getting together with Iron Woman they worked with their beads and sinew thread and pretended that they were back in camp doing their rightful work. But sometimes she straightened up from hoeing in the garden and looked west toward the long horizon where endless flat plains masked the distant mountains. There was no use trying to keep the world in place. Nothing was as magical as the first time you saw it. After a while the lights stopped dancing in the sky and it was very dark.

Métis Politics

Not long before the Bird family returned to the Red River settlement, the former western fur trader Alexander Ross published a history of the colony. Lamenting the lack of political involvement, sheriff Ross hoped to see political conscious rise from the people. But next summer just 574, only a fifth of the total population, were willing to sign a petition favoring the extension of Canadian government.[1] After long careers under corporate dictation, those old hands were unready to accept the paternalistic direction of strangers.

Matters might have drifted along in the ennui of the prairie summer or the frozen beauty of the northern winter if gold had not been discovered in New Caledonia. That distant bonanza flooded the northern plains with a new breed of boomer. Some, like the New York lawyer James Wickes Taylor, stayed to politicize the community. Even the Sheriff's Toronto-educated son, James Ross, became a proponent of Canadian takeover.

The gold-fixated, apolitical Timoleon Love was content to remain at Red River through the winter 1861/62 giving interviews on bonanzas to The Nor'wester. By May the St. Paul visionary Taylor was disillusioned, but Love was just getting his second wind. He saw that the real money was supplying others. During the winter, Love bought into the store that Edmund

Barber operated near Fort Garry. When their suppliers, Burbank Brothers of St. Paul, would only accept cash, Barber and Love convinced Mr. Bird to dip into those savings still riding on HBC account books.[2] In readily accepting Jemmy Jock's drafts Burbank Brothers optimistically expounded that, "the trade for the Gold districts must be large and you who are prepared for it will make money."[3] On 11 June Love succumbed to his own propaganda, sold his interest in E. L. Barber, and went off hoping to wash out five dollars a day on the upper Saskatchewan. Presumably Barber did well supplying miners and overlanders, and the capitalist Bird did not suffer financially from his investment. But it was quite a step from collecting buffalo hides to collecting dividends.

Opportunities for investment were limited. "The major occupation of the mixed-bloods and Métis was freighting, in boat brigades to York Factory and up the Saskatchewan; in Red River cart trains to the south, to St. Peter's and St. Paul, and west by the Carlton Trail and other traditional overland routes; and in winter with dog trains carrying the winter packet or other urgent freight."[4] Until the steamboats eased the cart traffic, it was a five-hundred-mile overland haul from St. Paul. With the upper Red River near a railhead, the company finally gave up hauling goods over the old York Factory mainline, which cost the young men with strong arms their jobs.

James Bird had lived too long in the delicate, potentially fatal, balance between ambitious young Indian warriors and stolidly calculating elders. Now he just wanted to live in peace on his little bit of the increasingly bounded earth. That title was unique because Lord Selkirk had misunderstood the territorial concepts of seminomadic hunters and actually bought the land from local Ojibwa. No one questioned that they were also immigrants. For fifty years Bird had owned 126 acres of what some now intended to redesignate as the Province of Manitoba.

Although he helped divide the Blackfoot country Jemmy Jock Bird was not impressed by boundaries. He had run with the Gens du Large for so long that he almost believed that the earth belonged to everyone, and to no one. The imperial pretensions of a distant abstraction called Great Britain were fantastic. Those foolish diplomats had agreed to an invisible line drawn across the northern plains without regard for the meandering rivers and drainage divides that made better landmarks. Buffalo didn't recognize that border and why should men. Bird's sentimental attachments were to the Sturgeon River where he was born, or to old Edmonton House where he spent a brief childhood. The other special places that he held in his heart were high in the mountains or beside mirror lakes on the headwaters of the Bow.

Surveyors measured out the dark earth along the banks of the Red with iron chains. In time, the block of ten lots that Lord Selkirk awarded to acting Governor

Bird had been broken up. After the old trader's death, the widow Bird still lived at White Cottage. Her educated son, Doctor Curtis James Bird, had a house in town to be nearer his practice. Others were relatively confident in the possession of their little lots. If a neighbor's cow wandered into the cornfield, it was a matter between individuals. But some were agitating for a connection with the Canadians, and the Catholic Métis were rightfully worried how a new regime would treat them.

In 1859, the exclusive License to Trade lapsed. A year later, on 7 September 1860 Governor Sir George Simpson died. His career had been devoted to keeping a lock on Rupert's Land which the Red River community had resisted. But with his death many of those former opponents feared that the company was about to sell out its children. Before their homeland slipped from under their moccasins, apprehensive Métis had to insure their future.

There was a smell of annexation in the air. That had been forecast by the Ross book, and underlined by the British and Canadian exploring parties. Canadians were just as land hungry as their rapacious neighbors to the south, and after the best part of Ontario was taken up expansionists began making up folk songs about "a little piece of ground." Those eastern dudes who could not bring themselves to take the trail across those plains to the goldfields were already scheming of ways to pan valuable acreage from Métis. A new class of boomers and exploiters infiltrated the dozy settlement.

Jemmy Jock had already been part of that process in the Blackfoot Treaty. He didn't see much difference between an Issac Stevens and a Canadian "annexer" like John Christian Schultz.[5] From a bully pulpit of the only newspaper, what editor Schultz wrote read like another treaty of cession. But it would be Métis instead of Indians who stood to lose. Another opportunist from St. Paul was a legless fellow named Enos Stutsman who hopped about on short crutches and dreamed of prairie empires.[6] Some of the recent arrivals from Ontario were English-speaking Protestants known as Orangemen or Fenians who dragged along their ancient resentment of Catholics. To a retired Piikani like Jemmy Jock, Red River politics were becoming as intrusive as a party of Flathead buffalo hunters. No surprise that his name is missing from daily accounts of the political powder keg recorded in the journal of Alexander Begg.[7]

Carters returned from St. Paul infected with democratic illusions.[8] That gathering resistance spoke with a distinctly French accent and most Anglophone half-breeds were uncertain if a demonstration was any of their business. Although it was a bit late in the game for the democratic tactic of a filibuster, Bird's St. Paul connection, James W. Taylor, was one of the sixty-nine or so Americans in the settlement who were waiting to see how the situation turned out. American ambitions centered around the U.S. Consul, Oscar Malmros, the deformed Enos Stutsman, and Taylor, but the best they could do was to stiffen Métis resistance to the Canadian party.[9] After his restrained description of the leader of the Canadian annexationists as unscrupulous, Taylor left the hard criticism to others.[10]

During a difficult time when half-tribesmen should have listened to the conservative wisdom of their elders, the Métis responded to the reckless energy of a twenty-five year old fledgling. Louis Riel's father led previous eruptions against the overbearing company. Patriot and instinctive demagogue, young Riel's downstream education had made him a true believer, a powerless intellectual capable of seizing the minds of others. In their greater wisdom, both the opposition and the establishment dismissed him as a mere saloon loafer.

There was still the buffalo hunt. If the former plainsman found an excuse for a summer outing, Jemmy Jock's fun was spoiled by stiffening joints and failing eyesight. And each year the buffalo were farther away. Accustomed to real meat, the best in the world, the Bird family was learning to appreciate moldy pemmican. It may have been to avoid the looming quarrel, that in the autumn 1867 the Bird family left the settlement to winter at Qu'Appelle. Two years before, their eighteen-year-old son Tom Bird married Anne McKay, a daughter of the little bearskin McKays who frequented the Qu'Appelle area.[11]

But living on the plains was not so easy. During the winter 1869/70 so much snow lay on the prairies that there was no certainty of finding buffalo next summer. In 1871/72 fire blackened the plains around Qu'Appelle and also kept the herds out of reach on the South Branch. As that winter closed in, shivering hunters could only hope that glacial winds from the mountains would drive the buffalo east.

In early 1870, the Ancient and Honorable Company of Adventurers executed a Deed of Surrender and Prince Rupert's Land passed to the Dominion of Canada. Militant Métis blocked the Canadian surveyors and stopped Lieutenant-Governor William McDougall at Pembina. The situation began to look like 1816 all over again. On 16 November 1869 the Red River dissidents organized *Le Comité National des Métis de la Rivière Rouge* with John Bruce as president and Louis Riel as secretary. By the end of the month they boldly seized Fort Garry in a generally orderly takeover. From that base of operations young Riel devised a balanced coalition of French- and English-speaking mixed-bloods and called a convention where he proposed a provisional government.

Jemmy Jock was among the thousand people who assembled in the fort compound on 19 January 1870. Attempting to ease the transition, HBC Chief Factor Donald Smith assured them that the new Canadian government would be liberal and fair. That failed to derail the provisional government that elected Riel as its head. One member of Riel's new council was Bird's half brother, Doctor Curtis James Bird.

In the melodramatic exchanges that followed in February, some men were apprehended at the home of John Schultz. They were still being held as prisoners when one of the frustrated Canadian surveyors, an Ontario Militia Captain named C. A. Boulton, took it upon himself to raise a war party and force their release. Tromping about in the snow half-drunk, those heroes were more dangerous to each other than to the Métis who wisely holed up in comfortable old Fort Garry.

The gang that assembled in the Kildonan schoolhouse fed on false reports and outrageous rumors. As they became more threatening, a terrified young Métis prisoner named Parisen made a break for it. In his hysterical flight, the boy inadvertently killed seventeen-year-old Johnny Sutherland.

As the Kildonan women went to pieces, the men from the lower parish simply melted away leaving Boulton's war party up in the air. The best that they could do was escort Schultz as far as Doctor Bird's house. When last seen Schultz was headed in the general direction of Duluth on snowshoes.

It is possible that Jemmy Jock threw in with the Portage la Prairie men to make sure that his nephew William G. Bird got safely back to his Poplar Point home. As the party was crossing the open prairie well clear of the settlement, their hearts sank. A force marched from Fort Garry to intercept them.[12] Fifty Métis were enough to cow forty-one loyalists. The rebel Richot came forward offering his hand and, except for a little scuffling when the heroes gave up their arms, harmony prevailed.

The prisoners were conducted to the fort by the forces of the Provisional Government and installed in six rooms of the officer's quarters. Chaining the less than impressive Captain Boulton so embarrassed Susie Delorme, the captain of the guard, that he was brought to tears. Given the circumstances, cooperation was the better course, but the pugnacious Fenians were determined to create trouble. When Tom Bunn and James Ross were delegated to represent the "English" element in the new government, the protests of Thomas Scott and another vocal prisoner resulted in their being ironed.

After threatening to execute Boulton, Riel was driven to make an example of the obnoxious Scott. By 4 March the adamant "Yankee Fenian" was taken out into the yard and shot. That telling demonstration led to the release of the other prisoners. Jemmy Jock returned home to find his neighbors still grieving over the death of young Sutherland and convinced that revolutions weren't that much fun.[13] On 15 July 1870, the Province of Manitoba was proclaimed at Ottawa. Most of the demands of the Métis for responsible government, provincial status, denominational schools, and guarantees of land title and Indian title were at least considered. A total of 1.4

million acres of land were set aside for the children of the country who were not already in possession of plots. Before long, river lot residents went to the banks, to see the Sixtieth Rifle Regiment rowing up to Point Douglas in the rain.[14]

After the government of Canada confirmed Bird's right to lot sixty-three, he was free to sell it. Property close to the growing town of Winnipeg had become valuable. Bird placed his upstream lot in the hands of an attorney who sold it to the land speculator Schultz. The Bird family relocated on lots 280 and 287 in St. Andrew's Parish. As lot 281 was a Schultz property, a land swap may have been part of the deal.[15]

Threading through the maze of the Provisional Government Jemmy's half brother, Dr. Curtis J. Bird was elected to the new legislature of Manitoba. When Winnipeg boosters attempted a shortcut to incorporation, as Speaker, Bird felt obliged to uphold the law. In revenge he was ambushed on a dark night, hauled from his carriage, and brutally tarred. Losing enthusiasm for Manitoba politics, Dr. Bird went to England in 1876 where he contracted pneumonia and died. After eighty-eight years in Rupert's Land, the brightest promise of old chief factor Bird's mixed flock returned to a Chiswick parish grave.

There is no indication what became of the beautiful girl, Letitia, Bird photographed in 1858. Several of Jemmy Jock and Sally's children died in the mountains and records are missing that might have provided clues to what became of Edward, Charles, Joseph, Mary, Maria, and Catharine. Now the youngest were flying away.[16]

Tom Bird married Anne McKay of the little bearskin Qu'Appelle family in 1865, but five years later smallpox claimed the young mother and her baby at Edmonton. Nancy Bird may have had a daughter by Peter Lang before they were married at Winnipeg in 1866. Agnes Bird, a dusky beauty with fine features and olive cheeks, found a good husband in big Thomas Hourie, called Tommack. They drifted to the Métis settlement between the forks of the Saskatchewan.[17] After their youngest son Philip married Mary Kipling at St. Andrew's on 8 September 1871, James and Sally Bird turned the family home over to the newlyweds. The new couple was still living there three years later when they buried a son in that churchyard.[18] Not long after, Philip Bird and Mary Kipling went on the plains.[19]

Eighteen years of a settled life disproved sniffy claims that the Bird family were mere plains roamers. Since coming to the community Jemmy Jock had helped capitalize a modest flyer in mercantilism, provided geographical advice that helped route the Fraser and Saskatchewan River gold rushes, and contributed ethnological data to advance outside understanding of the mountain tribes. Seventy-three-year-old men don't just ride away into the sunset. Perhaps aging Sally longed to see her tribesmen again. But that wasn't going to be easy for the old couple. Jemmy Jock's joints had stiffened until he had to lead a horse to a high point to get on. The unrelenting sun had clouded his vision and his teeth were worn down by a nearly complete meat diet. At his age, old Bird should have been content to sit in the sun with his neighbors retelling familiar lies.

Prairie Calling

There was still room to roam, but the northern plains were far from the wilderness suggested by tardy discovery literature.[1] If not exactly teeming, those vast expanses were a vital tribal range where young Indians still rode to capture horses or keep the neighbors upset. Jemmy Jock left that life after helping the Americans make a peace treaty that was supposed to blunt the self-destructive contests for buffalo. But the *iinii* had become a commodity and Fort Benton entrepreneurs were not going to let the lucrative robe trade escape them.

Along the Upper Missouri, tribesmen saw their way of life slipping away and looked to recover spirit power from the bottle. Inebriated warriors took out their frustrations on intruders who responded in kind. How could anyone have foreseen that miners would flood into Montana giving young warriors new enemies to fight. The country was tortured by mutual murder until January 1870 when a detachment of United States troopers was sent to punish troublemakers. Instead, they slaughtered the wrong band of Piikani.[2]

After the attack on Heavy Runner's smallpox-ravaged camp, many of Jemmy Jock's old friends fled north of the border. In their charred hearts they carried deadly coals of dreaded smallpox. The Northern Piikani lost a thousand and the Siksika and Kainaa about six hundred people. Searing the country as far north as Edmonton, the conflagration claimed Tom Bird's wife Anne and their baby Abraham.

There was another deadly visitor to the band camps. Yankees crossed the Medicine Line with deadly kegs of whiskey. In the first months of 1869 the Fort Benton opportunists, Johnny Healy and Al Hamilton, drew $50,000 from their Fort Whoop-Up operation. Grimly recounting the deaths of forty-two Indians killed in drunken orgies the horrified missionary to the Stoney Indians wrote:

> Some terrible scenes occurred when whole camps went on the spree, as was frequently the case, shooting, stabbing, killing, freezing, dying. Mothers lost their children. These were either frozen to death or devoured by the myriad dogs of the camp. The birth rate decreased and the poor red man was in a fair way toward extinction, just because some white men, coming out of Christian countries, and themselves the evolution of Christian civilization, were now ruled by lust and greed.[3]

Beliefs were as deadly as smallpox or chemicals. There was a famous stone on a hilltop near the Battle River that seemed to be made of iron. That spirit power had been respected for years beyond recall. Then Methodist missionaries from Victoria on the Saskatchewan River below Edmonton decided that was an ungodly object of pagan worship, and hauled it off. The desecration meant bad times for the outraged Cree. Within three years, the blow fell when Bird's old friend, Maskepetoon, risked going to a Blackfoot camp on another peace mission. The northern plains diplomat was treacherously assassinated. In revenge, a Cree and Assiniboine army moved toward the Oldman River in the fall 1860. Ignoring a nearby Piikani camp, they fell on a small camp of Bloods. Piikani riding to the sound of the fight were armed with new repeating rifles and turned the invasion into a rout. Actual loses from the battle of the Oldman River were probably closer to seventy-five slain Cree and Assiniboine, balanced against forty dead Blackfeet. But exaggerated claims of three or four hundred casualties, combined with the losses from smallpox, were hard lessons that could not be ignored. Next spring the humiliated Cree sent tobacco and made conciliatory gestures leading to the peace that was agreed at the Red Deer River.

The northern plains were the last resort of the mixed-blood children of the country. Adding to the pressure upon the tribes and their resources, seasonal tides of Métis cart men bumped along the trails from Fort Carlton or Fort Benton. Columns of a hundred or more carts snaked across the western grasslands, their roads cutting the rutted buffalo trails, the shrieking of ungreased cartwheels a death song for diminishing herds. Disengaged grandchildren of the fur trade seemed to be camped beside every pond, or in every sheltering coulee. Métis hunters lived by making pemmican or taking hides for a little cash. The distance they had to go to find the herds drew Métis hunters into dangerous proximity with increasingly desperate tribes.

The Bird family was part of that increasingly anachronistic population. In company with their son Philip and his wife Mary Kipling, Jemmy Jock and Sally must have left the Red River settlement in 1874. That community was in the flush of intensified development and those relics of a lost past hoped to escape into expanses that the Canadians had not engrossed. The family group had the ability to speak to Cree kinsmen, Stoney associates, or displaced Peigans. In encounters with Métis Bird could speak French or Michif, while retaining a distinctly English accent.[4] They would get along but returning to that sun-blasted world cost old Bird the last of his sight. Increasingly, he bumped along in a cart, sealed in an envelope of remembered places. Beyond speaking, what good was a blind old man on the prairies? Past seventy and almost blind, he was too old to rope a pony, fork a bronco, or even identify an approaching rider. Dependent on his dutiful son Philip, or later Tom, Jemmy Jock's last wanderings would be traced to the places where grandchildren were born.[5]

Although the Hudson's Bay Company had relinquished its grip on Rupert's Land, it reserved large tracts of land around the trading posts. That acreage was certain to increase in value as development in-filled around them. Reduced to mere businessmen and real estate salesmen, the once lordly traders continued to broker provisions and buy buffalo robes. When the Métis rebellion briefly blocked shipping on the old road to the bay, the company devised an alternative. Goods shipped up the Missouri by steamboat were already being accepted and hauled north to the posts. It was only reasonable to send down heavy bales of hides by the returning boats.[6] When Saskatchewan traders sent cart trains laden with northern robes south to Fort Benton, the infamous Whoop-Up Trail became a two-way street.

Liquor from the Fort Benton fountain was the great consumable of the robe trade. It was illicitly dispensed from several notorious *whiskihagens* by what might be generously called an unreliable element. In late May 1873 wolfers festering in the beleaguered Indian heartland concocted an excuse to attack a band of Stoneys in the Cypress Hills. In the resulting shoot-out twenty Indians were killed and five captured women were raped.

The atrocity was intolerable, but plans had already been implemented for the extension of Canadian authority. That autumn the North West Mounted Police rode west to impose order.[7] Before long, the green logs of Fort McLeod became the western bastion of the queen's law.

Being driven back across the line by redcoats gave the obnoxious whiskey traders an inverse legitimacy. Montana Territory made the former liquor peddler Johnny

Healy sheriff. No surprise that around the old Blackfoot agency in 1874 from fifteen to twenty Piikani, including several chiefs, were killed in drunken brawls.

The treaty Bird helped negotiate nineteen years ago had been altered several times. A series of lusterless, rather than outright corrupt, Indian agents permitted the subdivision of the huge tract originally reserved for the Blackfeet. Ten years after the peace treaty of 1855, the chiefs, head men, and delegates of the several tribes of the "Blackfoot Nation" were assembled at Fort Benton to meet special commissioner Gad E. Upson and acting governor of Montana Thomas Meagher. After reaffirming perpetual peace, friendship, and amity they convinced the tribesmen to cede half of the territory reserved to them previously. No Indian office employee was going to stand in the way of that.

When a more responsible appointee tried to block additional land cessions by refusing to move the agency, he was replaced by an Iowa lawman with blind enthusiasm for frontier law and order. The new broom assembled five thousand Indians and demanded that they elect a new leader. In this exercise of imposed democracy, Little Plume emerged as chief with Generous Woman and White Calf as his assistants. The codes of law that were drawn up smelled more of agent than Indian, but it gave the reservation council authority to punish murder, threatening, theft, assault, wife beating, polygamy, rape, sale of female relatives, and the buying, selling, or even keeping of liquor.[8] After that repudiation of ancient excesses was signed on 23 April 1874, a new agency was established on Badger Creek just fourteen miles inside the reservation.

There were signs that outmoded habits were softening. When Bird's Piikani brother-in-law, Three Suns, ran some Sioux horse thieves to ground in the Cypress Hills, instead of taking their scalps he turned them over to the Mounties at Fort Macleod. But that also showed that the wards of both powers were ignoring the Medicine Line. The north Peigans learned to work the system by drifting south to get in on United States annuities and then ingenuously complained about the shrinking rations. They recalled how the Americans initially provided flour in large sacks. Each year those bags got smaller. What that really meant was increased dependence on a potentially corrupt system.

An unconfirmed hint suggests that James and Sally Bird crossed the line during the winter 1873/74 to receive rations at the new Assiniboine and Gros Ventre Agency.[9] But they were back at a more familiar place by fall as the daughter of Philip and Mary Bird was born at the Bow River on 10 October 1874. The baby was named in honor of Philip's sister, Nancy.

The place favored by the Bird clan was known as the Blackfoot Crossing. A gravel bar across the swift-running Bow River made a convenient ford that the

Blackfeet used. A small Métis settlement had developed. The Bird's daughter Nancy had been born on the plains and married at the Red River settlement in 1866. Ten years later she married a Blood named Medicine Shield. That connection gave the Birds a degree of acceptance among bands that usually resented Métis.[10]

There was no place to go to escape the relentless march of progress. The well-intentioned missionary John McDougall was going around to the Cree camps preaching a gospel of fair play, justice, and liberty that owed as much to English history as it did to Christian doctrine. Good works were part of the process of softening the impact of what the Dominion of Canada had in mind for the northwest.[11] The first Canadian prime minister had already expressed the dilemma. "I would be quite willing to leave the whole country a wilderness for the next half century, but I fear that if Englishmen do not go there, Yankees will."[12]

On 15 September 1874 Treaty Number Four was concluded with the Cree, Salteaux, and others. During the negotiations at Qu'Appelle it became apparent that the Indians were getting more sophisticated in the politics of cession. Claiming that the Hudson's Bay Company had stolen their lands by taking £300,000 for surrendering the northwest, they claimed that money should have been paid to them.[13] Fat chance.

Tom Bird's second wife Anne Gabriel died in 1874, perhaps as a consequence of the birth of a daughter named Laura. With a baby to care for, next year Tom married Isabelle Flammard. The wedding took place in the vicinity of Touchwood Hills and Qu'Appelle, close to where the Canadians made two attempts to engross another large area of Indian territory.[14] When a daughter Mary was born to the couple in 1876, old James Bird and Sally were living at Battle River. That was not all that far from where his life's odyssey began.

The trails across the plains were crowded with traders and freighters. In mid-August Lieutenant-Governor Alexander Morris was on his way to negotiate another treaty when he found over a hundred carts and wagons stacked up waiting for the scow at Dumont's Crossing of the South Branch. During the rest of August and into September Treaty Number Six with the Plains Cree and Assiniboine was negotiated at Forts Carlton and Pitt. The ceded area of 120,000 square miles stretched as far west as the mountains and down the Red Deer River to the South Branch. All that was remained to be engrossed was the Blackfoot Country.

South of the Medicine Line, the politics of dispossession had turned hot. The Americans were at war with the Indians. The Lakota Sioux emphatically rejected reservations when they left 219 dead bluecoats on the Little Big Horn. After defeating the horse soldiers the tribes fled north. Sitting Bull's followers appeared at Wood Mountain in fall 1876 as hunted fugitives. By the following spring there were as many as five thousand of those unwelcome intruders there, or at Frenchman Creek and Pinto Horse Buttes.

The appearance of former enemies coincided with the realization that the buffalo herds were thinning on the northern plains. Too many were competing for a declining resource. Although the mounted police had closed down the worst of the whiskey traders, the demand for hides drew Cree and Métis hunters to the remaining animals. In the face of a threat to their livelihood, the bands of the Blackfeet gathered at the Hand Hills. The grave councils included a French Canadian named Jean L'Heureux who had been living with the bands for the last twenty years. The chiefs asked him to write a letter asking for a meeting with the Canadians.

Treaty Number Seven

The Canadian government took two years to respond to the letter from the Blackfeet. Even then, the meeting scheduled to be held at Fort Macleod had to be shifted. Tribal politics imposed when the Siksika leader Crowfoot insisted that the proceedings be moved to the Blackfoot Crossing. Whatever his reason, that was sure to put off his brother-in-law, the Kainaa leader Red Crow, as most of the Bloods were hunting near the border. There was no guarantee that they would attend. By 1 September scattered bands began setting up lodges beside the Bow. A narrow band of cottonwoods along the south side of the clear stream set off a beautiful mile-wide meadow stretching for three miles. There was good grazing for the pony herds on the hills behind.

The recently designated Lieutenant-Governor David Laird was one of the two commissioners. On his way to Fort Macleod to coordinate with his associate, Lieutenant-Colonel James Macleod of the mounted police, Laird stopped at the Blackfoot Crossing. Although it was early, he met the Blood leader Rainy Chief, and Jean L'Heureux who had written the letter calling for a meeting. Although there were disquieting rumors that L'Heureux was a spoiled priest who had been run out of Montana for an indiscretion, Laird thought that he might be a useful channel to the bands.[1] The sometime missionary provided Laird with "an elaborate list of the different Chiefs and minor Chiefs of the Blackfeet, Bloods, Piegans, and Sarcees, with the principle [*sic*] families of their respective tribes and clans of divisions."[2]

Laird came primed by an analysis provided last year in a letter from Father Constantine Scollen. The oblate of Mary Immaculate came to St. Albert in 1862 to work with Father Lacombe among the Cree. His knowledge of that language qualified him as an interpreter at Treaty Number Six where the minister of the interior David Mills asked his opinion of the Blackfeet. As a "civilizer" with humanitarian sensitivities, Scollen had developed a Cree bias. He warned that the Blackfeet were jealous of their lands and might concoct an alliance with the refugee Sioux. The ethnocentric descriptives he employed included terms like sullen, superstitious, and dangerous, coupled with such extremes as "thirst for blood" or "barbarous passions."[3] Those briefing notes were unlikely to quiet Commissioner Laird's preconceptions of what he had to accomplish. He went on to Fort Macleod to confirm arrangements with Lieutenant-Colonel Macleod and insure that there would be an adequate guard of the mounted police.

On Saturday 15 September Lieutenant-Colonel James Macleod appeared at the head of eighty officers and men of the mounted police. Along with the wheeled guns and supply wagons they drove a herd of cattle; rations on the hoof. Next day Lieutenant-Governor Laird trailed in and the commission prepared to begin business on Monday.

The chiefs came forward and were introduced to the commissioners. Sitting down around the treaty pavilion they passed the pipe. What followed is grand in the descriptions; a performance worthy of the glory and greed of the British Empire. Lieutenant-Governor Laird repeated the worn words about brotherhood and the great queen's love for her children. He reminded that it was the government that had stopped the whiskey trade and was making laws to save the buffalo. But he only stated in a general way why the tribes should sign a treaty. Laird's carefully worded speech of welcome was spoiled by the difficulties of translation. Jerry Potts, the NWMP interpreter, was notorious for cutting florid speeches to the bare bone. His version of what Lieutenant-Governor David Laird said did not live up to the flourishes of Victorian rhetoric.

The initial meeting was disappointed that very few of the Bloods, Sarcees, or Peigans had arrived. Unwilling to proceed until there was better attendance, the commissioners put off business until Wednesday. Meantime, the tribes could apply to the mounted police for rations. The Stoneys and one Blood chief took flour, tea, sugar, and tobacco, but the Siksika spokesman, Crowfoot, refused a gift that might later compromise his position. That was an ominous development so early in the gathering.

Without responding, the tribal leaders went off to consider what they had heard. There was no consensus in the lodges that evening. Although Crowfoot was already drifting toward agreement, he warned that nothing could be finalized until Red Crow arrived. Next day there were questions about hunting and fishing rights. Laird assured that they were free to hunt anywhere as long as that did not interfere with settlers. One matter left over from Treaty Number Six was cleared up on the second day. Those Cree who adhered to Bobtail frequented the upper Bow but were not included in the previous agreement. On Tuesday they confirmed their acceptance. But the usual long-winded replies of Indian leaders seemed curiously abbreviated. The treaty makers might have appreciated the brevity of Potts' translation, but this was important business.

Concern over Potts' ability to accurately describe the terms of the treaty increased, but the commissioners were reluctant to rely too much on L'Heureux. After two days of preliminaries, it was obvious that Potts had to be replaced. The ghost dredged up from the past was blind Jemmy Jock Bird. As Lieutenant-Governor Laird reported, "The Commissioners at first had not a good interpreter of the Blackfoot language, but on Wednesday they secured the services of Mr. Bird, a brother of the late Dr. Bird of Winnipeg. He has been for many years among the Piegans and Blackfeet, and is a very intelligent interpreter."[4]

The old man's presence may not have been entirely fortuitous. Earlier, in mid-June, the HBC trader at Fort Carlton wrote to the Edmonton district factor Richard Hardisty concerning the accounts of several Edmonton freemen. For reasons unspecified, he was trying to locate the Bird brothers. "Will you please inform me whether Thomas & Phillip Bird was in your neighborhood or at Fort McLeod."[5] As Hardisty planned to go for the scheduled treaty at the Bow River, he should able to relocate them. Another bayman, John Bunn, was already operating at the Elbow River in competition with an independent trader named French. There was little doubt that other traders would show up to skim expected treaty payments.[6] On the opening day, the Métis living at the Blackfoot Crossing wasted no time in addressing a letter expressing their concerns to Sir John Macdonald. They wanted to be confirmed in their holdings. Old Bird also had an interesting connection to the Bloods. His daughter Nancy was the wife of the Blood, Medicine Shield. When old Bird rose to interpret, would he be speaking for the Crown, for his Blackfoot friends or for the Métis?

On the morning of Wednesday 19 September heralds circulated the camps calling the tribes to assemble at two o'clock. A half hour before that time, the gun placed on commanding high ground fired and the band of the mounted police struck up "Hold the Fort" and "The Maple Leaf Forever."[7]

What followed was a performance worthy of the glory and greed of the British Empire. But, if the difficulties of translation and interpretation are considered, the resounding speeches were a little suspect. There was no way of insuring what Lieutenant-Governor David Laird said and what Crowfoot and the other chiefs heard, was correct. First, there was a broadcast problem. Bird's words may not have carried far beyond the chiefs seated on blankets before the commissioner's field desk. His old voice wasn't strong enough to carry through an audience of four thousand. At best, increasingly misunderstood repetitions rippled away through the crowd like the children's pass-it-on game gone awry. Those listeners, like the speaker, also suffered from a kind of blindness, when men from different worlds cannot see each other for what they really are.

Jemmy Jock had been an interpreter for most of his life; a calling based on the authenticity of the words he translated, committed to keeping as close to the intended meaning as his vocabulary permitted. He knew that the phrases that he repeated touched on subjects as deep as wounds; the end of the buffalo, the limitation of ranges, the restriction of old ways.

Documents of important national interest do not originate on a field desk in the wilderness. They are the product of careful homework and it is unlikely that the commissioners came to the Blackfoot Crossing unprepared for what they intended to accomplish. At the very least there was a carefully worded, legally correct draft treaty modeled on previous agreements. That was an instrument of Canadian intention rather than a mutual agreement between "political equals." If the Indians expected answers to their two-year-old petition, Lieutenant-Governor Laird was prepared to provide them. But discussion was not going to change the inevitability that the tribes were being prepared for a massive territorial cession. They were being asked to give up autonomy and become wards of Queen Victoria.

From the available evidence, it appears that the actual text of the treaty was not read. The reader must have paraphrased the document in a general way, very likely carefully skirting around the central point of land cessions and acceptance of reserves. The gifts and annuities that the tribes would receive were emphasized. The trustworthy Colonel Macleod confirmed his previous guarantee that the tribal territories would be protected. The audience expressed no doubts about what amounted to a blatant contradiction. For over a hundred years, the British Empire had pretended a sympathetic concern for native peoples, in contrast to the ruthless methods employed by its former colonies. Truth was, the tribal nations of North America were toppling like dominoes, as their inheritors scrambled to get a bit more than a fair share. The British Empire, masked as the Dominion of Canada, wanted something from native folk and as cheaply as possible.

Although an area of about 35,000 to 50,000 square miles was under consideration, only one square mile would be reserved to every five Indians. The tribesmen were giving that up for the munificent payment of twelve dollars the first year, and five dollars annually thereafter. There was no way that a tottering old blind man could make them realize that they were expected to live on a little piece of ground growing potatoes, herding cattle, and sending their sons and daughters away to be taught by strangers. The words must have rasped in Bird's throat. The chiefs were not expected to respond until tomorrow. Meantime, they were invited to partake of the rations without being committed. Most of the chiefs, including Crowfoot, took meat and other good things.

On Thursday the meeting convened at the usual afternoon hour with a further explanation of the previously outlined terms. The commissioners emphasized that under Canadian law Indian *reserves* could not be taken from them without their consent. The Kainaa, Medicine Calf came early and threatened to upset the proceedings. Bird remembered Medicine Calf at the Judith Treaty when he was a fine looking, but inconsequential young man. After smallpox claimed Seen-From-Afar and Calf Shirt was murdered by whiskey traders, that little button chief spoke for the Many Tumors band. As one of the last surviving Bloods who signed the American paper, he now complained that under the terms of the Judith Treaty the country between the Missouri and the international border had been reserved for the exclusive use of the Blackfeet. But in a later treaty with the Americans, Little Dog had foolishly given away half of that for nothing. Losing those ranges meant increased pressure on the buffalo north of the line, herds that were already under attack by intruding Cree, Métis, and Lakota.

When Medicine Calf recalled how the promised gifts had diminished and nearly dried up, it was clear that he understood the true meaning of the term "annuity." He was prepared to bargain for specific points like a peltry seller at the trade shop window. That included a demand to be paid for the timber that the redcoats used to build Fort Macleod. The bemused lieutenant-governor's response that the tribes should pay the queen for protecting them drew a grim laugh from old warriors who earned their reputations in war games.

But Medicine Calf had hit on a sore spot. What had been unjustly imposed upon the American Blackfeet was being proposed to British tribes now. That nearly incomprehensible concept involved a good deal more than merely agreeing to mutual use of the land, and the tribal leaders went off for more private discussions. It was after dark when the Bloods finally rode in. Although the chiefs had heated talks through the rest of the night, there is no record of what was said. The following afternoon the cannon called them to the awning. As the final speeches were shouted, Jemmy Jock stood in his personal darkness, translating sad words of containment and irrevocable change. Drawn into the role of a marginal man, the old plains roamer was a victim of his duality, trying to broker a reconciliation between the forces that had shaped his life.

The inescapable fact was that the buffalo were going and they had no choice except to give up their hunting ranges and become wards of the queen. Those words were like arrows driven into the hearts of the forty-four hundred listening Indians. The former fellow traveler could sense how the murmuring audience received that wound. In their hearts they were responsible men, they had dependents to think about. Standing in turn, Crowfoot, Rainy Chief, Red Crow, and the north Peigan leader Eagle Tail responded with their hopes and swallowed regrets.

What was subject to negotiation was the location and size of the reserves. According to the maps, the Siksika and Sarci would be contained within a twenty-mile by four-mile area along the north side of the Bow from the Blackfoot Crossing to the mouth of the Red Deer. The *aapatohsipikani* (north Peigans) were set apart at Crow's Creek on Oldman's River, near the foot of the Porcupine Hills where buffalo might run again if Napi heard their drumming. Kainaa eventually settled for the largest, most eastern reserve. The Stoneys located near the new town of Morleyville where the Wesleyan preacher McDougall held out. As long as they stayed out of trouble, tribesmen could continue to hunt on government lands, and would be supplied with ammunition. But the emphasis was on permanent settlement and a conversion to farming. The commissioners moved fast to confirm the reserved lands. Under the careful supervision of L'Heureux, the leading men stepped up and made their little marks on a paper. By that x, the *niitsitapi* ceased to be a free people.

The ambiguous oblate Father Scollen described the document as a pact of faith. As an expert about the power of belief, he was convinced that they really didn't understand what they had given up. As long as the treaty was just another level of obscurity, it was appropriate that a blind man interpreted it. The band might play "God Save the Queen," but it was Napi's indifference that had failed the people.[8]

The next days were devoted to payments and the distribution of medals, flags, and uniforms. There was a last meeting on Wednesday the twenty-sixth when the commissioners returned to the council tent to receive the thanks of the chiefs. Speaking on their behalf, L'Heureux expressed "their gratitude to the Commissioners generally for the kind manner in which they conducted the negotiations...." The officers responded that the Indians would not regret having agreed to the treaty.[9]

When the payments were completed on Friday, the accounts were totted up. A total of 4,392 head chiefs, minor chiefs and councillors, men, women, and children had received $52,954. That was rapidly being spent with the traders who had been waiting to begin business.

The half-breeds were not behindhand in inquiring if restrictions on buffalo hunting would be immediately enforced. As it turned out to be a mild winter, the buffalo failed to retreat into the shelter of wooded foothills. In their hungry winter camps, those who had agreed to the paper worried that they had made a grave mistake. Starvation drove the Canadian Blackfeet to the Sand Hills north of the Cypress Hills where they had to hunt in competition with Sitting Bull's refugee Sioux. By then, those intruders had been joined by what was left of the Nez Percé who'd made a 1,700-mile flight to avoid being put on an American reservation. To bad that Chief Joseph had stopped a bit too short of the Medicine Line.

After the gifts and commemorative medals were distributed and the tribes dispersed, the Bird family moved away from the Blackfoot Crossing. On 10 October, old Sally helped Philip's wife deliver a baby girl in the family lodge pitched near Fort Porcupine. That winter old Hugh Munroe wintered at Joe Kipp's Cow Creek trading post. The lodge tales and war stories that young James Willard Schultz began collecting there, and in time published, became the lasting image of the tribes.

In a Gathering Darkness

Buffalo in the Cypress Hills attracted Blackfeet, Bloods, Cree, Assiniboine, Gros Ventre, and Sioux and that was good for the business of the robe traders. In the summer 1878 most of the Canadian bands returned to the Blackfoot Crossing to hold the sun dance and collect five dollar annuities. In the winter 1879/80 Big Bear's Cree crossed Milk River to hunt in United States territory as far south as the Bear Paw Mountains. Next summer the Fort Walsh and Fort McLeod traders took in 13,000 buffalo robes, only half as many as the previous year. Then the Cypress Hill herds were gone. From Moose Jaw to the Blackfoot Crossing, the country was covered with the bleaching remains of the buffalo. It had only taken half a century to do it.

Treaty Number Seven did not inhibit passages across the border. As the herds vanished the American Blackfeet were dependent on agency rations. They would never forget the winter of 1883/84. Cattle were replacing winter-resistant buffalo on the plains, but the Blackfoot agency failed to obtain enough beef to feed the people. In Three Sun's camp on Two Medicine Creek that bureaucratic ineptitude caused five hundred people to starve to death. Even then, some tribesmen could not give up the old ways. Crows laying up on Heart Butte took the opportunity to sweep away the thin Piikani ponies.

There was another lost tribe that followed the well-defined cart trails from Fort Ellice and Qu'Appelle to Wood Mountain. After the Canadian takeover, Métis became a paper people, officially recognized as authentic inhabitants whose children were guaranteed a fair share of the only land they knew. But that meant holding their own in a world rapidly being given over to newcomers. Wood Mountain was almost astride the line and as many as twelve hundred Métis may have been around there, supplied by American traders operating from the Milk and Missouri rivers. According to the reminiscences of the plainsman Louis Goulet, Métis worked for American traders or even hired on as scouts for the bluecoats. The nomads were connected by easy family ties. "If two grandfathers traded dogs one day, that was enough for their grandchildren to call themselves relatives. Children of cousins two or three times removed turned into uncles and aunts. The in-laws of children united by marriage were called dittawawuk."[1] But differences of language and religion may have kept the Anglican Birds to the edge of those migratory Catholic flocks.

Joe Kipp was the half-Mandan son of the man who initiated the robe trade at the mouth of Maria's River. He moved his post to the steamboat wooding station at Carroll thirty miles above the mouth of the Musselshell, There were a large number of Métis families living in log shanties about a hundred miles downstream. On 6 August 1880 the leader of the Métis, Louis Riel, addressed a petition asking for a half-breed reservation to Major General Nelson A. Miles. One of those who signed was Thomas Bird, but it is uncertain if that was old Bird's son.[2]

During the winter, one beaming Carroll saloon keeper sold two thousand gallons of liquor to thirsty Métis. Drunkenness and prostitution in the camps destroyed families. Those rowdy neighbors led the Fort Belknap Assiniboine and Gros Ventre to complain. Next spring, U.S. Army Major Klein led a campaign to drive unwelcome Canadians back across the border. In mid-March the soldiers spent two days at the Métis camp near Medicine Lodge where they burned 150 cabins. The discouraged Métis trudged north.

During those terrible times, Jemmy Jock and Sally Bird wandered from band to band, dependent on their children, the hospitality of former friends, or the toleration of old enemies. Contemporary caregivers discommoded by aged parents might take a lesson from the responsibility that Tom or Philip Bird accepted for blind Jemmy Jock and old Sally. Unable to hunt for themselves, the old couple might have only a few days reserve of fresh meat. Leaving them for very long with an indulgent Indian band risked resentment, mistreatment, or hunger. In a new world of imposed Christian morality and institutionalized indifference, the ancient nomadic solution of merciful abandonment was no longer a consideration.

Non-treaty Cree coming to Fort Macleod were denied rations until their leader Big Bear took treaty. He finally agreed to accept a reserve to be determined in the north, and at the end of June 1883 moved to the Eagle Hills and Frog Lake. Selecting a permanent location upset next summer's band gathering. Big Bear's eldest son, Twin Wolverine and his friend Woodpecker, initially tried Buffalo Lake but spent the next winter at his father's choice for a reserve at nearby Spotted Creek. Most of Big Bear's followers favored a location at the mouth of Dog Rump Creek (now Atimoswe) between Frog and Saddle Lakes. An observer reporting to the Edmonton papers wrote from the Bear's Hill Reserve on Battle River in March 1885. C. B. had recently visited Buffalo Lake by making an eight-day journey on snowshoes through three feet of snow. He found seventy or eighty Indians living in squalid, starving conditions. During the muskrat hunt they ate those tiny morsels as fast as they were caught and skinned. Failing to kill many rabbits, they were forced to fish under the ice for pike. Eight lodges of cold, ragged people were under the tutelage of Tatwasin (going through the ice). Another four or five lodges of Saulteurs from Qu'Appelle followed Thunder, "an inveterate old wizard who holds the traditions of his fathers to be far more philosophic than all the wisdom of the white man."

> Amongst the other curiosities which I met with, were the impressive ruins of a quasi-white man who had seen better days. He is known to many readers of the *BULLETIN*. He is now 85 years old and stone blind. He lives near the lake in a little hut with the wizened old Blackfoot squaw who had been his partner through weal and through woe for many long years. He descends from an honorable stock. His father was a governor of the H.B.Co. His name is James Bird, commonly known by the name of Jimmy Jock. He has many afflictions, but his greatest are the loss of his eyesight and the want of 'eatables.' He converses fluently in English and the bright intelligence flashes now and then through the rusty enamel with which it has been overlaid during a long contact with Indian habits. I consider this old couple a worthy object of charity.[3]

There is no indication that went beyond publication.

When Louis Riel was called north to lead the Métis, rebellion became a threat. Big Bear's Cree might be drawn into it. The blind old man at Buffalo Lake wanted no part in those politics. There was an option. In order to keep Crowfoot's wavering Blackfeet in line, the Canadians increased their rations. By mid-March, the Bird family was headed south to relocate near the iron road station of Gleichen. None too soon.

Ten days later the Métis seized the store at Duck Lake and next day defeated the force sent from Fort Carlton to restore order. By the last week of April, the Alberta Field Force commanded by the Gleichen rancher, Major General Thomas Bland Strange, and made up of Calgary area cowboys was marching toward Edmonton.[4] Because Cree were implicated in some killings at Frog Lake, the disturbance was also inflated into an Indian rebellion. The overwhelming forces sent west from Canada marched and countermarched, made incompetent but impressive martial displays, and gradually corralled the rebels. On 12 May the Canadian Northwest Field Force ended four days of mutual sniping by killing at least six Métis, one ninety-three and another seventy-five years of age.

Although the heroes of that outing went home bragging that they had settled the Métis problem once and for all, the conquest of Riel's decrepit Métis cost the Dominion five million dollars.[5]

Old Bird was willing to settle for $160 in Métis scrip. Nine years after taking over Manitoba, the Dominion finally got around to addressing the half-breed claims. The legislation to implement it had been passed on 30 March 1885, too little and too late to muffle dissatisfaction already out of hand. The Bird family came to the frontier town of Calgary on 21 May 1885 to authenticate their claims. Grants were being made to qualified half-breeds living in the North West Territory as heads of family, but that required a declaration.

Three commissioners were sent out to conduct the survey; P. R. Street from London, Ontario, A. E. Forget of Regina, N. W., and Roger Goulet of St. Boniface, Manitoba. During that spring the commission began sittings at Fort Qu'Appelle followed by Regina, Maple Creek, and now Calgary. From there they would go on to Fort Macleod, Pincher Creek, and Edmonton. In six frantic months the commissioners received 1,694 applications, heard and recorded the statements of 1,815 half-breeds, including 300 who had died of smallpox.

In Goulet the Dominion found a marvel who continued as the sole commissioner, next year hearing an additional 1,414 statements and allowing 256 claims. Clearly, Goulet should have been the man to write the history of the children of the fur trade. Close on his heels stalked the speculative buyers who meant to acquire script at well below the face value.[6]

In the declaration that Mr. Bird made at Calgary, he stated that he was living near Gleichen post office along the Canadian Pacific Railway and had resided at the Crowfoot Crossing for the last two years. That misstatement was followed by his recollection of the date and place of his birth, which he gave as 1800 at the Sturgeon River. This was a tense time on the northern plains and Bird's reason for leaving the Red River settlement might have been suspect. Was the old man trying to gloss any participation in the troubles of the first Métis rebellion? Bird swore that he had lived at the Red River settlement for eleven years, until 1867, when he put his land in the hands of an attorney and went to winter at Qu'Appelle. Later he lived at Riding Mountain.

Commissioner Goulet suspected that when the Manitoba Act came into effect on 15 July 1870, Bird already had land in the province. But he had probably never received scrip.

Whatever Jamey wanted them to swear to was just fine with his witnesses. They were his father's old associate James Sandison and Alexander McKay, both from Medicine Hat.[7] Based on the evidence, and some humanity, the chairman of the script commission authorized a certificate for $160.[8] Questioned if he was known by any other name, the blind old man nodded that he was sometimes called James Joke.

Whoever guided the blind old man's hand to draw the x surrendered him to a new west of elitist ranchers, railroad magnates, and the red-coated illusion of Victorian order. The brawlers who drove the half-breeds out of Winnipeg, and the prairie settlement boomers, imagined that they typified the frontier spirit. Most actuality looked backward to the outdistanced and outmoded loyalist traditions of the Canadas or were fugitives from the perpetual mess of Ireland with sullen disrespect for entrenched class. The Métis were the real new people. They should have been an undeniable element, but like their Indian kinsmen, those sons and daughters of the country were just chaff blowing ahead of bonanza wheat farms, spinning dizzily in whirlwinds of change over a land they could no longer call their own.

In the winter 1888/89 the old man and his wife lived on the north Peigan reserve where the supervising Mountie, W. H. Cox, recognized Bird. He had been a significant contributor to the accomplishment of Treaty Number Seven and Cox wanted to do something special for him. The old woman with Bird had dutifully pre-chewed Jemmy Jock's meat until a sympathetic friend in Prince Albert supplied them with the convenience of a food chopper. Although Cox occasionally slipped them a piece of liver, what could a man who lived on real meat feel about surviving on pap.[9]

The country union of James and Sally had lasted over sixty-five years. When Bird completed his half-breed script application, she was named as the only mother of their eleven children. Most were dead by then: Charles, Edward, Joseph, Mary, Letty, Maria, and Catharine. The old couple was unaware that Agnes had died near Duck Lake. Only Thomas, Philip, and Nancy survived. Thomas and Philip also filled out half-breed claims for themselves or for their deceased children. Because she was living on the American Blackfoot Reservation Nancy did not file an application.[10]

Cree and Shoshone Women. Courtesy of Arthur H. Clark & Company.

The old man, or the son assisting him in filing the application, neglected to mention four other daughters. In keeping with tribal custom, Sarah had been the sits-beside-wife and James might have married her younger sisters. It is uncertain if Sally was the same as the Hawk Woman who Eli Gardipee mentioned to John B. Ritch of the Montana Historical Society in 1940. When Ritch took a statement from Jamey's grandson next year, Thomas Bird named Sally as his grandmother. In his suspect story, "The Theft of the Sacred Otter Bow-Case," James Willard Schultz added to the puzzle by naming Mad Wolf, who was born around 1820, and his brother Bear Head, as Bird's brothers-in-law.[11]

The four other daughters claimed to be the children of two other Piikani or Inuk'sik wives. Susan or Susie Bird Ear Rings was born sometime before 1855. She is remembered on the Blackfoot reservation as living with her son in 1907 when she gave her mother's name as Crane, a full Pikuni, and her father's name as Bird or Bear Sitting Up, a deceased white man. In another statement, Good Coup named Susie Ear Rings and Flag Woman as her half sisters. That was supported by Flag Woman's (or Flying Woman's) declaration listing Long Time Good Success, Annie the wife of Gambler, and Susie Ear Rings as her full sisters, and Tom and Philip Bird as her half brothers.

Annie, the wife of Gambler, was born around 1847 and gave her parents as James Burd, a deceased white man, and Kills in the Water. In her understanding, Flag Woman was a full sister while Tom Burd, Philip Burd, Susan Ear Rings, and Good Success were half brothers or sisters.

Those relationships were really matters of family and band, the convoluted interweaving of a mobile, flexing world where names did not have to be permanent, and could be changed at will.

When he left Fort Conrad in 1885, the trader/writer James Willard Schultz moved to the Blackfoot reservation and built a home five miles north of the agency on Two Medicine Lodges River. Next year old Hugh Munroe came to live with his son-in-law, William Jackson. Four years later Hugh got together with Jemmy Jock. The two relics were trying to promote a reward for their services to the Steven's Treaty where Munroe had been the Gros Ventre interpreter and Bird spoke to the Blackfeet.

According to newspaper accounts Hugh was living with his two sons and getting around "quite vigorous." In contrast, the feeble Bird had to use a stick and rely on his wife's support to get around. Hugh confided to a visiting reporter that he thought Bird was a pitiful case hobbling across the agency compound on Sally's arm. Blind in one eye from a past exchange with the Sioux, Hugh could still ride a horse or go fishing at the mountain lakes. It was his imperfect recollection of past events that had slipped.[12] Neighbor Schultz had a connection with an eastern editor and published the stories he heard from old Hugh.

Bird was not so infirm, as he showed up north of Prince Albert the following summer. The couple was living in a camp of "a dozen tepees with the usual number of half-starved dogs, half-naked children and general squalor" when the Winnipeg writer G. H. Gunn found them. Gunn wanted to see a character that his grandfather and his brother had described to him. The visitor felt qualified to indulge in a philosophically laced description of the last camp of the famous renegade.

Nothing distinguished the lodge of the former great chief of the Peigans. An old Indian wearing white man's clothing and moccasins sat in the darkness. Although his frame was bent and shrunken from the cramped posture of tent life, and his eyes were blind from too many smokes, the face of Jemmy Jock was still bronze and seamed by the sun. The English accent that had persisted through two generations was passing to a third.

The Reverend Gunn made a pious speculation about social or moral degeneration by alluding to the four wives who once graced Bird's lodge. Affectionately bantering his companion, Bird said, "this ugly old thing you see here is the only one that is left." Ever the Victorian gentleman, Gunn thought that the bent old woman, as wrinkled as her consort, had an air of intelligence and gentle kindness about her.

For native American couples, bonding had always been a matter of survival. Perhaps that denied open expression of deeply held emotions. But through many trying times Sally's quiet love had been faithful and consistent. That attachment had lasted almost seventy years and if it was not romantic love, then it may have represented something even finer.

Pleased by the visit of the son and grandson of former acquaintances, Jemmy Jock told a few of his practiced lodge tales. From those dusty memories old Bird drew verbal pictures of his illustrious former state as a Peigan chief, of his pony herd, and of a splendid lodge large enough to be divided into rooms. Sewn from hides attesting to his skill as a hunter, it had been elaborately decorated with pictures of warfare, hunting, and tribal traditions.[13]

> ... as he recounted those former glories, he seemed to live them over again in fancy. His face, with the sightless eyes took on a new expression, his bent and shrunken form seemed to regain something of its youthful bearing, and the old cracked voice range once more with the vibrant resonance of confidence and command.

As the afternoon shadows lengthened, Gunn left the old man who seemed like an artifact of a vanished time. "On that strip of green that fringes the river's lip the leaves still whisper on the summer zephyrs, the river still murmurs as it flows. But somewhere, long since under those mild Saskatchewan skies the kindly mother earth that knows no difference of white or red, rich or poor, humble or great, has gathered them again to her bosom. God rest their souls."[14] Gunn's epitaph was premature.

Tom Bird came to find his father and mother. After the death of Mary Kipling, his brother Philip Bird remarried. But Louise Lussier was a harsh stepmother for Philip's son, Thomas. The boy was better off living with his Uncle Tom.[15] At some point that family moved west of the mountains to the Fort Colvile area.[16] In spring 1891 they left the Tobacco Plains, driving their horses through the snow on Kutenai Pass. After vigilant mounted police held them for a month at Fort Macleod calculating the import duty on livestock, they trailed northeast to old Fort Carlton. About sixty miles above Prince Albert they found old Bird living near the place of his birth.

Still hoping to receive a reward from the United States, old Jemmy Jock wanted to return to the Montana Blackfoot reservation. Passing St. Paul de Métis they followed the Saskatchewan to Edmonton to visit William Bird and his two sons, Jim and Nicolas. The city of Edmonton had grown up around the old fort. The factory grounds had been subdivided into mill sites, stores, and even a combination dance hall and opera house, and the company was planning to build a new brick store on the corner of Jasper Avenue and 103rd Street.

Bird's sightless eyes could still see the great fort on the hill and the places where he spent his childhood. In his memory, long lines of warriors dressed in elaborate costumes rode up the trails from the river and a dazzled young man followed them to find his destiny.

An item in the Edmonton paper for 16 May 1892 reported the death of James Bird, who had returned from British Columbia some years previously. But this was a nephew of Jamey's who entered the service of the HBC in 1860 and whose descendants still live around Fort St. James in British Columbia. Another news item noted, "Thomas Bird of Macleod and his father, James Bird, arrived from Egg lake east of Saddle Lake last week on a visit to Wm. Bird of Edmonton. James Bird, better known as 'Jimmy Jock' is a native of Red River; who has lived nearly all his life with the Blackfeet Indians, and is now nearly 100 years of age. His father was an officer in the H.B.Co service, and Dr. Bird of Winnipeg, now deceased, was his half brother. He is a man of good education and address and was interpreter for the Hudson's Bay Company for many years, but afterwards lived not only amongst the Indians but became one of them. He was interpreter for Lieutenant-Governor Laird at the making of the treaty with the Blackfeet in 1877. He has been stone blind for many years."[17]

With old Bird sitting in the back of the springless Red River cart, the travelers headed south. Twelve-year-old Tom was so impressed by his exotic grandfather that he imitated his English accent. This last trip proved too much for old Sarah. She sickened of what they called the summer fever and died in camp. Going into Calgary, Uncle Tom sold a fine trotting horse in order to buy a fancy coffin that had a glass window in the lid. As the grieving old man sagged over the box, he broke the glass. The resulting uproar was something that young Tom never forgot. Rejecting the air burials that some Blackfeet still practiced, grandfather was emphatic that he wanted to be buried in a coffin.

Young Tom was apprehensive about the "redcoats." He was driving the cart as they approached Fort Macleod. Suddenly the gates suddenly swung open and the mounted police band marched out tooting. Tom wanted to turn away, but his grandfather told him that you should never show fear when approaching a strange camp. Go boldly forward.

Authorities on both sides of the line were trying to discourage the last horse raiders so reporting was required. The pill-box-hat-lidded Mounties came late to the plains, but after almost three decades most of the corners had been knocked off. Unfortunately the Fort Macleod command failed to note the passage of a mythic character and old Bird slipped through their gauntlets without a handshake. By now he was just a figment of the looking glass, someone whose atoms were so loosely connected that he could pass from one wonderland to another without a blink of recognition.

The trail south from Fort Macleod led to its United States counterpart, Fort Shaw. Stopping on the Blackfoot reservation, the Bird family found a place to settle on Two Medicine Creek. Not far down the canyon there was an ancient piskan where buffalo had been driven over the bluff and slaughtered. But just across the creek was the recently established Holy Family Mission and school. That was a Catholic boarding school where about a hundred Indian children were being trained in skills useful in the white world. That education also intended to root out traditional native ways through isolation from all that was familiar to the children. The priests and nuns replaced it with a new dependence on the white Napi. Those who could not tolerate alienation from their families ran away. Blind to all that, old Bird heard the children's voices echoing across the valley. When the wind blew right he smelled fresh bread baking.

In the role as his grandfather's eyes and caretaker, young Tom often sat in the shade of the trees along the creek listening to the old man's lodge tales. Grandfather spoke seven languages; French, Blackfoot, Gros Ventre, Stoney, Cree, and Sarsi, but it was the lingering echo of Middlesex English that Tom aped until the Fort Shaw school teachers beat it out of him.[18]

Grandfather spoke of traveling to places so far north that it was six months day and six months night. Those snows had blinded him and his eyes never fully recovered. Another time he traveled south for forty days with his kinsman Mad Wolf to recover a sacred object left by a dead Piikani warrior. There were ancient Indian dwellings clinging to the sides of red stone cliffs. When it was finally dedicated at the next sun dance, the artifact had caused the deaths of nine men. They left the otter skin swinging in the prairie winds.[19]

Unable to give up the idea that the Americans owed them something for services at the Stevens Treaty, Bird and old Munroe found excuses to get together and discuss the matter. There were wild expectations about what they could do with a little cash. Their lives had vanished up the smoke hole, but the money might benefit their children and grandchildren.

James Willard Schultz, the literary squawman lived five miles up Two Medicine Creek. He knew the Munroe and Jackson families, appreciated a good yarn, and had the talent to restate it. That rich fund of material included Hugh's son-in-law, Billy Jackson, who was a guide for the bluecoats during the Custer fight. Later he rode from the post at Wolf Point as a government policeman.[20] Schultz wrote down those yarns and sent them off to eastern sports magazines. In the stories that boys read in their magazines the Piikani and their fellow traveler lived on.[21]

Last fall another lodge tale collector had visited. A sportsman as well as a sports editor, George Bird Grinnell liked to climb around in the mountains naming peaks.[22] He hired Billy Jackson to carry his camera and took a photo of old Hugh in front of his cabin. But none of old Bird. Next spring, another western writer, Emerson Hough also overlooked the local patriarchs.

On 7 December 1892, Hugh Munroe reached the end of his long mountain ramble. He was some distance away on the Milk River when he died, but the body was brought back to the Holy Family Mission for burial in consecrated ground. The Montreal boy whose imagination had been captured by the Blackfeet was put on the hilltop just east of the mission.

A week later grandfather Bird was lying in his bed in a corner of the cabin when young Tom noticed that he was gasping for breath. By the time Uncle Tom came running, it was too late. The Master of Life had called the old renegade to the Sand Hills. The white man's date was 15 December 1892.

According to his father's wish, Uncle Tom was determined to provide a coffin. But there were no boards available and the best he could do was take the old Red

River cart apart and fashion a box from the crudely-hewn planks. Although the family was Protestant, Tom asked the understanding priest to baptize the body posthumously, so the old plainsman could be buried next to his friend. James Bird Jr rests in the Holy Family Mission cemetery. There was no stone and after the prairie grass grew over for a few years, the graves were lost.

Man or Myth?

Biography is acquired intimacy and it is difficult to leave someone you have come to know if not completely, then pretty well. The last twenty years of Jemmy Jock's life were spent in a gathering darkness. Sitting close to the smoldering little fire in the smoky cone of an aging buffalo skin tipi, he must have thought about his unique heritage and eventful life. But there are no clues to suggest introspection or regret. He had lived for the moment, always going forward and rarely looking back in a direct experience that engrossed the nineteenth century on the northern plains.

During that long life, James Bird Jr knew the beaver trade intimately. By mid-century the demand for felting fibre had passed. Strategically situated Americans shifted the Upper Missouri River business to buffalo skins and robes. Few could have foreseen what that would mean to the apparently endless herds. Bird's vision had darkened before all there was left to see was bleaching bones.

His mixed English and Cree parentage allowed Bird to operate in the electric margin between cultures in collision. Business, religion, and government offered opportunities for interpreters or brokers, but this study has not discovered that James Bird Jr deliberately pursued those roles. Most of his early experience was as a functionary in the rivalries of others; tribes or intruders, Nor'westers or baymen, British or Yankees, Canadians or Métis.

There is the intellectualized temptation to recast Bird as a marginal man and extract some symbolic racial or social ambiguity. But the clues to racial sensitivity mostly apply to Sally, the Piikani wife and her experience with the tortured zealot Rundle. The difficulty of adjusting to transplanted social order may have been the reason that the family preferred to return to more familiar tribal relationships. Being Indian by habit is no small compliment.

Bird spent the first forty-one years of his life as a complete outdoor man, always on the move, living by the hunt, accepting responsibility for the well-being of his family and the security of his band. But during the mountain years, Jemmy Jock never completely withdrew from the trader's world. Although he was on the payroll as a "confidential servant" of the Hudson's Bay Company, attacks on Bird's character came from those first corporate men and the institutions they served. Business demanded predictable people who could be efficiently manipulated. To Bird's credit, he didn't fit that model and managed to teach the field managements of two giant business organizations telling lessons in the value of an individual.

His reaction to missionary Christianity was ambiguous. As a Piikani fellow traveler he seems to have tried to deflect then moderate the impact of imposed belief systems. Joining the church may not have eased the Birds transition into Victorian community, and after fourteen years of trying Jemmy Jock and Sally gave up and returned to the plains. Their wandering became the basis for the myth that was invented to explain an outrageous half-breed. Creeping gentility required drawing distinctions between the new visions of prairie empire and the inconvenient embarrassment of Métis and half-breeds. In that the myth the renegade had more to do with the imitation of the stilted proprieties than it did with a man who had lived his life as he felt he should. Two occasions document Bird's role in the extension of a "civilized" frontier. Those spanned a period of twenty-two years while the Indian world was being overwhelmed. Bird used his facility in languages to ease the process. It is beyond the available data or the author's intention to speculate on the metaphysical aspects of Bird's life with the Indians. Turned in upon himself by blindness the old man's last years must have been like a dream. In that darkness, an old warrior reconsidered his deeds and re-evaluated what he had done in a world that had vanished.

Bibliography

Archival Sources

Alberta Provincial Archives, Edmonton.

British Columbia Archives, Victoria.

Joslyn Art Museum Center for Western Studies. Szmrecsanyi translation of "Journals of Prince Maximilian in North America," Volume II.

Public Archives of Manitoba, Hudson's Bay Company Archives Winnipeg.

Manitoba Provincial Archives, Winnipeg. Red River Settlement Papers, 1814–20.

Missouri State Historical Society, Columbia, Missouri.

Montana State Historical Society, Helena, Montana.

National Archives of Canada, Ottawa. Selkirk Papers (Public Archives of British Columbia microfilm copy), Métis claims files, record group 15, volume 1325.

Oregon Historical Society, Portland, Oregon. Microfilm 1502, John Stuart Letterbook.

St. Louis Missouri Historical Society. Robert Campbell Collection, Chouteau Collection, American Fur Company Account Books 1831–33, Fur Trade Collection.

Yale University Library. Coe Collection, Harriot, J.E., "Memoirs of John Edward Harriot."

Hudson's Bay Company Archives

Hudson's Bay Company London Records

A5/4-5	London General Correspondence Outward
A11/17	York Factory Correspondence Inward
A11/76	York Factory Correspondence
A16/34	Officers and Servants Ledger
A16/35	Officers and Servants Ledger
A16/111	Servants Commissions 1787–1802
A30/15	
A32/3	Servants Contracts
C1/423	
E8/5	Red River Settlement Papers 1815-19
E8/6	Red River Settlement Papers 1814-20

Hudson's Bay Company Post Journals

B239/a/89	York Factory Journal 1788–89
B239/a/90	York Factory Journal 1789–90
B213/a/1	Swan River Journal 1790–91
B213/a/2	Swan River Journal 1791–92
B213/a/3	Swan River Journal 1792–93
B121/a/7	Manchester House Journal 1791–92
B24/a/1	Buckingham House Journal 1792–93
B121/a/8	Manchester House Journal 1792–93
B205/a/8	South Branch House Journal 1793–94
B148/a/1	Nippoewin House Journal 1794–95
B27/a/1	Carlton House Journal 1795–96
B27/a/2	Carlton House Journal 1796–97
B27/a/3	Carlton House Jornal 1797–98

B197/a/1	Carlton House and Setting River Journal 1798–99
B60/a/5	Edmonton House Journal 1799–1800
B60/a/6	Edmonton House Journal 1806–07
B60/a/7	Edmonton House Journal 1807–08
B60/a/8	Edmonton House Journal 1808–09
B60/a/9	Edmonton House Journal 1810–11
B60/a/10	Edmonton House Journal 1811–12
B60/a/11	Edmonton House Journal 1812–13
B60/a/12	Edmonton House Journal 1813–14
B60/a/13	Edmonton House Jouranl 1814–15
B235/a/3	Winnipeg (Brandon crossed out) Journal 1814–15
B60/a/15	Edmonton House Journal 1815–16
B27/a/6	Carlton House Journal 1816–17
B235/a/4	Winnipeg Journal 1820–21
B235/a/5	Fort Garry, Lower Red River Journal 1822–23

Hudson's Bay Company Correspondence Books and Reports

B42/b/55	Churchill Correspondence 1811
B42/b/57	Churchill Correspondence
B49/b/1	Cumberland House Correspondence 1817–18
B49/b/2	Cumberland House Correspondence 1818
B60/e/1	*Edmonton Report 1815*
B60/e/2	*Edmonton Report 1816*
B60/f/1	*Saskatchewan Servants List 1815–16*

Private Collections

J. C. Bird, of Waltham Abbey, Essex, England. Collection of Bird family information.

John C. Jackson. Collection of Bird Family Letters and Documents.

T. R. McCloy. MacKay family collection.

Government Documents

U.S. Senate. *Report of Exploration of a Route for the Pacific Railroad near the 47th and 47th Parallels, from St. Paul to Puget Sound by Isaac I. Stevens.* vol. 1. 33rd Cong., 1st sess, *SED129.*

———, *Canada. Indian Treaties and Surrenders from 1680 to 1890* II (Ottawa: Brown Chamberlin, Printer to the Queen's Most Excellent Majesty, 1891; Toronto: Coles Publishing Company, 1971).

———, Great Britain Parliament, *Select Committee on Hudson's Bay Company Territories* Appendix 15 (London: 1857).

The Dictionary of Canadian Biography

Alexander Begg, 12:81–84, by D. R. Owram

James Bird, 8:90–91 by John E. Foster

James Bird, 12:110–11, by David Smyth

Curtis James Bird, by W. D. Smith

Jacques-Raphael Finlay, 6:253–54, by Eric J. Holmgren

John James Hargrave, 12:408–09, by Glen Makahonuk

John Edward Harriott, 9:366–67, by Sylvia Van Kirk

William Kittson, 7:473, by Eric J. Holmgren

Donald McKenzie, 8:557–58, by Slyvia Van Kirk

John McLoughlin, 8:575–81, by W. Kaye Lamb

James McMillan, 8:583–84, by Gregory Thomas

Nicolas Point, 9:636, by Joseph P. Donnelly

Peter Skene Ogden, 8:660–62, by Glydwr Williams

Robert Terrill Rundle, 12:931–32.

Sir George Simpson, 8:812–18, by John S. Galbraith

James Sinclair, 8:819–20, by Irene M. Spry

John Work, 9:850–54, by William R. Sampson

Books

Arima, Eugene Y. *Blackfeet and Palefaces: The Pikani and Rocky Mountain House: A Commemorative History from the Upper Saskatchewan and Missouri Fur Trade*. Ottawa: Golden Dog Press, 1995.

Barker, Burt Brown, ed. *Letters of Dr. John McLoughlin written at Fort Vancouver 1829–1832*. Portland, OR: Binfords and Mort, 1948.

Bennet, Ben, *Death Too, For the Heavy Runner*. Missoula, MT: Mountain Press, 1982.

Berry, Don. *A Majority of Scoundrels: An Informal History of the Rocky Mountain Fur Company*. New York: Harper & Brothers, 1961.

Binnema, Theodore. *Common & Contested Ground: A Human and Environmental History of the Northern Plains*. Norman, OK: University of Oklahoma Press, 2001.

Bonner, T. D. *The Life and Adventures of James P. Beckwourth*. 1856. Reprint New York: Alfred Knopf, 1931.

Bowsfield, Hartwell, ed. *The James Wickes Taylor Correspondence 1859–1870*. vol. 3. Winnipeg: Manitoba Record Society Publications,1968.

———. *The Letters of Charles John Brydges 1879–1882*. Winnipeg, MN: Hudson's Bay Record Society, 1977.

Brown, Jennifer S. H. *Strangers in Blood: Fur Trade Families in Indian Country*.

Vancouver, BC: University of British Columbia Press, 1980.

Camp, Charles L.Camp, ed. *James Clyman Frontiersman*. Portland, OR: Champoeg Press, 1960.

Catlin, George. *Letters and Notes on the manners, customs, and conditions of the North American Indian*. vol. 1. 1844. Reprint New York: Dover Publications, 1973.

Charette, Guillaime. *Vanishing Spaces: Memories of Louis Goulet*. Winnipeg, MN: Editions Bois Brules, 1976.

Cline, Gloria Griffin. *Peter Skene Ogden and the Hudson's Bay Company*. Norman, OK: University of Oklahoma Press, 1974.

Coues, Elliott, ed. *The Manuscript Journals of Alexander Henry and of David Thompson, 1799–1814*. 2 vols. Minneapolis: Ross & Haines, 1965.

Crawford, John C. "What is Michif?: Language in the Métis tradition." *The New Peoples: Being and Becoming Métis in North America*. Lincoln, NE: University of Nebraska Press, 1985.

Davies, K. G., and A. M. Johnson, eds. *Peter Skene Ogden's Snake Country Journal 1826–27*. London: The Hudson's Bay Record Society, 1961.

Demarce, Roxanne, ed. *Blackfoot Heritage: 1907–1908*. Browning, MT: Blackfoot Heritage Program, 1980.

Dempsey, Hugh. *Crowfoot: Chief of the Blackfeet*. Norman, OK: University of Oklahoma Press, 1972.

———. *Red Crow: Warrior Chief*. Lincoln, NE: University of Nebraska Press, 1980.

———, ed. *The Rundle Journals 1840–1848*. Calgary: Historical Society of Alberta, 1977.

de Smet, Pierre-Jean, S. J. *Life, Letters and Travels*. 4 vols. Edited by Hiram Martin Chittenden and Alfred Talbert Richardson. New York: F. P. Harper, 1905.

———. *Letters and Sketches, 1841–42*. Edited by Rueben Gold Thwaites in *Early Western Travels*. vol. 29. Cleveland, OH: Arthur H. Clark, 1906.

DeVoto, Benard. *Across the Wide Missouri*. Boston, MA: Houghton Mifflin, 1947.

Diettert, Gerald A. *Grinnell's Glacier: George Bird Grinnell and Glacier National Park*. Missoula, MT: Mountain Press, 1992.

Dippie, Brian W. *Catlin and His Contemporaries: The Politics of Patronage*. Lincoln, NE: University of Nebraska Press, 1990.

Donnelly, Joseph P., and S. J. Donnelly, trans. *Wilderness Kingdom: Indian Life in the Rocky Mountains: 1840–1847*. New York: Holt, Rinehart and Winston, 1967.

Dunn, John. *History of the Oregon Territory and British North American Fur Trade*. London: Edwards & Hughes, 1844.

Ewers, John C. *The Blackfeet: Raiders on the Northern Plains*. Norman, OK: University of Oklahoma Press, 1958.

Fraser, Marian Botsford. *Walking the Line: Travels Along the Canadian/American Border*. Vancouver, BC: Douglas & McIntyre, 1989.

Friesen, Gerald. *The Canadian Prairies: A History*. Toronto: University of Toronto Press, 1984.

Fryer, Harold. *Alberta: The Pioneer Years*. Langley, BC: Stagecoach Publishing, 1977.

Galbraith, John S. *The Little Emperor*. Toronto: Macmillan of Canada, 1976.

Giraud, Marcel. *The Métis in the Canadian West*. Translated by George Woodcock. 2 vols. Lincoln, NE: University of Nebraska Press, 1986.

Glover, Richard, ed. *David Thompson's Narative, 1784–1813*. Toronto: The Champlain Society, 1962.

Gray, John Morgan. *Lord Selkirk of Red River*. Toronto: Macmillan of Canada, 1963.

Gray, W. H. *History of Oregon 1792–1849*. Portland, OR: The Author, 1870.

Grazebrook, G.P. de T., ed. *The Hargraves Correspondence, 1821–1843*. Toronto: The Champlain Society, 1938.

Gunn, J. J. *Echoes of the Red*. New York: Macmillan, 1930.

Haid, Bruce, ed. *A Look at Peter Fidler's Journal: Journal of a Journey over Land from Buckingham House to the Rocky Mountains in 1792 & 3*. Lethbridge, AB: Historical Research Centre, 1991.

Haines, Francis D., ed. *The Snake Country Expedition of 1830–1831: John Work's Field Journal*. Norman, OK: University of Oklahoma Press, 1971.

Harper, J. Russell, ed. *Paul Kane's Frontier: Including Wanderings of an Artist among the Indians of North America by Paul Kane*. Fort Worth, TX: The Amon Carter Museum, 1971.

Healy, W. J. *Women of Red River*. Winnipeg, MN: The Woman's Canadian Club, 1923.

Hind, Henry Youle. *Narrative of the Canadian Red River Exploring Expedition of 1857 and the Assiniboine and Saskatchewan Exploring Expedition of 1858*. Edmonton, AB: Hurtig, 1971.

Howard, James H. *The Canadian Sioux*. Lincoln, NE: University of Nebraska Press, 1984.

Huel, Raymond, ed. *The Collected Writings of Louis Riel*. Edmonton, AB: University of Alberta Press, 1985.

Huyda, Richard J. *Camera in the Interior: 1858: H. L. Hime, Photographer: The Assiniboine and Saskatchewan Exploring Expedition*. Toronto: The Coach House Press, 1975.

Jackson, John C. *Children of the Fur Trade: Forgotten Métis of the Pacific Northwest*. Missoula, MT: Mountain Press, 1995.

———. *The Piikani Blackfeet: A Culture Under Siege*. Missoula, MT: Mountain Press, 2000.

——. *Shadow on the Tetons: David E. Jackson and the Claiming of the American West*. Missoula, MT: Mountain Press, 1993.

Johnson, Alice M., ed. *Saskatchewan Journals and Correspondence, Edmonton House 1795–1800, Chesterfield House 1800–1802*. London: The Hudson's Bay Record Society, 1967.

Johnson, Donald R., ed. *William H.Gray: Journal of his Journey East, 1836–1837*. Fairfield, WA: Ye Galleon Press, 1980.

Joslyn Museum. *Karl Bodmer's America*. Lincoln, NE: University of Nebraska Press, 1984.

Kane, Paul. *Wanderings of an Artist among the Indians of North America from Canada to Vancouver's Island and Oregon through the Hudson's Bay Company's territory and back again*. 1859. Reprint Edmonton, AB: Hurtig, 1974.

Killoren, John J., and S.J, Killoren. *Come Blackrobe: De Smet and the Indian Tragedy*. Norman, OK: University of Oklahoma Press, 1994.

Lavender, David. *The Fist in the Wilderness*. Albuquerque, NM: University of New Mexico Press, 1979.

Lent, D. Geneva. *West of the Mountains: James Sinclair and the Hudson's Bay Company*. Seattle: University of Washington Press, 1963.

McDonald, Lois Halliday. *Fur Trade Letters of Francis Ermatinger*. Glendale, CA: Arthur H. Clark Co., 1980.

McDonnell, Anne, ed."The Fort Benton Journal. 1854–1856 and The Fort Sarpy Journal. 1855–1856." *Contributions to the Historical Society of Montana*. vol. 10. 1940. Reprint Boston, MA: J. S. Canner & Co., 1966.

McDougall, John. *In the Days of the Red River Rebellion*. Edmonton, AB: University of Alberta Press, 1983.

Macgregor, J. G. *John Rowand: Czar of the Prairies*. Saskatoon, SK: Western Producer Prairie Books, 1978.

MacLeod, Margaret A., ed. *The Letters of Letitia Hargrave*. Toronto: The Champlain Society, 1947.

Maximillian, Prince, zu Wied-Nuwied. *Travels in the Interior of North America*. Edited by Rueben Gold Thwaites in *Early Western Travels*. vols. 22–24. Cleveland, OH: Arthur Clark, 1909.

Merk, Frederick, ed. *Fur Trade and Empire: George Simpson's Journal Remarks Connected with the Fur Trade in the Course of a Voyage from York Factory to Fort George and back to York Factory 18240 1825; together with Accompanying Documents*. Cambridge, MA: Harvard University Press, 1931.

——. *The Oregon Question: Essays in Anglo-American Diplomacy and Politics*. Cambridge, MA: The Belknap Press of Harvard University Press, 1946.

Morgan, Dale L. *The West of William H. Ashley*. Denver, CO: The Old West Publishing Company, 1964.

Morton, W. L., ed. *Alexander Begg's Red River Journal and Other Papers Relative to the Red River Resistance of 1869–70*. Toronto: The Champlain Society, 1956.

Morton, Arthur S. *A History of the Canadian West to 1870–71*. Toronto: University of Toronto Press, 1973.

Morgan, Lewis Henry. *The Indian Journals 1859–62*. Edited by Leslie A. White. Ann Arbor: University of Michigan Press, 1959.

Munnick, Harriet Duncan, and Mikell DeLores Wormell Warner, ed., and trans. *Catholic Church Records of the Pacific Northwest: Vancouver and Stellamaris Mission*. St. Paul, OR: French Prairie Press, 1972.

Nicandri, David L. *Northwest Chiefs: Gustav Sohon's View of the 1855 Stevens Treaty*

Councils. Tacoma: The Washington State Historical Society, 1986.

Oliver, E. H. *The Canadian North-West: Its Early Development and Legislative Records*. Vol. 2. Ottawa, Government Printing Bureau, 1914.

Pambrun, Andrew Dominique. *Sixty Years on the Frontier of the Pacific Northwest*. Fairfax, WA: Ye Galleon Press, 1978.

Phillips, Paul C., ed., *Life in the Rocky Mountains by W. A. Ferris*. Denver, CO: Old West Publishing Company, 1940.

Ray, Arthur J. *Indians in the Fur Trade: their role as trappers, hunters and middlemen in the lands southwest of Hudson Bay, 1660–1870*. Toronto: University of Toronto Press: 1974.

Rich, E. E., ed. *Part of Dispatch From George Simpson, Esqr., Governor of Ruperts Land to the Governor and Committee of the Hudson's Bay Company, London*. London: The Hudson's Bay Record Society, 1947.

Rich, E. E., ed. *Peter Skene Ogden's Snake Country Journals 1824–25 and 1825–26*. London: The Hudson's Bay Record Society, 1950.

Roe, Frank Gilbert. *The North American Buffalo: A Critical Study of the Species in its Wild State*. 1951: Toronto: University of Toronto Press, 1970.

Ross, Alexander. *The Red River Settlement: Its Rise, Progress and Present State*. 1856. Reprint Minneapolis: Ross and Haines, 1957.

Schultz, James Willard. *My Life as an Indian*. 1907. Reprint New York: Fawcett Columbine, 1981.

Seele, Keith C., ed. *Blackfeet and Buffalo: Memories of Life among the Indians by James Willard Schultz (Apikuni)*. Norman, OK: University of Oklahoma Press, 1962.

Simpson, George. *Narrative of a Journey Round the World During the Years 1841 and 1842*. London: Henry Colburn, 1847.

Sprague, D. N., and R. P. Frye. *The Genealogy of the First Métis Nation*. Winnipeg, MN: Pemmican Publications, 1983.

Spry, Irene M., ed. *The Papers of the Palliser Expedition 1857–1860*, Toronto: The Champlain Society, 1968.

Sunder, John E. *Joshua Pilcher: Fur Trader and Indian Agent*. Norman, OK: University of Oklahoma Press, 1969.

Tanner, Ogden. *The Canadians*. Alexandria, VA: Time Life Books, 1977.

Thomas, Davis and Karin Ronnefeldt, eds. *People of the First Man: Life Among the Plains Indians in Their Final Days of Glory: The Firsthand Account of Prince Maximilian's Expedition up the Missouri River 1833–34*. New York: E. P. Dutton, 1976.

Townsend, John Kirk. *Narrative of a Journey Across the Rocky Mountains to the Columbia River*. 1838. Reprint Lincoln, NE: University of Nebraska Press, 1978.

Tyrrell, J. B., ed. *David Thompson's Narrative of his Explorations in Western American, 1784–1813*. Toronto: The Champlain Society, 1916.

Van Kirk, Sylvia. *"Many Tender Ties": Women in Fur Trade Society, 1670–1870*. Winnipeg, MN: Watson and Dwyer, 1980.

Fuller, Francis. *River of the West*. 1870. Reprint Columbus, OH: Long's College Book Co., 1950.

West, John. *The Substance of a Journal during a residence at the Red River Colony, 1820–23*. London: 1827.

Williams, Glyndwr, ed. *Hudson's Bay Miscellany, 1670–1870*. Winnipeg, MN: Hudson's Bay Record Society, 1975.

———. *Peter Skene Ogden's Snake Country Journals, 1827–28 and 1828–29*. London: Hudson's Bay Record Society, 1971.

Wisler, Clark, and D. C. Duvall. *Mythology of the Blackfoot Indians*. Introduction by Alice Beck Kehoe. Lincoln, NE: University of Nebraska Press, 1995.

Wright, Richard Thomas. *Overlanders 1858 Gold*. Saskatoon, SK: Western Producer Prairie Books, 1985.

Serials and Periodicals

Bradley, Lieutenant James. "Affairs at Fort Benton from 1831 to 1869." *Contributions to the Historical Society of Montana*. vol. 3.

Bradley, Lieutenant James. "Establishment of Ft. Piegan as told me by James Kipp." Bradley Manuscript Book F, *Contributions to the Historical Society of Montana*. vol. 8. (1917).

Blegen, Theodore. "James W. Taylor, A Biographical Sketch." *Minnesota Historical Bulletin* 1 (November 1915).

Brown, Jennifer S. H. "A Colony of Very Useful Hands." *The Beaver* (Spring 1977): 39–45.

Cox. W. H. "Diary of a Mountie, from 1880 to '85." *Lethbridge Herald Golden Jubilee Edition* (11 July 1935): 67–76.

Deland, Charles E. and Doane Robinson, eds. "Fort Tecumseh and Fort Pierre Journals and Letterbooks." *South Dakota Historical Collections*. Vol. 9 (1918).

Doty, James. "A Visit to a Blackfoot Camp." Edited by Hugh A. Dempsey. *Alberta Historical Review* 14:3 (Summer 1966): 17–26.

Edmonton Bulletin. (16 May 1892).

Elliott, T. C. "Journal of Alexander Ross – Snake Country Expedition." *Oregon Historical Quarterly* 14 (December 1913).

———. "The Journal of John Work, July 5–15 September 1826." *Washington State Historical Quarterly* 6:1 (January 1915).

Ewers. John C. "Identification and history of the Small Robes Band of the Piegan Indians." *Journal of Washington Academy of Sciences* 37:12 (15 December 1946).

Farr, William E. "When We Were First Paid" The Blackfoot Treaty, The Western Tribes, and the Creation of the Common Hunting Ground, 1855." *Great Plains Quarterly* 21 (Spring 2001).

Goldring, Philip. "Governor Simpson's Officers: Elite Recruitment in a British Overseas Enterprise, 1834–1870." *Prairie Forum: The Journal of the Canadian Plains Research Centre* 10:2 (Fall 1985).

Grinnell, George Bird. "A White Blackfoot," *The Masterkey* 46:4 (October–December 1972); 47:1 (January–March 1973).

Gunn, G. H., "Jimmy Jock, the Story of the Englishman Who Turned Indian in the Palmy Days," *Winnipeg Free Press* (8 November 1930).

———. "Hugh Monroe 1784–1892, A Brief Sketch of the Life of the Oldest Man in Montana – Still Vigorous at 106 Years of Age." *The River Press* (19 February 1890).

Jackson, John C. "Old Traders in a New Corporation: The Hudson's Bay Company Retreats North in 1822." *North Dakota History* 55:3 (Summer 1988): 23–28.

Johnstone, Barbara. "Big Donald of the Blackfeet." *The Beaver* (Winter 1959).

McLeod, J.E.A. "Old Bow Fort." *Canadian Historical Review* 12:4 (December 1931).

Mattison, Ray H. "Kenneth McKenzie." *Fur Traders, Trappers and Mountain Men of the Upper Missouri*. Lincoln, NE: University of Nebraska Press, 1995.

Merk, Frederick. "The Snake Country Expedition Correspondence, 1824–5." *Mississippi Valley Historical Review* 21 (June 1934).

"Minutes of Council 1836." *North Dakota Historical Collections* 4 (1913).

Mitchell, Elaine A. "Red River Gossip." *The Beaver* (Spring 1961).

Nasitir, Abraham P. "The International Significance of the Jones and Immell Massacre and of the Arikara Outbreak of 1823." *The Pacific Northwest Quarterly* 30 (January 1939).

Owram, Doug. "Conspiracy or Treason: The Red River Resistance: From an Expansionist Perspective." *Prairie Forum* 3:2 (1978).

Pannekoek, Frits. "Demographic Structure of Nineteenth Century Red River." *Essays on Western History*. Edited Lewis H. Thomas. Edmonton: University of Alberta Press, 1976.

Smyth, David, "The Struggle for the Piegan Trade: The Saskatchewan Versus the Missouri." *Montana: The Magazine of Western History* 34:2 (Spring 1984): 2-15.

Stewart, Donald M. "The Land Script Issues of Canada." *The Canadian Paper Money Journal* 15:1 (January 1979).

Tessendorf, T. C. "Red Death on the Missouri." *The American West* 14:1 (January–February 1977).

Wickman, John E. "James Bird, Jr." *The Mountain Men and the Fur Trade of the Far West*. vol. 5. Glendale, CA: Arthur H. Clark Co., 1968.

Notes to Chapter 1

1. This composite description is drawn from Alexander Morris, *The Treaties of Canada with the Indians of Manitoba and the Northwest Territories* (1880; Reprinted Saskatoon, SK: Fifth House, 1991); Treaty Seven Elders and Tribal Council with Walter Hildebrandt, Dorothy First Rider, and Sarah Carter, *The True Spirit and Original Intent of Treaty Seven* (Montreal and Kingston: McGill-Queen's University Press, 1996); Hugh A. Dempsey, *Crowfoot: Chief of the Blackfeet* (Norman, OK: University of Oklahoma Press, 1972) and *Red Crow: Warrior Chief* (Lincoln, NE: University of Nebraska Press, 1980).
2. According to Dempsey, *Crowfoot*, 209–10, Medicine Shield drove the ailing Crowfoot to Fort Belknap in fall 1888.

Notes to Chapter 2

1. Contract dated 23 April 1788, Hudson's Bay Company Archives, Provincial Archives of Manitoba (hereafter HBCA) A32/3, fol. 202.
2. Gens du Large expressed the mobility of the northern plainsmen. The *Nitsitapi* are now generalized as Blackfeet but were distinct as Siksika (Blackfoots), Kainaa (Blood) and *Piikani* (Piegan, Peigan, or Muddy River Indians). Their neighbors were Atsiina (Gros Ventre, Minnetari of the Plains, Big Bellies, or Flying Falls Indians) and *Sarci*.
3. For more about the silty streams of the northern foothills see John C. Jackson, *The Piikani Blackfeet: A Culture Under Siege* (Missoula, MT: Mountain Press, 2000), 5–7.
4. Peter Bakker, Institute of General Linguistics, University of Amsterdam, to the author, 2 October 1991. "In eastern Saskatchewan and Manitoba Woods Cree and Swampy Cree are spoken. If this [name] would be Swampy Cree, I would suggest it is ... 'well-dressed woman.' ... The late Lily MacAuley suggested something like ... 'digging woman.' I was also thinking maybe ... 'good rowing woman,' but there are some problems with the vowels and women do not usually row among the Cree."
5. Baptism number 221, Mitcham parish register, Surrey, 22 January 1815 baptism of George Bird, aged twenty years. Courtesy of Mr. James C. Bird of Waltham Abbey, Essex.
6. Carlton House Journals, 1795/96, HBCA B27/a/1; 1796/97, B27/a/2; 1797/98, B49/a/28. Setting River Journal, 1798/99, HBCA B197/a/1.
7. "Declaration of James Bird concerning his claim to participate in an grant to Half-Breeds living in the North-West Territories as a Head of family" given at Calgary, 21 May 1885, National Archives Canada, record group 15, volume 1325, half-breed claim number 285, courtesy of Trudy Nicks.
8. Leaving Jacco Finlay across the mountains Montour returned to Rocky Mountain House on 31 December. He went to Fort Augustus and returned from there on 11 January 1807. Journal of the Rocky Mountain House Occurrences, 1806/07 by David Thompson, MS notebook 18, microfilm reel 2, Archives of Ontario.
9. Nicholas Montour was born and baptized in Albany, New York and spent his early life among the British traders at Michilimackinac.
10. For a discussion of the persistence of michif see John C. Crawford, "What is Michif?: Language in the Métis tradition," *The New Peoples:*

11   *Being and Becoming Métis in North America*, edited by Jacqueline Peterson and Jennifer S. H. Brown (Lincoln, NE: University of Nebraska Press, 1985), 231–41.

11   Saskatchewan Servants Accounts in 1815/16 list George Bird, Joseph Bird, and James Bird. Charles Bird is the trader's younger brother. HBCA B60/f/1, items 1, 6, 7, 8, 70.

12   Alice M. Johnson, ed., *Saskatchewan Journals and Correspondence, Edmonton House 1795–1800, Chesterfield House 1800–1802* (London: The Hudson's Bay Record Society, 1967), 124 n.2, 140 n.3.

13   Raymond Beaumont of Winnipeg found that James Bird Jr was entered as an apprentice and enrolled in the York Factory school on 5 August 1809, along with William Sinclair and Richard Colen. York Factory Journal 1809–10, HBCA B239/a/119, fol. 21d. The York school apparently began in 1808. Sylvia Van Kirk, *Many Tender Ties: Women in Fur Trade Society, (1679–1870)* (Winnipeg: Watson and Dwyer, 1980), 104–5.

14   The "School Instructions" in 1808 specified enrolment of all children of currently employed servants to be admitted at age five, as well as the children of chiefs of friendly tribes. No York School book seems to survive, but the York officers in September 1809 sent home schoolwork as "Samples of Progress." Jennifer Brown, "A Colony of Very Useful Hands." *The Beaver*, (Spring 1977), 41–2.

15   Marcel Giraud, *The Métis of the Canadian West*, 2 vols. (1945; Translated by George Woodcock. Lincoln, NE: University of Nebraska Press, 1986) 1:339–44.

16   Raymond Beaumont found that James Bird was enrolled in the York Factory School on 5 August 1809. York Factory Journal 1809–10, HBCA B239/a/119, fol. 21d. The "School Instructions" in 1808 specified the enrolment of all children of currently employed servants to be admitted at age five, as well as the children of chiefs of friendly tribes. See also Sylvia Van Kirk, *Many Tender Ties: Women in Fur Trade Society, 1670–1870* (Winnipeg: Watson and Dwyer, 1980), 104–05.

17   See Arthur J. Ray, *Indians in the Fur Trade: their role as hunters, trappers and middlemen in the lands southwest of Hudson Bay, 1660–1870* (Toronto: University of Toronto Press, 1974), 137–38.

18   HBCA B60/a/10, 14; B60/a/11, 3d, 4d. The Astorian overland party took the precious experiences of Andrew Henry and his men at the Three Forks to heart and reached the Columbia by a more southern route.

19   Broadly drumming up trade, but also a way to subsist spare men in the winter camps.

20   Edmonton House Journal, HBCA B60/a/13, 12, 13, 22.

Notes to Chapter 3

1   Edmonton House Journal 1806/07, HBCA B60/a/6, fol. 6. Contrary to accepted belief, only one Piikani was killed.

2   Edmonton House Journal 1807/08, HBCA B60/a/7, fols. 6–8.

3   Ibid., fol. 12.

4   Edmonton House Journal 1814/15, HBCA B60/a/13, fol. 7d.

5   Glasgow men were in the first colonial party of 1811. The second group sailed from Sligo on 24 June 1812 with hired Irish servants, chiefly recruited from western Ireland and led by Owen Keveny. The recruiting must have been instigated by Lord Selkirk who went

to Sligo in May. John Morgan Gray, *Lord Selkirk of Red River* (Toronto: Macmillan, 1963).
6   Johnson, ed., *Saskatchewan Journals*, 98.
7   Edmonton House Journal, 1815/16, HBCA B60/a/15, fol. 23.
8   Ray, *Indians in the Fur Trade*, 205–6.
9   Two excellent previous studies of mixed-blood children of the fur traders have concentrated on material drawn from family data of company officers. Those are Sylvia Van Kirk, *Many Tender Ties: Women in Fur Trade Society, 1670–1870* (Winnipeg: Watson and Dwyer, 1980) and Jennifer S. H. Brown, *Strangers in Blood: Fur Trade Families in Indian Country* (Vancouver: University of British Columbia, 1980).
10 "Deposition of Pierre Pamburn," Red River Settlement Papers, 1815–9, HBCA E8/5,36.
11 "Statement of James Bird Jr" HBCA E8/6, 91 (Red River Settlement Papers, 1814–20).
12 Brandon House Journal, 19 May 1816, HBCA B22/a/18, fol. 33d.
13 It may have been a measure of Bird's self-possession in a moment stolen from the concerns of his temporary government, that he remembered a promise made to the Muddy River Indians. He wrote asking an undoubtedly puzzled London purchasing agent to send out a few light, ornamented brass shields which he intended to use as a gratuity to important Indian leaders. Edmonton District Report, HBCA B60/e/2,6d.8d.
14 Edmonton House Journal, B60/a/15, 49d.
15 James Bird Edmonton Report 1816, written at York Factory, 20 September 1816, HBCA B60/e/2, fol. 6.
16 Carlton House Journal 1816/17, HBCA B27/a/6, fols. 1, 2, 4d.
17 Francis Heron was one of two Donegal brothers brought into the HBC in 1812. After beginning as a steward at York Factory, Herron progressed to the responsibility of Cumberland House by 1815/16. Following the death of Governor Semple, James Bird used Heron as a disposable around Carlton House. The twenty-two-year-old Irishman gained enough experience to be appointed Edmonton District master from outfit 1817/18 until 1821.
18 Carlton House Journal 1816/17, fols. 7, 7d.
19 Fol. 9. This is an interesting suggestion that the plan to bring together the half-breeds had included the upper Saskatchewan. Another clerk, Thomas McKay, came from the Columbia Department but that may have been a coincidence.
20 Fol. 15d.
21 Fol. 17d, 25 February 1817.
22 Fols. 33, 34.
23 Edmonton House Journal, HBCA B60/a/17, fols. 6, 7d, 16.
24 No matter how closely associated with tribal kinsmen, freemen would not have been able to continue in the country without relying on the traders. In the competition for productive trappers, the traders forced advances on families that locked them into obligations that were difficult to escape.
25 David Smyth, "James Bird Jr," *Dictionary of Canadian Biography*, 8.
26 HBCA A6/42, fols. 8, 125.

Notes to Chapter 4

1   Snakes is the name usually applied to Eastern Shoshones, but the term may have been more general at that time and applied to other southern peoples.

2. This depends on the version that David Thompson obtained from the aged Saukamapee and included in his famous *Narrative*. As actual fact it should be approached with caution.
3. Ibid., 2:495. Passing Battle Mountain in summer 1808 Alexander Henry learned that Cree had killed three Peigans and were determined to prevent the traders from resupplying their enemies.
4. Before the introduction of the steel trapping method traders usually waited for Indian hunters to bring in their catch, or in the case of the debt system, returns from advances made previously based on set standards of trade. But that method was increasingly inconvenient in the new corporate world.
5. A. P. Nasitir, "The International Significance of the Jones and Immell Massacre and of the Arikara Outbreak of 1823," *The Pacific Northwest Quarterly* 30 (January 1939), 77–108.
6. See John E. Sunder, *Joshua Pilcher; Fur Trader and Indian Agent* (Norman: University of Oklahoma Press, 1969), 37–40. Emphasis mine. Edmonton House Journal, 1822/23, HBCA B60/a/21, fol. 7. This suggests that the Piikani were already in contact with trappers or traders from the Missouri Fur Company on the Yellowstone at the mouth of the Big Horn. The traders Robert Jones and Michael Immell carried instructions "to obtain a friendly interview with the Blackfoot Indians...."
7. HBCA B60/a/21, fols. 2, 11d, 20d, 22d, 24.
8. HBCA A12/1, fol. 186d.
9. HBCA E2/2, fols. 2–39. A somewhat unofficial publication of this important document was made to celebrate the southern Alberta bicentennial. See Bruce Haig, ed., *A Look at Peter Fidler's Journal: Journal of a Journey over Land from Buckingham House to the Rocky Mountains in 1792 and 3* (Lethridge: Historical Research Centre, 1991).
10. Edmonton House Journal 1811/12, HBCA B60/a/10, fol. 14; B60/a/11, fols. 3d, 4d.
11. Typescript MS, "Munro Family," in possession of descendants of James Bird living on the Blackfoot Reservation in Montana.
12. Colin Robertson or the HBC Montreal hiring agents, Maitland, Gardens, and Auldjo.
13. Saskatchewan Servants, B60/f/1, number 70.
14. Edmonton House Journal, HBCA B60/a/18, fols. 9, 10d, 14.
15. Edmonton House Journal, HBCA B60/a/22, fol. 26.
16. The best consideration of this incident and its documents is Nasatir, "The International Significance...."
17. Edmonton House Journal, HBCA B60/a/22, fol. 26d–28.
18. Caches were the safe-deposit boxes of the wilderness. A bottle shaped hole was usually dug in an obscure place, lined perhaps, goods deposited, and then covered over and concealed. Property upon which lives depended was left to the mercy of the elements. Although there were examples of failure due to leakage or discovery, in general this security system worked well.
19. McDonald to McTavish, Spokane, 4 April 1824, HBCA B239/c/1, York Correspondence, 1807–1828, fol. 140d.
20. Cokalarishkit, the Salish road to the buffalo followed the Blackfoot River.
21. Ranging south and west, and dedicated to beaver trapping, the Inuk'sik or Small Robe band of the Piikani were most inclined to seek

22 accommodations with their Salish neighbors. By 1832 the Inuk'sik had grown to 250 lodges.
22 Edmonton Journal 1823/24 (written by Duncan Finlayson) HBCA B60/a/22, fol. 40–41.
23 The term is explained in Governor Simpson's Dispatch, 10 August 1832, HBCA A12/1, 460.
24 Arima, 211 n.54.

Notes to Chapter 5

1 Edmonton District Report 1824/25, B60/e/8. See also J. G. MacGregor, *John Rowand Czar of the Prairies* (Saskatoon: Western Producer Prairie Books, 1978), 65.
2 The Inuksiks (Small Robes) were a considerable band of Piikani operating close to the mountains. See John Ewers, "Identification and history of the Small Robes Band of the Piegan Indians," *Washington Academy of Sciences* 36:12 (15 December 1946), 397–403. The Mr. Bird who Ogden and Work met in September 1823 must have been brother George.
3 For the development of this challenge see John C. Jackson, *Shadow on the Tetons: David E. Jackson and the Claiming of the American West* (Missoula, MT: Mountain Press, 1993).
4 "Journal of Alexander Ross – Snake Country Expedition, 1824" edited by T. C. Elliott, *Oregon Historical Quarterly* 14 (December 1913), 388.
5 Frederick Merk, ed., *Fur Trade and Empire: George Simpson's Journal Remarks Connected with the Fur Trade in the Course of a Voyage from York Factory to Fort George 1824–1825, together with Accompanying Documents* (Cambridge: Harvard University Press, 1931), 27, 47. Long accepted as a primary source for HBC operations, this document requires closer scrutiny and deeper critical analysis.
6 E. E. Rich, ed., *Peter Skene Ogden's Snake Country Journals, 1824–25 and 1825–26* (London: The Hudson's Bay Record Society, 1950).
7 Rich, ed., *Ogden's Snake Country Journals 1824–25*, 10,19, 23, 28, 34.
8 Company records include; "Snake Journal pr. Mr. Ogden 1824/25," HBCA B202/a/2; "Journal of Occurrences in a Trapping Expedition to and from the Snake Country in the Years 1824 and (25) kept by William Kittson," HBCA B202/a/3.
9 George Bird Grinnell, "A White Blackfoot," *The Masterkey*, 47:1 (January–March 1973), 12–7.
10 Hugh's memory was faulty, it had been three months before.
11 Rich, *Ogden's 1824–25 Journal*, 240–1.
12 Rich, *Ogden's 1824–5 Journal*, 64.
13 Rich, "Kittson's Journal"*Ogden's 1824–25 Journal*, 241. Between the Ogden and Kittson journals it is possible to come up with a total of 221 beaver traded from the Blackfeet between 21 and 29 June 1825 near Camas Creek. That compares favorably with the 240 beaver that Munroe remembered when he described the event to Grinnell.
14 Merk, *Fur Trade and Empire*, 171–4.
15 Rich, *Ogden's 1824–25 Journal*; McKay to Stuart.
16 These trappers apparently remained at the old fort at the mouth of the Big Horn last fall and were working up the Yellowstone before crossing to the upper Green River and joining the American rendezvous planned for Henry's Fork of the Green. On their way they were attacked by Indians who killed a man named Le Brache. Charles L.Camp, ed., *James Clyman Frontiersman* (Portland: The

17 Champoeg Press, 1960), 37–8; T. D. Bonner, ed., *The Life and Adventures of James P. Beckwourth* (New York: Alfred A. Knopf, 1931), 38–40.

17 "McKay to John Stuart, Missouri Forks, 11 July 1825," John Stuart Letterbook, Oregon Historical Society Microfilm 1502.

18 Rich, "Kittson's Journal," 241; Grinnell, "White Blackfoot", 16–7.

19 Ogden to HBC, East Side, 27 June 1825 in Frederick Merk, *The Oregon Question* 92–3.

20 Ogden to HBC, East Fork, Missouri, 10 July 1825, Merk, *The Oregon Question*, 86–92.

21 Munroe, Picard, Bird, and Ward who was never mentioned by name.

22 Ogden to HBC, East Fork, Missouri, 10 July 1825.

23 Rich, *Ogden's 1824–25 Journals*, 67–8, 243. Kittson headed over Gibbon pass driving twenty animals laden with seventeen packs and four pactons holding 744 large and 248 small beaver of poor quality. Beyond the 221 pelts traded from the Peigans, Ogden's men were taking less desirable summer skins.

24 Given the extent of Piikani penetration several rivers in the region carried that name. The Big Blackfoot was the channel of Cokarishkit, the road to the buffalo, and came in near the Hellgate. Yet another Blackfoot River entered the Snake near the present Blackfoot, Idaho.

25 This must have been the trapping brigade led by Captain John Weber returning after the American rendezvous.

26 Rich, *Ogden's 1824–25 Journal*, 75, 78, 82, 83.

27 Francis Fuller Victor, *The River of the West* (Hartford: The Author, 1870: reprinted Columbus: Long's College Book Store, 1950).

28 Ogden to Simpson, Fort Nez Percés, 12 November 1825 in Merk, ed., *The Oregon Question*, 94.

Notes to Chapter 6

1 J. G. Macgregor, *John Rowand: Czar of the Prairies* (Saskatoon: Western Producer Prairie Books, 1978), 65. Long distance estimates were unreliable. Just two years before, Francis Heron counted 600 Peigan, 400 Blood and 600 Gros Ventre lodges.

2 Edmonton House Journal, HBCA B60/a/23, fols. 2d–3.

3 Edmonton House Journal, HBCA B60/a/23, fol. 4.

4 Folios 9, 10d, 11–11d.

5 Folios 6d, 10d, 11–11d; "Stuart to HBC, Carlton, 7 February 1826," OHS Microfilm.

6 Edmonton House Journal 21 April 1824, HBCA B60/a/22; Edmonton District Report 1824/25, B60/e/8, fols .2–2d.

7 Edmonton House Journal 1826/27, B60/a/24, fol. 7.

8 Folio 17.

9 Edmonton Journal, B60/a/24, fols. 7, 17. Munroe turned in just thirty skins; not much for a year of trapping.

10 George Bird Grinnell, "A White Blackfoot," *The Masterkey*, vol. 46:4 (October–December 1972), 142–51; vol. 47:1 (January–March 1973), 12–22. Eugene Y. Arima *Blackfeet and Palefaces: The Pikani and Rocky Mountain House: A Commemorative History of the Upper Saskatchewan and Missouri River Trade* (Ottawa: Golden Dog Press, 1995), 21 n.54 states that Munroe was the subject of a disparaging remark in 1822 and after serving for eight years was discharged on 25 November 1823. He left on 1 December in company with the interpreter Charles McKay and the Métis Primeau. When they

returned on 12 April 1824, Munroe remained with the Peigans.

11. Grinnell, "A White Blackfoot," 17–19. The incident was likely a consequence of the liquor the Indians carried away with them to drink at the first camp.

12. These developments are followed in Dale L. Morgan, *The West of William H. Ashley* (Denver: The Old West Publishing Company, 1964).

13. For American activities see Jackson, *Shadow on the Tetons*, chapters 9 and 10.

14. T. C. Elliott, "The Journal of John Work, July 5–15 September 1826,"*Washington State Historical Quarterly* 6:1 (January 1915), 38–41, 43–44.

15. Evidence of a meeting with Blackfeet at the old location of Andrew Henry's winter post on Henry's Fork rests on a statement by the less than reliable trapper James Beckwourth.

16. Edmonton House Journal, 17 November 1826, B60/a/24, fol. 19d.

17. "A Narrative of Col. Robert Campbell's Experiences in the Rocky Mountain Fur Trade from 1825 to 1835," Missouri Historical Society MSS.

18. Thomas McKay was as mythic a figure in the Pacific Northwest as James Bird Jr should be on the northwestern Canadian plains. The mixed-blood son of Alexander McKay came to the Columbia River with the Astorians and passed through the NWCo to the HBC. Simpson initially appreciated McKay's tough-minded qualities in dealing with the Indians.

19. Glydnwr Williams, ed., *Peter Skene Ogden's Snake Country Journals, 1827–28 and 1828–29* (London: The Hudson's Bay Record Society, 1971) 8 n.4, 80–81. By then Ogden had taken over 2,000 MB while McKay's party added another 440. The Americans lost about four thousand dollars worth of beaver which at the price of five dollars each could have been about 800 skins.

20. Sending advance agents to the house was an old practice to insure a proper welcome, which meant tobacco or an advance gift of liquor. Distributing this gratuity provided a means of gaining respect and influence for the heralds.

21. Edmonton House Journal, 4 August 1828, HBCA B60/a/26, fol. 8.

22. Folio 29.

23. Rocky Mountain House Journal 1828/29, HBCA B184/a/1.

24. Rocky Mountain House Journal 1829/30, HBCA B184/a/2.

25. Culled from MacGreggor, *John Rowand*.

26. For a discussion of this problem as it related to the business see Philip Goldring, "Governor Simpson's Officers: Elite Recruitment in a British Overseas Enterprize, 1834–1870," *Prairie Forum: The Journal of the Canadia Plains Research Center* 10:2 (Fall 1985).

27. Perhaps *onistaipokaa* or Calf Child?

28. David Lavender, *The Fist in the Wilderness* (1964: reprint Albuquerque: University of New Mexico Press, 1979), 393, puts this figure at ninety-two Peigan men and thirty-two women.

29. Fort Edmonton Correspondence Inward, 1831/60, HBCA B60/c/1, fol. 1.

30. Fort Edmonton Correspondence Inward, 1831/60, HBCA B60/c/1, fol. 2.

Notes to Chapter 7

1. About 4,000 skins. There are two printed versions of Kipp's statements to Bradley, the most

detailed being James Bradley, "Establishment of Ft. Piegan as told to me by James Kipp," Bradley MS, Book F, *Contributions to the Historical Society of Montana* (1917) 8:244–50.
2. Rocky Mountain House Journal 1830/31, HBCA B184/a/3.
3. Ibid., 249.
4. John Work's Snake brigade encountered the invasion but the description of the attack comes from the recollection of an American trapper. See W. A. Ferris, *Life In The Rocky Mountains*, Edited by Paul C. Phillips (1940; Revised edition Denver: Old West Publishing Company, 1983), 216–17, 222.
5. "Treaty of Trade and Peace Between the American Fur Company and the Blackfeet," vol. 24, *Early Western Travels*, Edited by Reuben Gold Thwaits, 317.
6. Charles E. DeLand and Doane Robinson, "Fort Tecumseh and Fort Pierre Journals and Letterbooks," *South Dakota Historical Collections*, vol. 9 (1918), 155–57.
7. George Catlin, *Letters and Notes on the manners, customs, and conditions of the North American Indians*, 2 vols. (London: 1844; reprint New York: Dover Publications, Inc., 1973), 1:23, 35, 46, 223.
8. Catlin, *Letters and Notes*, 51–52.
9. James H. Bradley, "Affairs at Fort Benton, 1831–1869," *Contributions to the Historical Society of Montana*, vol. 3 (Helena, 1900), 201–03.
10. Journal of Occurrences at Fort Sanspariel from 23 May 1832 to —, by Patrick Small Jr, HBCA B60/a/27, fol. 1d.
11. Ibid.
12. Fols. 10d–11.
13. Simpson's Dispatch to London, York Factory, 10 August 1832, HBCA A12/1, para. 418.
14. Para. 460. Curiously, the Saskatchewan servants accounts show payments to Hugh Munroe up to 1828, but the account for James Bird Jr stops on 30 November 1823 showing a balance carried forward of 5/19/11. HBCA A6/42.
15. Ibid.; Simpson to HBC, York Factory, 10 August 1832, HBCA D4/99. This seems to confirm Kipp's recollection of 6,450 pounds of beaver.
16. London Correspondence Inward, 1823–1843, HBCA A12/1, para. 460–61.
17. Ibid., para. 460d.
18. Moose Incoming Correspondence, 1789–1861, HBCA B135/c/12, folder 2, 94–7.
19. J. E. Harriot to governor, chief factors and chief traders, Peigan Post, 6 January 1833, Simpson's Correspondence, 1831–1837, D5/4.
20. Ibid.
21. Bradley was told that the employees of Fort McKenzie observed the sun dance that year so it must have been held in the vicinity of the post.
22. Ferris, *Life in the Mountains*, 241–44.
23. Hiram Martin Chittenden, *The American Fur Trade of the Far West*, 2 vols. (1902: Reprinted Lincoln, NE: University of Nebraska Press, 1986), 1:355–63.
24. Smith, Jackson, and Sublette foresaw that, and had closed business in 1830.
25. This steers away from Blackfoot cosmogony to avoid dealing with a complex subject in a limited space. For one version of Napi see Clark Wisler and D. C. Duvall, *Mythology of the Blackfoot Indians*, Introduction by Alice Beck Kehoe (Lincoln, NE: University of Nebraska Press, 1995), 5–12.
26. Simpson to Aitkin, 2 July 1834, HBCA D4/20; Minutes of a tempo-

27   McLoughlin to Heron, 9 September 1831, 14 March 1832, Burt Brown Barker, ed., *Letters of Dr. John McLoughlin written at Fort Vancouver 1829–1832* (Portland, Oreg.: Binfords and Mort, 1948), 212, 263. The plan was to send Montour or Rivet traveling with the Indians much as Bird did east of the mountains. An American, Warren Ferris, who turned up at Flatheads Post was engaged to cover Montour's attempt to break into the rendezvous.

28   E. H. Oliver, *The Canadian North-West: Its Early Development and Legistlative Records*, vol. 2 (Ottawa: Government Printing Bureau, 1914), 690, 693, 704.

29   Citing Simpson's Report to HBC, York Factory, 25 July 1827, HBCA D4/90, fols. 24–5.

30   Ibid.

31   Journal of Fort Sanspareil 1832–3, HBCA B60/a/27, 2v., fols. 10–11; D4/100,17–8, Simpson's Report, 21 July 1834, HBCA D4/100, fols. 17–18; Simpson's Report, Red River Settlement, 10 June 1835, HBCA D4/102, fol. 39; Rowand to Simpson, Edmonton, 7 Jan 1835, HBCA D4/127, fol. 34; 15 January 1839, HBCA D5/5, fol. 88–89; Edmonton House Journal, September 1833–February 1834, HBCA B60/a/28, fols. 15, 28, 41–2.

32   Simpson to Rowand, London, 28 February 1838, HBCA D4/23, fol. 117.

33   Symth, "James Bird Junior," *DCB*, vol. 8.

Notes to Chapter 8

1   Peter Fidler observed Kutenai trading horses in the same area in 1793. A friendly Kutenai intervened on Munroe's behalf in his dispute with Tete que Leve. A Kutenai married to a Piikani woman was painted by Bodmer in 1833. All point to friendly, as well as hostile relationships.

2   J. E. A. McLeod, "Old Bow Fort," *Canadian Historical Review*, 12:4 (December 1931), 407. The location was just a long day's ride north of favorite winter camps.

3   Edmonton Journal, HBCA B60/a/27, fols. 11d–12d.

4   Edmonton Journal, 8 December 1832, HBCA B60/a/27, fols. 27d–28.

5   This statement and those that follow are from the Szmrecsanyi translation of Prince Maximilian's field journal. "Journals of Prince Maximilian in North America" (Center for Western Studies, Joslyn Art Museum, unpublished) vol. 2, 475; through the courtesy of Dr. Joseph C. Porter.

6   The initial publication of the prince's observations was *Reise in das Innere Nord-America in den Jahren 1832 bis 1834*, 2 vols. (Koblenz: J. Holscher, 1839–41) with an English translation appearing in 1843. *Maximilian, Prince of Wied's Travels in the Interior of North America* appeared as volumes 22 to 25 of *Early Western Travels, 1748–1846* edited by Reuben Gold Thwaits (Cleveland: Arthur H. Clark Company, 1906). The Karl Bodmer art has been the subject to several recent books including Davis Thomas and Karin Ronnefeldt, eds., *People of the First Man: Life Among the Plains Indians in their Final Days of Glory* (New York: E.E. Dutton, 1976), and *Karl Bodmer's America* (Lincoln, NE: University of Nebraska Press, 1984).

7   Bird took two young Red River men to Fort Union on his way back from the settlement, one of them the son

of the recently deceased chief factor Alexander Kennedy. Harriot to HBC, 10 January 1834, HBCA D4/126/63. The educated Kennedys were a family that did not entirely buy into the new society being promoted by Simpson, who disparaged them. A grandson, A. K. Isbister, later became the advocate of Métis rights in London.
8   *Bodmer's America*, 237.
9   The liquor trade had been lamented for half a century, but as long as government wasn't watching, Americans used it. By July 1833 it became so difficult to convince hunters to go to the Bow River that Edmonton broke the standing rule against trading liquor during the summertime. Fort Sanspariel (Edmonton) Journal 1832/33, HBCA B60/a/27.
10 Maximilian Field Journal, 2:477.
11 Thomas and Ronnefeldt, *People of the First Man*, 105–04.
12 Apparently, he Red Horn who retrieved Bird's horse from Fisher.
13 The experienced baymen at Peigan Post mistook him for a white man.
14 Bodmer Field Journal.
15 Davis and Ronnefeldt, eds. *People of the First Man*, 109.
16 The description is backed up by Bodmer's vivid impression of the battle.
17 It was forty-six years since David Thompson met the famed Piikani war leader Kutenape. It is unlikely this was the same individual, as famous names were often passed down to younger men.
18 Extracted and paraphrased from Reuben Gold Thwaites, ed., "Maximilian's Travels," *Early Western Travels*, 23:147–53.
19 The quotation from the published version in Thwaites has generated considerable speculation over Maximilian's meaning, but the field notes do not contain the statement in that form. While calling Bird "pernicious" and "a very bad, insincere man" whom nobody trusts the Prince does not suggest extrajudicial assassination.
20 Sixty-one/ Rowand to governor, chief factors and chief traders of Northern Department, Edmonton, 10 January 1834, HBCA D4/126, fol. 61.
21 Fort Edmonton Journal 1833/34. HBCA B60/a/28, fols. 8d, 14.
22 Folio 15.
23 James J. Bird to J. E. Harriot, Badger River, 23 October 1833, HBCA D4/126, fol. 13d.
24 Rowand to governor, chief factors and chief traders of Northern Department, Edmonton, 10 January 1834, HBCA D4/126, fols. 61–64d.
25 The Edmonton prohibition against selling liquor during the summer probably had more to do with maintaining tranquility around a post with a reduced summer compliment.
26 Ray H. Mattison, "Kenneth McKenzie," *Fur Traders, Trappers and Mountain Men of the Upper Missouri*, edited by Leroy R. Hafen (Lincoln, NE: University of Nebraska Press, 1995), 21–28.
27 Lavender, *Fist in the Wilderness*, 414–17.
28 Simpson's Report to HBC, 21 July 1834, para. 17, HBCA D4/100, fols. 17d–18.
29 HBCA B21/a/1, fols. 3d, 4, 4d–5, 9–11.

Notes to Chapter 9

1   Simpson's Correspondence, HBCA D5/4, fol. 143.
2   "Rowand to HBC, Edmonton, 7 January 1835," Simpson's correspondence, HBCA D5/4, fol. 99d.
3   Ibid. The emphasis is mine.

4   Andrew D. Pambrun, "The Story of his life as he tells it", typescript manuscript paraphrased by Eva Emery Dye, *McDonald of Oregon*. This is published as Andrew Dominique Pambrun, *Sixty Years on the Frontier of the Pacific Northwest* (Fairfax, Wash.: Ye Galleon Press,1978). Pambrun stayed at Red River as a student and then as a teacher for six years before returning to the west about 1841.

5   Minutes of Council 1836, *North Dakota Historical Colletions*, vol. 4 (Fargo: 1913). That was the same salary that clerks like William Kittson, Thomas McKay, Francis Ermatinger, Pierre Pamburn, or even the governor's ambitious cousin, Thomas Simpson, were receiving.

6   Johnson, ed., *Saskatchewan Journals*, 311–14 and notes.

7   The joint Flathead/Mountain Man revenge was visited upon relatively innocent Gros Ventres who happened to be passing, but it was meant as a response to the Peigan/ Blood invasion of the previous spring.

8   John Kirk Townsend, *Narrative of a Journey Across the Rocky Mountains to the Columbia River* (1839; Reprinted Lincoln, NE: University of Nebraska Press, 1978), 243–45. Antoine Godin was killed across the Portneuf River from Fort Hall on 22 May 1836.

9   Rowand to HBC, Edmonton, 4 January 1837, Simpson's Correspondence, HBCA D5/4.

10 W. H. Gray, *History of Oregon 1792–1849* (Portland: The Author, 1870), 171–2; Donald R. Johnson, ed., *William H. Gray: Journal of his Journey East, 1836–1837* (Fairfield, Wash.: Ye Galleon Press, 1980), 42–7.

11 Johnson, ed., *Gray Journal*, 43, 46.

12 T. C. Tessendorf, "Red Death on the Missouri," *The American West*, 14: 1 (January–February 1977), 48–53. The original sources are in Abel, *Cardon's Journal at Fort Clark*; and Denig, *Five Indian Tribes*.

13 Rowand to Hargraves, Edmonton House, 31 December 1838, in G. P.deT. Grazebrook, ed., *The Hargraves Correspondence, 1821–1843* (Toronto: The Champlain Society, 1938). The dead wife may have been Crane Woman whose daughter was Susan Bird.

14 At Edmonton the priests baptized three of Hugh Munroe's children, so he had also returned from the Blackfoot country.

15 A5/23, London Correspondence Outwards, HBC official, 1833–1848. Reel 41 HBC to Gentlemen Traders, London, 7 March 1838, para. 21. "In the prosecution of the trade with the Piegans and other Plain tribes inhabiting the country between the Saskatchewan and Missouri, we have to desire that no establishment be formed to the southward of the 49th parallel of latitude and that none of the companys engaged servants be sent across the boundary for the purposes of trade."

16 Simpson to Bird, 6 January 1841, HBCA D4/25, in Hugh Dempsey, ed., *The Rundle Journals 1840–1848* (Calgary: Historical Society of Alberta, 1977), 27.

Notes to Chapter 10

1   It is speculative, but that individual seems to be the same as Makuie Poka whom Bodmer painted at Fort McKenzie in mid-August 1833. He was later of considerable service to Father Point.

2   Mikell DeLores Wormell Warner and Harriet Duncan Munnick,

trans. and eds., *Catholic Church Records of the Pacific Northwest: Vancouver and Stellamaris Mission* (St. Paul, Oregon: French Prairie Press, 1972), sixth through tenth pages of manuscript. Interesting to compare the birth dates to the biography of Munroe by Schultz, or Hugh's own statements at various times.

3. Hugh Dempsey, ed., *The Rundle Journals, 1840–1848* (Calgary: Historical Society of Alberta, 1977).

4. Rowand to Simpson, 4 January 1841, HBCA D5/6, in Dempsey, *The Rundle Journals*, 24.

5. Dempsey, ed., *The Rundle Journals*, Appendix, 346.

6. Rundle sometimes used an "x" standing for a cross, as shorthand for Christianity.

7. Dempsey, ed., *Rundle Journals*, 66–67, 69–72.

8. The migrants have been treated in D. Geneva Lent, *West of the Mountains: James Sinclair and the Hudson's Bay Company* (Seattle: University of Washington Press, 1963); and in John C. Jackson, *Children of the Fur Trade: Forgotten Métis of the Pacific Northwest* (Missoula, MT: Mountain Press, 1995).

9. Goldring, "Governor Simpson's Officers," 251–81.

10. Simpson to James Evans, Edmonton, 27 July 1841, HBCA D4/113, fol. 324; Wesleyan Missionary Society Archives, Box 12/1 in Dempsey, *Rundle Journals*, 29. Simpson missed meeting Rundle but was convinced that he could do no good wandering about in the care of the Indians and exposing himself to danger. "This was the case with a scamp named Jamey Jock, one of the most villainous of his brand in the Country as an interpreter...."

11. Dempsey, *Rundle Journals*, 136. Four years later Bird refused the hand of his daughter to Piche's son.

12. Ibid., 137.

13. The Jesuit mission is beautifully illustrated in the catalog of the de Smet Project, Jacqueline Peterson and Laura Peers, *Sacred Encounters: Father De Smet and the Indians of the Rocky Mountain West* (Norman, OK: University Oklahoma Press, 1993).

14. Ibid., 197.

15. Ibid., 199.

16. De Smet's letter, 30 October 1845 in *Life, Letters and Travels of Father De Smet*, 2 vols., edited by H. M. Chittenden and A. T. Richardson (New York; Francis P. Harper, 1905), 2:526–27. See also Thwaits, ed., *Early Western Travels*, vols. 27, 29.

17. Ibid.

18. Ibid., 2:524. Letter dated 31 December 1845.

19. Ewers, "Small Robes Band," 397.

20. Joseph P. Donnelly, S.J. trans., *Wilderness Kingdom: The Journals and Paintings of Nicolas Point* (New York: Holt, Rinehart, and Winston, 1967).

21. Keith C. Seele, ed., *Blackfeet and Buffalo: Memories of Life among the Indians by James Willard Schultz (Apikuni)* (Norman, OK: University of Oklahoma Press, 1962), 179–93. Schultz came into the country in 1886 as a young trader just as the buffalo were disappearing but while the tribes were still trying to live as they had for decades. His marriage to a Piikani woman gave Schultz access to the lodge tales of her relatives. Over the next sixty years Schultz produced a remarkable body of Blackfoot stories. Unfortunately, most are an almost indecipherable mix of recalled truth and suspect fiction. He met Bird and Munroe as old men and incor-

22 The dates seem improbable. According to the Rundle journals Bird was around Edmonton at this time.
23 The Stoney (Assiniboine) were Siouan speakers.
24 Ibid., 272–74.
25 Ibid., 306–07.
26 The Methodist Board of Inquiry excused Evans from the charges "but found imprudence in aspects of his behavior." He died in England in November 1846.
27 J. Russell Harper, ed., *Paul Kane's Frontier: Including Wanderings of An Artist Among the Indians of North American by Paul Kane* (Fort Worth, Tex.: The Amon Carter Museum, 1971), 138. The 1847 Christmas dinner guests were Harriot, three clerks, Rev. Jean Baptiste Thibault, the Manitou Lake Catholic missionary, Mr. Rundell, and Kane.
28 Ibid., 301.
29 Ibid., 306.
30 Paul Kane, *Wanderings of an Artist among the Indians of North America from Canada to Vancouver's Island and Oregon through the Hudson's Bay Company's territory and back again* (1859: Reprinted Edmonton: Hurtig Publishers, 1974), 288–92.
31 Ibid., 313.

Notes to Chapter 11

1 Speculating on the children of James Bird Jr is risky as there may have been as many as eighteen. Charles and Edward who were baptized in 1841 were old enough to help out.
2 MacGregor, *John Rowand*, 109 citing *The Hargrace Correspondence*, 317.
3 Frank Gilbert Roe, *The North American Buffalo: A Critical Study of the Species in its Wild State* (1951; porated them into stories that do not always match recoverable fact. Toronto: University of Toronto Press, 1970) 309 n.135, 137.
4 In 1835 1,500 pounds of beaver were shipped compared to forty-five tons of robes. Lavender, *Fist in the Wilderness*, 412.
5 Taken from David A. Dary, *The Buffalo Book: The Full Saga of the American Animal* (Chicago, Ill.: Swallow Tail Press, 1974).
6 For the development of this problem see Theodore Binnema, *Common and Contested Ground: A Human and Environmental History of the Northern Plains* (Norman, OK: University of Oklahoma Press, 2001).
7 Fort Benton Journal, 47.
8 Jackson, *The Piikani Blackfeet*, 184–87.
9 Ewers, *The Blackfeet*, 69.
10 The drawings that Father Nicolas Point collected are a vivid record of the Indian impression of traders. Joseph P. Donnelly S.J., trans., *Wilderness Kingdom: Indian Life in the Rocky Mountains: 1840–1847* (New York: Holt, Rinehart & Winston, 1967), 96 through 113.
11 Anne McDonnell, ed. and annotator, "The Fort Benton Journal, 1854–1856," *Contributions to the Historical Society of Montans*, vol. 10 (Boston: J. S. Canner & Company reprint, 1966), 7, 9, 11, 21. However, in the entry for 29 June 1855 (p. 39) the journalist notes that Burd [sic] and Cadote had left to go to the Bearpaw Mountains to trap beaver.
12 Ibid., 240 n.2.
13 Maximilian Field Journal, 27 August 1833 in *People of the First Man*, 109. For the later often quoted relationship with Natawista see *Fort Benton Journal*, 243.
14 Ewers, "Small Robes Band," 397.
15 For a blow-by-blow description of this treaty see John J. Killoren, S.J., *Come Blackrobe: De Smet and*

the Indian Tragedy (Norman, OK: University of Oklahoma Press, 1994), chapter 6.

16 For a description of Stanley's interesting career see Brian W. Dippie, *Catlin and His Contemporaries: The Politics of Patronage* (Lincoln, NE: University of Nebraska Press, 1990), 295–6.

17 Doty to Stevens, Fort Benton, 28 December 1853, "Report of Exploration of a Route for the Pacific Railroad near the 47th and 49th Parallels, from St.Paul to Puget Sound," 33rd Congress 1st Session, *Senate Executive Document 29*, vol. 1 (Washington), 442.

18 Hector Finlayson to Thomas Taylor, Rocky Mountain House, 10 February 1854, Edmonton Correspondence Inward, 1831–1860, HBCA B60/c/1, fol. 17.

19 No longer the American Fur Company as the Astor sold his interest to Pierre Chouteau Jr and Company.

20 Day-to-day events are extracted from the Fort Benton Journal.

21 Anne McDonnell incorrectly identified the son as Thomas Bird, but he would have only been five or six at that time. Perhaps Charles or Edward.

22 Hugh Dempsey, "James Doty. A Visit to a Blackfoot Camp," *Alberta Historical Review* 14:3 (Summer 1966), 20.

23 "Fort Benton Journal," 269–70, n.73.

24 Benjamin Durocher was the twenty-eight year trader from St. Louis.

25 John Kirk Townsend, *Narrative of a Journey Across the Rocky Mountains to the Columbia River* (1839; reprint Lincoln, NE: University of Nebraska Press, 1978), 243–44; John Dunn, *History of the Oregon Territory and British North American Fur Trade* (London: Edwards & Hughes, 1844), 156–57.

26 The drawing is labelled 18 October 1855. It is now in the collection of the Washington State Historical Society and has been published, along with portraits of many of the other participants in David L. Nicandri, ed., *Northwest Chiefs: Gustav Sohon's View of the 1855 Stevens Treaty Councils* (Tacoma: The Washington State Historical Society, 1986), 35.

27 Manypenny to Cumming, Stevens and Joel Palmer, 3 May 1855, Indian Office Records, in Ewers, *Blackfeet*, 214.

28 William E. Farr, "When We Were First Paid: The Blackfoot Treaty, The Western Tribes, and the Creation of the Common Hunting Ground, 1855," *Great Plains Quarterly* 21 (Spring 2001), 139.

29 McDonald, ed., "Notes and references to the Fort Benton Journal," 260.

30 Ashley to *St. Louis Enquirer*, 17 November 1823 in Morgan, ed., *The West of William Ashley*, 63–64.

31 Farr, "When We Were First Paid," 131–54.

32 Significantly, another Blackfoot delegation appeared at Edmonton in September 1855 to conclude a peace agreement with the Cree. Edmonton Journal 1855/56 cited in Milroy, *Plains Cree*, 110 and Farr, "Blackfoot Treaty," 145–46 n.63.

33 Albert J. Partoll, "The Blackfoot Indian Peace Council," *Frontier Omnibus* (Helena: Historical Society of Montana, 1962), 197–207.

Notes to Chapter 12

1 For the legal report see John C. Jackson, "Red River Settlers vs. Puget Sound Agricultural

Company," *Oregon Historical Quarterly* 85, 3 (Fall 1984), 279–89.
2   Lent, *West of the Mountains*, 176–77.
3   Bird to Alexander Christie, 31 March 1846, Public Archives of Manitoba Red River Collection, 87.
4   A tip of the Stetson to Ian Tyson's "palaver" at Elco, Nevada in 1997.
5   Ann McDonald notes that Chambers, who knew the Crow language and was married to a Gros Ventre, had not tasted radishes or lettuce for six years. "Fort Benton Journal," 270 n.77.
6   Ibid., 166, 169–70.
7   Edwin Denig, *Five Indian Tribes of the Upper Missouri, Sioux, Arickaras, Assiniboines, Crees, Crows* (Norman, OK: University of Oklahoma Press, 1961), 24–25.
8   Will of James Bird, Oregon Historical Society.
9   Statement of Philip Vankougnet, president of the executive council in John S. Galbraith, *The Little Emperor: George Simpson of the Hudson's Bay Company* (Toronto: Macmillan of Canada, 1976), 194.
10 Ibid., 199, citing Simpson to governor and commissioner 26 July 1856, HBCA D4/76a.
11 The Irving brothers were country sons of an HBC Orkneyman. The wife of James Irving was Angelique St. Germain who L. H. Morgan variously identified as a Chipawyan, McKenzie River woman, Athapaskan Hare, and finally as a former resident of Fort Good Hope.
12 See Irene M. Spry, "The Métis and mixed-bloods of Rupert's Land before 1870," *The New Peoples* (Lincoln, NE: University of Nebraska Press, 1985), 95–118.
13 Irene M. Spry, ed., *The Papers of the Palliser Expedition 1857–1860* (Toronto: The Champlain Society, 1968). Delivered to the Red River by a *voyageur* named Montour, Palliser engaged an elite crew that may have included a descendant of one of the first two men to cross the Rocky Mountains. Others were named Ballenden, Ross, Sinclair, Sutherland, and Munroe.
14 Henry Youle Hind, *Narrative of the Canadian Red River Exploring Expedition of 1857 and the Assiniboine and Saskatchewan Exploring Expedition of 1858* (Edmonton: M. G. Hurtig, 1971), 176–77.
15 Richard J. Huyda, *Camera in the Interior: 1858: H. L. Hime, Photographer: The Assiniboine and Saskatchewan Exploring Expedition* (Toronto: The Coach House Press, 1975), plate 37. See also plate 36, John Mckay, plate 45, residence of C.F. Bird. Of the thirty-six photographs which Hime took thirty-five have survived.
16 From a population of 6,077 in the 1850 U.S. census in ten years Minnesota Territory grew to 172,000.
17 Galbraith, *Little Emperor*, 200–203.
18 Theodore Blegen, "James W. Taylor, A Biographical Sketch," *Minnesota Historical Bulletin*, vol. 1 (November 1915), 153–95, in Richard Thomas Wright, *Overlanders 1858 Gold* (Saskatoon: Western Producer Prairie Books, 1985), 9–11.
19 St. Paul *Pioneer and Democrat*, 14 July 1858 in Wright, *Overlanders*, 11.
20 Ibid. See Spry, ed., *Palliser Expedition*, 45–50 for the lack of geographical knowledge about the northern plains.
21 Although Bird did not include his old Inuk'sik friends, a traveler on the plains during the winter 1857/58 distinguished between the "Peakuns" and the Little Blankets. Spry, ed., *Palliser Expedition*, 214.

22 Here is a belated explanation why the Kutenai at Fort McKenzie in 1834 was married to a Piikani woman and their son Wolf Child found a wife among the Flatheads.

23 White, ed., *Morgan's Journals*, 128.

Notes to Chapter 13

1. Great Britain Parliament, *Select Committee on Hudson's Bay Company Territories*, Appendix 15 (London: 1857), 439.
2. Since 1858 Burbank Brothers had a covert agreement with Governor Simpson concerning the operation of the riverboat *The Pioneer* which gave the HBC a decided advantage in transportation expenses.
3. Wright, *Overlanders*, 189.
4. Irene M. Spry, "The Métis and mixed-bloods of Rupert's Land before 1870," *The New Peoples* (Lincoln, NE: University of Nebraska Press, 1985), 105.
5. For a discussion of Schultz of whom opponents said, "Fate had manufactured a scoundrel out of material meant by Nature for a gentleman" see Gerald Friesen, *The Canadian Prairies: A History* (Toronto: University of Toronto Press, 1984), 115–17.
6. Marian Botsford Fraser, *Walking the Line: Travels Along the Canadian/American Border* (Vancouver: Douglas & McIntyre, 1989), 122.
7. A condensed summation of this development is treated in the introduction to Hartwell Bowsfield, ed., *The Letters of Charles John Brydges 1879–1882* (Winnipeg: Hudson's Bay Record Society, 1977), 11–14.
8. Lewis Henry Morgan in 1861 recorded his debate with Joseph James Hargrave, the son of the former York Factory factor and nephew of the present Fort Garry chief factor William McTavish, on "The Theory of Democracy." *Morgan's Indian Journals*, 113. Saloon discussions along that line may have been less restrained.
9. Doug Owram, "Conspiracy or Treason: The Red River Resistance From an Expansionist Perspective," *Prairie Forum* 3:2 (1978), 157–74.
10. Hartwell Bowsfield, ed., *The James Wickes Taylor Correspondence 1859–1870*, vol. 3, (Winnipeg: Manitoba Record Society Publications, n.d.).
11. See Spry, "Métis and mixed-bloods of Rupert's Land," *The New Peoples*, 98–99 for a shorthand notice of this clan. Fuller data is contained in the collection of T. R. McCloy, The Glenbow Museum, Calgary, Alberta.
12. *Begg's Red River Journal*, 312–15. One of them was Thomas Hourie dit Tommack who the Red River historian Gunn wrote was the husband of Jamey's daughter, Agnes Jock.
13. W. J. Healy, *Women of Red River: Being a Book Written from the Recollections of the Women Surviving from the Red River Era* (Winnipeg; Women's Canadian Club, 1923), 221–36.
14. Friesen, *Canadian Prairies*, 125–27.
15. D. N. Sprague and R. P. Frye, *The Genealogy of the First Métis Nation* (Winnipeg: Pemmican Publications, 1983), tables 4 and 5.
16. Only Thomas, Agnes, Nancy and Philip were living in 1885.
17. Gunn, *Echoes of the Red*, 164.
18. The child was buried at St. Andrew's on 16 February 1874.
19. Land Records, Half-breeds and Original White Settlers 1870–1930, declaration number 285, 21 May 1885, National Archives of Canada, RG15, D118.

Notes to Chapter 14

1. Hind's narrative of the Canadian Red River exploring expedition was published in 1860, the Palliser reports from 1859 to 1863, Hargraves described the Red River community in 1871 and Captain Butler could still call the Canadian west "The Great Lone Land," in 1873.
2. The attack on the camp of Heavy Runner was really intended to strike that of Mountain Chief whose followers were suspected of what pioneer Montanans called depredations. The direct responsibility for the attack rested on the leader of the column, Colonel Eugene M. Baker, but the chain of culpability included many others. Ewers, *The Blackfeet*, 236–53. A popularized description of the attack of 23 January 1870 and useful bibliography of sources is in Bob Bennett, *Death Too, For The Heavy-Runner* (Missoula, MT: Mountain Press, 1981).
3. Ibid., 152, citing S. W. Horrall, *The Pictorial History of the Royal Canadian Mounted Police* (Toronto: McGraw-Hill Ryerson, 1973), 18.
4. Thomas J. Bird interview, 24 November 1941, Montana Historical Society.
5. Métis claims affidavits extracts [NWHB], RG 15, p. 113, National Archives of Canada.
6. The carefully edited letters of Walter Traill show how the trading system responded to the surrender of the charter. Mae Atwood, ed., *In Rupert's Land: Memoir of Walter Traill* (Toronto: McClelland and Stewart, 1970).
7. In 1873 Canada authorized the formation of a uniformed constabulary. By the following summer the North West Mounted Police rode west to establish divisional headquarters on the Oldman River.
8. Ibid., 274–75.
9. Ann McDonnell's notes to the *Fort Benton Journal*, 260. It is possible that the old man has been confused with Agent Wellington Bird of the Fort Peck agency.
10. Nancy was living at Calgary when she filed her NWHB #90.
11. John McDougall, *In the Days of the Red River Rebellion* (Edmonton: The University of Alberta Press, 1983) 124–25, reports that smallpox was on the plains in the summer 1870. It traveled from the Sioux, Gros Ventre, and Cross to the Peigan, Blood, Blackfeet, and Sarcee and on to the Mountain and Wood Stoney. All the missionaries could do was scatter the half-breeds and close the churches. McDougall blamed Father Lacomb at St. Paul and other Catholic priests for spreading the disease by continuing to congregate their followers.
12. Sir John Macdonald speaking on the Red River rebellion as cited in Ogden Tanner, *The Canadians* (Alexandria, VA: Time Life Books, 1977), 140.
13. Friesen, *The Canadian Prairies*, 141–45.
14. Métis claims index numbers 59, 60, NAC RG15.

Notes to Chapter 15

1. Treaty Seven Elders and Tribal Council with Walter Hildebrandt, Dorothy First Rider, and Sarah Carter, *The True Spirit and Original Intent of Treaty 7* (Montreal & Kingston: McGill-Queen's University Press, 1996), 56.
2. Alexander Morris, *The Treaties of Canada with the Indians of Manitoba and the Northwest Territories* (1880;

Reprint Saskatoon: Fifth House, 1991), 253.
3. Scollen to Governor of Manitoba, 8 September 1876 in Morris, *Treaties of Canada*, 249.
4. Morris, *Treaties*, 261.
5. L. Clark to Hardisty, 18 June 1877, Richard C. Hardisty fonds, series 16, M477/936, Glenbow Archives.
6. L. Clark to Hardisty, 18 June 1877, Richard C. Hardisty fonds, series 16, M477/936, Glenbow Archives.
7. This description is a composite drawn from Hugh A. Dempsey, *Crowfoot: Chief of the Blackfeet* (Norman, OK: University of Oklahoma Press, 1972) and *Red Crow: Warrior Chief* (Lincoln, NE: University of Nebraska Press, 1980).
8. What is written becomes a final word fixed in time: what slips into tribal memory is subject to revision. In recent years claims have been made that Bird misinterpreted the treaty and admitted as much in a deathbed confession. While deeply felt and sincerely repeated that is not supported by the record of the death scene which was unavailable to revisionists.
9. Morris, *Treaties*, 260.

Notes to Chapter 16

1. Guillaime Charette, *Vanishing Spaces: Memories of Louis Goulet* (Winnipeg: Editions Bois Brules, 1976), 43.
2. Raymond Huel, ed., *The Collected Writings of Louis Riel* (Edmonton: University of Alberta Press, 1985), 223–27.
3. *Edmonton Bulletin*, 28 March 1885, Provincial Archives of Alberta.
4. Harold Fryer, *Albert: The Pioneer Years* (Langley, B.C.: Stagecoach Publishing, 1977), 17–18.
5. Friesen, *The Canadian Prairies*, 231.
6. Donald M. Stewart, "The Land Script Issues of Canada," *The Canadian Paper Money Journal*, 15:1 (January 1979).
7. Orkneyman James Sandison built the first Carlton House in 1795 so Bird's witness, James F. Sanderson of Medicine Hat must have been his son. The other witness, Alexander McKay, was related to Bird's Oregon brother-in-law, Charles McKay.
8. Half-breed script certification 285 (indexed as 359), PAC RG15, National Archives of Canada.
9. W. H. Cox, "Diary of a Mountie, from 180 to '85," *Lethbridge Herald Golden Jubilee Edition* (11 July 1935), 67–76; in Gerald L. Berry, "Alberta-Montana Relationships," M.A. thesis, University of Alberta, March 1950, 39.
10. Registrations made after 30 March 1885 were worth $240 in script that could be spent or used to buy 240 acres of land. Script was also issued to Métis children born before 15 July 1870. Heads of families could receive $160 or 160 acres. Giraud, *Métis*, 454.
11. James Willard Schultz and his wife Fine Shield Woman were living at Cow Cree, in 1877–78 where he met Hugh Munroe. Schultz moved to the Blackfoot Reservation in 1885, hunted with Billy Jackson and Tom Bird and left in 1903 when his wife died.
12. "Hugh Monroe 1784–1892, A Brief Sketch of the Life of the Oldest Man in Montana – Still Vigorous at 106 Years of Age," *The River Press* (19 February 1890) in *Contributions to the Historical Society of Montana*, vol. 10 (1940), 255–56 n.22.
13. The lodge which may have been preserved until recently on the Blood Reserve.

14. G. H. Gunn, "Jimmy Jock, the Story of the Englishman Who Turned Indian in the Palmy Days," *Winnipeg Free Press* (8 November 1930) 7, 11; copy in Montana Historical Society Bird folder.
15. After Mary Kipling, the mother of Tom died, on 27 December 1881, Philip Bird remarried the widow Louise Lucier Dequire at Duck Lake, Saskatchewan. Their son Edward was born about 1885 and four years later Louises' son Harry Dequire was brought to the U.S. reservation to be educated. About the same time young Tom may have been turned over to his uncle. Philip and Louise traveled between places on the northern plains until she left him to live on the Browning Reservation in 1907 while he remained at Calgary. *Blackfoot Heritage*, 53–5.
16. Christina McDonald, a daughter of a Columbia District bayman, remembered that Mr. Bird attended her wedding at Fort Colvile and that he had a big son whom he was teaching to drive the oxen that hauled logs to the mill. Oregon Historical Society Eva Emery Dye collection. This must have been Tom Bird.
17. *Edmonton Bulletin* (16 May 1892), Alberta Provincial Archives.
18. Thomas J. Bird interview, Montana Historical Society.
19. Keith C Seele, ed., "The Theft of the Sacred Otter Skin Bow Case (Told by Chief James Bird)," *Blackfeet and Buffalo: Memories of Life among the Indians by James Willard Shultz (Apikuni)* (Norman, OK: University of Oklahoma Press, 1962), 179–93.
20. Charette, *Vanishing Spaces*, 90–91.
21. "The Quest of the Otter Skin Bow Case" serialized in *Boy's Life* from July to September 1935 was republished in part in *Blackfeet and Buffalo*. Bird's brothers-in-law were named as Mad Wolf and Bear Head, the sons of Lame Bull. Grinell visited the Munroe cabin on 5 September 1891 when he took the photo of old Hugh and his son-in-law. Emerson Hough visited the Glacier area in February 1902 and used Billy Jackson as his guide. Schultz lived with the Blackfeet until 1903. His grave is on the ridge overlooking the Bird cabin on Two Medicine Creek.
22. Gerald A. Diettert, *Grinnell's Glacier: George Bird Grinnell and Glacier National Park* (Missoula, MT: Mountain Press, 1992).

A

Absoroka (Crow), 59, 61
Acton House, 12
American Fur Company (Upper Missouri
 Outfit), 56, 68, 81
  Fort Union, 56, 59, 61, 65, 81, 120
  Fort McKenzie, 64, 73, 89
  Fort Tecumseh, 59, 61
  Fort Benton, 7, 109, 141
    robe traders from, 112, 120, 141
Ashley & Henry, 38, 39, 46, 116
Assiniboine, 59, 62, 86
Atsiina (Gros Ventre, Falls Indians), 45, 61,
 65

B

Baker, Col. E. M., 139
Baker Massacre, 139
Bear Chief (Nihoch-kieiu), 74, 77
Bear Paw Mountains, 71
Bear (Marias) River, 49
beaver trapping, 46
Berger, Jacques, 47, 49, 54, 56, 64
Berger, Pierre, 74
Big Bear, 153, 155
Bird, Curtis James (brother), 133, 136
Bird, Elizabeth Montour (step-mother), 14
Bird family, 69, 97, 104, 119, 135, 161
Bird, George (brother), 13, 15, 26, 28, 120
Bird, Chief Factor James, 12, 25, 68, 120–22
Bird, James Jr. (Jemmy Jock), 2, 15, 55
  birth, 13
  children, 68, 96, 99, 102–3, 107, 125, 136,
   147, 157
  death, 163–64
  employment HBC, 23, 24, 27, 28, 36, 37,
   50, 56, 70, 85, 92
  employment UMO, 56, 59, 61, 65, 67, 69
  interpreter, 95, 113, 118, 143, 147, 163
  marginality, 59, 69, 84, 85, 87, 91, 99, 104,
   124, 156, 160, 166
  name, 83
  Red River settlement, 124, 133
  salary, 50, 67, 70, 85, 92
  trade to south, 54, 56, 87, 115

wives, 49, 68, 96, 124, 129, 136, 157–59
Bird, John (brother), 95
Bird, Philip (son), 7, 136, 141, 147, 151, 161
Bird, Letitia (sister). *See* McKay
Bird, Thomas (grandson), 161–62
Bird, Thomas (son), 7, 134, 143, 147, 154, 161
Blackfeet (as generalization), 35, 45, 65, 153
   treaties, 113, 115, 117, 145
Blackfoot Crossing, 142, 156
Blackfoot River, 45
Bodmer, Karl, 73, 115
Bourdon, Michael, 35
Bow River, 1, 65, 96
Bow River expedition, 32, 33
buffalo, 49
   decline of, 108, 109, 118, 134, 139, 153
   uses, 108, 120
   numbers, 153
   robe trade, 59, 60, 67, 107–8, 120, 129, 153
Buffalo Lake, 155

C

carts, 162, 164
Catlin, George, 61
Chardon, Francis A., 61, 109
Chouteau Jr., Pierre, 60, 67, 81, 121
coalition of HBC and NWC, 28, 29
confidential servants, 36, 39, 41–42, 47, 64, 122
Clark, Malcolm, 110
Cree (Asinaa; Southerd Indians), 1, 19, 26, 31, 147, 153
   hostilities, 112
Crowfoot, 2, 146, 155
Culbertson, Alexander, 75, 84, 89, 109
Cummings, Alfred, 116

D

Denig, Edwin T., 89, 120, 128
de Smet, Pierre-Jean, 93, 99, 100, 102
Doty, James, 111
Duck Lake, 156, 157

E

Eagle Ribs (Petohpekis), 65
Edmonton House, 22
Ermatinger, Francis, 83, 86

F

Ferris, Warren, 83
Fisher, Henry, 37, 54, 57, 62, 71, 85
Flatheads Post, 38
Fort Chardon, 109
Fort Garry, 69
Fort Hall, 86, 87
Fort Lewis, 102
Fort Macleod, 141, 155, 162, 146
Forts des Prairies, 23
Fort Whoop-up, 140–41
Fraser, Colin, 79
freemen, 38, 40, 46
fur trade, Piikani, 47

G

Gens du Large (defined), 12
Gleichen on CPR, 155
Godin, Antoine, 86
Godin, Thyery, 86
Grant, Cuthbert, 25
Gray, William Henry, 88–89

H

Harriot, John Edward, 65, 69, 71, 79, 95, 126
Heron, Francis, 26, 27
Hind, Henry Youle, 126
Horse Prairie/Plains, 53
Hudson's Bay Company, 11, 22, 29, 134

I

Inuk'sik (Small Robes) band, 40, 49, 50, 67, 88
   leaders of, 109
   massacre of, 100, 102
   decline, 109, 110, 120, 128
Iron Shirt, 34
Iroquois, 35, 40, 85–86, 87, 95

Isham, Charles Thomas, 12, 13

J
Judith River, 5, 89, 109, 113

K
Kainaa (Bloods), 2, 49, 54, 59, 61, 71, 74, 79
   hostilities, 65
   leaders, 67, 145, 149
   resist trappers, 17, 22, 31, 35, 45, 47
   treaties, 2, 5
Kane, Paul, 104–5, 115
Kipp, James, 5, 56, 57, 59
Kipp, Joe, 154
Kittson, William, 39, 41, 45
Kutenai, 62, 71, 75, 79, 102

L
Laird, Lt. Governor David, 2, 145, 148
Lame Bull, 7
Lewis & Clark Expedition, 21
liquor, 154
Little Dog, 7
Lowman, Mary (stepmother), 122, 133
Love, Timoleon M., 128, 131

M
McDonald, "Big" Donald, 56, 57
McDonald, Finan, 35, 46
McKay, Charles (HBC), 36, 37, 39
McKay, Charles (brother-in-law) 98
McKay, John Richards 25, 98, 134
McKay, Letitia Bird (sister), 16, 96, 120
McKay, Thomas, 46, 53, 83, 115
Mackenzie, Kenneth, 5, 56, 57, 59, 61, 67, 81
MacLeod, Col. James, 2, 145, 146, 148
McLoughlin, Dr. John, 46, 63
McMillan, James, 69
Marias River (Bear River), 33, 45
Maskepetoon (Broken Arm), 112, 140
Maximillion, Alexander Phillip, Prince zu
    Weid, 73, 77
Medicine Calf, 7, 149
Medicine Shield, 7, 147, 154

Metis, 23, 25, 97, 140, 156
Metis script payments, 156, 157
Missouri Fur Company, 34–35
Missouri River, 19, 34, 45
missionaries, 87, 99, 166
   Catholic, 91, 93, 95, 98, 99, 146, 150, 162
   Protestant, 88, 93, 95, 104, 143, 160
Mitchell, David Dawson, 62, 67, 77–78, 110, 140
Montour, Robert dit Bonhomme, 14, 26
Montour, Nicholas 14
Montour, Nicholas the younger 14, 17, 33, 50, 68, 83
Morgan, Lewis Henry, 128
Mountain Chief, 7
Munroe, Hugh, 28, 34, 36, 37, 40, 42, 49, 51, 73, 79, 95, 151, 159, 163

N
Nez Perce, 2, 151
Niitsitapi (the People), 5
North Peigan, 157
North West Company, 21, 22, 24

O
Ogden, Peter Skene, 38, 39, 124
Ojibwa (Saulteur) companion, 73, 75, 79–80
Oomenahowish (mother), 13

P
Pacific Fur Company (Astorians)
Palliser, Captain John, 126
Pambrun, Andrew C., 85, 91
Pambrun, Pierre C., 24
Pemmican war, 23, 25
Picard, Maurice, 41, 44, 49
Peigan Post, 71, 79, 82, 98
Piikani (Muddy River Indians), 5, 34, 47
   bands and numbers, 56, 61, 82, 111, 118, 128, 139, 142
   beaver hunting, 32, 34, 47, 49, 79
   fur trade, 19, 44, 54, 59, 80, 107
   leaders, 56, 78, 110, 112, 120, 142
   seasonal round, 55, 56

territory and ranges, 44, 51, 55, 71, 109, 118
wars, 53, 54, 55, 59, 65, 77, 80, 82, 102, 111, 139–40
Point, Nicholas, 99, 102, 109
Potts, Jerry 7, 147
Prince Albert, 157, 160

R
Red Crow, 7, 147
Red River settlement, 27, 124
Red River rebellion, 133–35
Riel, Louis, 134, 154, 155
Rising Head. *See* Tete que Leve
Rivet, Francois, 83
Rocky Mountain Fur Company, 67, 81
Rocky Mountain House, 32, 49, 54, 59, 73, 95
Ross, Alexander, 38, 131
Rowand, John, 36, 47, 49, 62–63, 69, 84, 91, 97, 124
Rundle, Rev. Robert T., 95–99, 103–5
Rupert's Land, 23

S
St. Andrews parish, 126, 136
St. Paul's parish, 125
St. Paul, Minnesota, 126–27, 132–33
Saahsi (Sarcee), 1, 61, 96
Sahaptan Indians (Nez Perce)
Salish (Flathead), 49, 115
   buffalo hunts, 49, 117
   hostilities, 75, 79, 86, 102
   trade, 88
Sand Hills, 5
Saskatchewan River (North Branch), 29
Saskatchewan River (South Branch or Bow), 37
Schultz, James Willard, 103, 151, 159
Schultz, John Christian, 133, 135
Selkirk, Lord (Thomas Douglas), 19, 26
Semple, Governor Robert, 22–23
Shoshone (Snakes), 86
Siksika (Blackfeet), 2, 61, 71, 146
Simpson, Francis, 68–70

Simpson, Governor George, 32, 36, 37, 63, 68, 82, 97, 98, 122, 127
   discharges old hands, 33, 35, 39, 46
Simpson, Thomas, 95
Sinclair, James, 97, 119
Sioux (Lakota, Dakota), 2, 61, 143
Sly Shooting River, 102
Small, Patrick, 49
smallpox, 89, 91
Small Robes, 50. *See also* Inuk'sik
Smith, Jackson & Sublette, 50, 61
Smith, Jedediah, 39, 50
Snake River and plain, 35
Snake River Hunting Brigade, 35, 38, 40, 41, 51, 53, 84
Sohon, Gustav, 115
Southerd (Southern) Indians, 34. *See also* Cree
Stevens, Isaac Ingels, 110, 112, 116
Stanley, John Mix, 110, 115
Sublette, William, 39
Sweetgrass Hills, 71

T
Taylor, James Wickes, 127, 131, 133
Tete que Leve (Rising Head), 41, 49, 50, 112
Thompson, David, 17, 21, 32
Three Forks of Missouri River, 34, 35
trader/trappers, 36
treaties, 5, 110, 143
Treaty Seven, 1, 144, 145, 150
Two Medicine Lodges River, 159, 162

V
Vaughan, Alfred J., 110

W
Work, John, 63
Wyeth, Nathaniel J., 81, 86, 87

Y
York Factory, 15

www.ingramcontent.com/pod-product-compliance
Lightning Source LLC
Chambersburg PA
CBHW051051230426
43666CB00012B/2644